THE
STRUGGLE
FOR A FREE
EUROPE

DEAN ACHESON

THE
STRUGGLE
FOR A FREE
EUROPE

W · W · NORTON & COMPANY · INC · NEW YORK

Library of Congress Catalog Card No. 70-152306

SBN   393 09983 0

1 2 3 4 5 6 7 8 9 0

CONTENTS

1

THE CRISIS OF SURVIVAL

Nature Deals a Cold Hand

In Europe no one could remember such a winter as January 1947 ushered in. The one before had been bad enough, a winter of freezing drought. This was one of freezing blizzards. Since the surrender of Germany, the life of Europe as an organized industrial community had come well-nigh to a standstill and, with it, so had production and distribution of goods of every sort. Only in Britain and Russia did people have any confidence in government, or social or economic organization, or currencies. Elsewhere governments had been repudiated, or abolished by the conquerors; social classes were in bitter enmity, with resistance groups hunting out and executing, after drumhead trials, collaborators with the late enemy. The prewar economy had been taken over by Hitler and bombed out by the allies. Agricultural production was lower than at any time since the turn of the century, as the cities had little to exchange for produce of the country. Peasants produced only to nourish and clothe themselves.

Currency was worthless, the popular attitude toward it reflected by a remark made by Edward Playfair (later Sir Edward), who was then with His Majesty's Treasury, when the form of currency to be issued by the Anglo-American forces invading France in 1944 was being considered. There was much talk of who the issuer should be—Banque de France, République Française, or National Committee of Liberation. Playfair suggested that more thought be given to the obverse side. The Americans, he said, had had a good idea for their coins—"In God We Trust." He advanced a quotation from the Book of Job for the new invasion currency—"I

Young boys in London grubbing through the snow for coal bits during the fuel shortage, February 1947. WIDE WORLD

know that my redeemer liveth." In Europe the people were not so sure.

Then came that awful winter. It is enough to say of it that perhaps its most crushing blows fell on Britain, our chief ally and collaborator, to whom we looked to take the lead in maintaining the eastern Mediterranean and sharing with us the burdens of occupation and defense of Europe. Week after week blizzards battered England, stopped production of fuel, transportation, electric power —until finally nearly all industry was shut down, as electricity was cut off from it and furnished for domestic use only for a few hours in the morning. Unemployment rose to over six million, rations were cut to below wartime levels, and the workless millions relegated to their freezing homes. British monetary reserves were running out.

The Stuff of Command

In this situation General George C. Marshall took the oath of office as Secretary of State on January 21, 1947. Five months later in presenting him with an honorary degree of Doctor of Laws at Harvard, Harvard President James B. Conant described him as "an American to whom freedom owes an enduring debt of gratitude, a soldier and statesman whose ability and character brook only one comparison in the history of this nation."

It was a gifted citation. No other American in our history can be imagined who could have taken over command from General Washington at Valley Forge. It was, indeed, an act of God that made him chief adviser to the President and head of the State Department in the no less critical winter of 1947.

The General and I—at that time I was Under Secretary of State—walked across the street from the White House to my office, adjoining his new one.

"Will you stay?" he asked.

"Certainly," I answered, "as long as you need me, though before too long I ought to get back to my profession if I'm to have one."

"Would six months be too long?" he asked again. "That would get me started and give us time to find your successor." I agreed and we settled on June 30 as my retiring date. When asked what he expected of an Under Secretary, he said that he should be chief of staff and run the Department. Everything would come to the Secretary through the Under Secretary with his recommendation, unless the Under Secretary chose to decide the matter himself; everything from the Secretary would go, as his order, to the Department through the Under Secretary. There would be no other channel. He asked me why I was smiling. I replied that the incidence of heart attacks in the Department was due for a sharp increase, and that while the system could not work quite as he described it, we would try to approximate it. He sketched out the Central Secretariat to be installed and operated by Colonel Carlisle Humelsine from the Army General Staff. It would weld our offices into one and keep the unified office informed of all that was going on. From me he would expect complete and even brutal candor; he had no feelings, he said, "except those which I reserve for Mrs. Marshall."

Were there matters, he asked, awaiting decision? I said there was one that had been tearing the Department apart for six months for lack of it—whether we should move into the quarters built for the War Department before the war and abandoned for the Pentagon or attempt to stay where we were. Asked for the reasons for and against it, I outlined them. For, the White House wanted our building for the countless branches of the Executive Office of the President; the building was hopelessly insecure for our cryptographic work; both buildings were too small, but the other had plenty of ground about it for expansion.

"Against?" he asked.

"Tradition."

"Move!" said the General. Orders were issued to move. I never mentioned it to him again, nor did anyone to me, because I would not listen.

In addition to getting lines of command straight and clear, and setting up the Central Secretariat as an instrument of information and control, General Marshall created another institution—the Policy Planning Staff. He picked to head it George F. Kennan, the Foreign Service officer whose penetrating dispatches from Moscow in 1946 attracted so much attention among the higher officials in the Administration and who was currently lecturing at the War College. The General conceived the function of this group as being to look ahead, not into the distant future, but beyond the vision of the operating officers caught in the smoke and crises of current battle; far enough ahead to see the emerging form of things to come and outline what should be done to meet or anticipate them. In doing this the staff should also do something else—constantly reappraise what was being done. General Marshall was acutely aware that policies acquired their own momentum and went on after the reasons that inspired them had ceased.

These two tasks are extremely difficult to perform. Distraction lurks on two sides: on one, to be lured into operations; on the other, into encyclopedism, into the amassing of analyses of the problems of every area and country with the various contingencies that might arise and the courses of action that might be taken to meet them. Those who practice it seem to believe they are writing a "do-it-yourself" book of instructions for desk officers who would be enabled by looking up a country and a particular problem to find the answer. Under its first two chiefs, George Kennan and Paul Nitze, with whose work I am familiar, the staff was of inestimable value as the stimulator, and often deviser, of the most basic policies.

It may be noticed that I have thus far referred to the Secretary of State as General Marshall. I shall continue to do so. It was his own way of referring to himself. On picking up the telephone, he always said, "General Marshall speaking." All of those close to him, in and out of the Department, always so addressed him, including the President. Only a handful outside of his family—I can only recall Major General Frank R. McCoy—called him George. Perhaps those inveterate first-name users, President Roosevelt and James Forrestal, did, but certainly not even old associates such as Colonel Henry L. Stimson or General Omar Bradley. This was not because General Marshall had a trace of arrogance or stiffness popularly attributed to high military personages. Rationing his

none-too-ebullient energy to meet the great demands upon it led
to an aloofness, an ungregariousness, which was not ungraciousness.
When a situation was of his own choosing, he had warmth and a
strong social response.

The Decision to Help Greece and Turkey

The situation in Greece, bad at the end of December, de-
teriorated rapidly during January and February 1947. All three of
our scouts in Greece—Ambassador Lincoln MacVeagh, Paul Porter, chief of the economic mission, and Mark Ethridge, who had
been reporting to Secretary of State James F. Byrnes on conditions
in the Balkans—sent back increasingly alarming reports of imminent collapse due to mounting guerrilla activity, supplied and
directed from the outside, economic chaos, and Greek governmental
inability to meet the crisis. MacVeagh reported rumors of impending British troop withdrawals; Waldemar J. Gallman, Minister
in London, that the British Cabinet had met to discuss Greece,
and would be asking for help from the United States. All signs
pointed to an impending move by the Communists to take over
the country. The Director of the Department's Office of Near
Eastern and African Affairs, Loy Henderson, discussed this possibility in a memorandum entitled "Crisis and Imminent Possibility
of Collapse," which I edited and sent on to General Marshall. It
urged that only a national coalition government and substantial aid
could save Greece. Before leaving the next day—Friday, February 21,
1947—to speak to Princeton's bicentennial celebration, the General
instructed me to prepare the necessary steps for sending economic
and military aid.

Shortly after the General had gone, the British Ambassador's
private secretary asked urgently that his chief might see the Secretary of State to deliver "a blue piece of paper," the trade name for
a formal and important message from His Majesty's Government,
which Lord Inverchapel had been instructed to deliver personally
to General Marshall. The Ambassador and I were close friends. He
told me that the note contained important information about a
crisis in British aid to Greece. I explained that unless he went to
Princeton or North Carolina he could not catch General Marshall
until Monday morning; that if he did the General would turn the
note over to me; and that if he sent his First Secretary over with a
copy and presented the ribbon copy to the General on Monday,
the letter and spirit of his orders would have been meticulously
obeyed. He agreed.

Henderson shortly received not one but two documents. They were shockers. British aid to Greece and Turkey would end in six weeks. Henderson and John D. Hickerson, Deputy Director of the Office of European Affairs, brought them to me. They were brief and all too clear. One described the state of the Greek economy and army, which we all knew. It estimated Greece's current foreign-exchange needs at from two hundred forty million to two hundred eighty million dollars and, in addition, substantial sums over several years. The other reported Turkey as stronger but still unable to handle the financing of both the modernization and maintenance of the large army that Russian pressure demanded and the economic development of Turkey, which since Kemal Ataturk's time had been its first priority. The British could no longer be of substantial help in either. His Majesty's Government devoutly hoped that we could assume the burden in both Greece and Turkey.

I instructed Henderson and Hickerson to get the European and Near Eastern Division people together that evening and assign tasks for preliminary reports the next day on (1) facts as seen by United States representatives; (2) funds and personnel currently available; (3) funds and personnel needed; (4) significance of an independent Greece and Turkey to Western Europe. They should also confer the next day with Admiral Forrest Sherman, Deputy Chief of Naval Operations, and General Lauris Norstad, Army Director of Plans and Operations, so that they might brief the Secretaries of Navy and War on military-aid needs and available supplies for a meeting with the Secretary on Monday morning. Then, by telephone, I explained to the President and General Marshall what had happened, what had been done, and asked for further orders. They had none.

Reports kept coming in to me on Saturday from various working groups. These were studied, discussed, and sent back for further development and documentation. On Sunday they were brought to my house in Georgetown for final review. They were in good shape. Henderson asked me whether we were still working on papers bearing on the making of a decision or the execution of one. I said the latter; under the circumstances there could be only one decision.

General Marshall found the early-morning hours, before the place got cluttered up, his most productive time. Then he read the papers that Colonel Marshall (Pat) Carter had arranged for him and noted instructions for me. On Monday, February 24, although I came in early, he had already read the British notes and our memoranda preparatory to his meeting with Lord Inverchapel at ten o'clock. As usual, probing the essential points, he wanted to know whether we were sure of our facts about Greek and Turkish financial weakness; how long British troops could be induced to stay in Greece; what military forces would replace them; how we proposed to get an effective governmental organization in Greece; what were our estimates of cost and over how long? The consequences of inaction were clear enough. Of the answer to the first question I was sure; to the others, the answers had to be tentative, subject to further work. As we ended, the General said that I must continue to take the principal responsibility in this matter. He would be going to Moscow for the foreign ministers' meeting in a little over a week and had a lot of preparatory work to do. It would be essential to have continuity of direction. He would do everything possible to get us started.

The meeting with Lord Inverchapel, which I did not attend, was brief, performing its essential function of convincing the Ambassador of the General's grasp of the situation and its critical importance. Later the General went off to a Cabinet luncheon at the White House, staying afterward for a discussion with the President, the Secretaries of War and Navy, Admiral Sherman, and General Norstad. At its end the service secretaries and officers resumed it with Henderson, Hickerson, and me in my office. We agreed that the President and his principal advisers seemed convinced that it was vital to the security of the United States for Greece and Turkey to be strengthened to preserve their national independence, that only the United States could do this, that funds and authority from Congress were necessary, and that State would prepare for concurrence by War and Navy specific recommendations for the President. General Marshall approving, Henderson and his staff worked with me preparing the recommendations.

The next day, the three secretaries concurring, the President approved the paper for action. This moved us from consideration through decision by the Executive. The President set up a meeting for the following day to begin the all-important next step of consultation with the legislative branch, now controlled by the opposite political party. The actual planning had advanced only to the extent of a decision to send as soon as possible such funds and equipment as existing legislative authority permitted, to give Greece priority in assigning military aid, and to find out at once what British military help we could expect and for how long. A Pentagon proposal, voiced by General Eisenhower, to include in our request funds for other countries in need of bolstering was rejected because we already had more to deal with than the time available permitted.

When we convened the next morning in the White House to open the subject with our congressional masters, I knew we were met at Armageddon. We faced the "leaders of Congress"—all the majority and minority potentates except Senator Robert Taft, an accidental omission to which Senator Arthur Vandenberg swiftly drew the President's attention.

My distinguished chief, most unusually and unhappily, flubbed his opening statement. In desperation I whispered to him a request to speak. This was my crisis. For a week I had nurtured it. These congressmen had no conception of what challenged them; it was my task to bring it home. Both my superiors, equally perturbed, gave me the floor. Never have I spoken under such a pressing sense that the issue was up to me alone. No time was left for measured appraisal. In the past eighteen months, I said, Soviet pressure on the Straits, on Iran, and on northern Greece had brought the Balkans to the point where a highly possible Soviet breakthrough might open three continents to Soviet penetration. Like apples in a barrel infected by one rotten one, the corruption of Greece would infect Iran and all to the east. It would also carry infection to Africa through Asia Minor and Egypt, and to Europe through Italy and France, already threatened by the strongest domestic Communist parties in Western Europe. The Soviet Union was playing one of the greatest gambles in history at minimal cost. It did not need to win all the possibilities. Even one or two offered immense gains. We and we alone were in a position to break up the play. These were the stakes that British withdrawal from the eastern Mediterranean offered to an eager and ruthless opponent.

A long silence followed. Then Arthur Vandenberg said solemnly, "Mr. President, if you will say that to the Congress and the country, I will support you and I believe that most of its members will do the same." Without much further talk the meeting broke up to convene again, enlarged, in a week to consider a more detailed program of action.

The President's Message

With the President and both the executive and legislative leaders agreeing in principle to our assumption of responsibility in the eastern Mediterranean, we turned to the task of preparing a concrete program of operation and explaining it to the Congress and the country. Francis Russell, Director of the Office of Public Affairs, would take on the campaign of public information, and other assignments in the political and economic fields had to be

made and meshed. Believing that everyone involved should understand the full crisis and its importance, I got them all together,
told them what I had told the legislators and their response, gave
them the President's and the Secretary's orders for urgent action
and General Marshall's magnificent instruction about himself. On
March 5 he was going to Moscow, where he would be when our
whole program became public. We were to go forward, he instructed me, with utmost vigor and without regard to him and his
meeting. Events had relegated that to secondary importance. The
prime necessity was to save the pivotal position occupied by Greece
and Turkey. Many years would go by before an officer commanding
in a forward and exposed spot would call down his own artillery
fire upon his own position to block an enemy advance. The spirit
which inspired us all at the time has been well put by Joseph M.
Jones of the Office of Public Affairs, who was both a participant in
and the historian of all this effort: "All . . . were aware that a
major turning point in American history was taking place. The
convergence of massive historical trends upon that moment was so
real as to be almost tangible, and it was plain that in that carrefour
of time all those trends were being to some degree deflected."

Groups were appointed by Henderson, who was in charge,
with Hickerson as his second, to draft the legislation, to organize
and recruit the civilian group to exercise control and direction in
Greece, to set up with the Pentagon the military training and advisory teams, to order supplies and weapons, and to procure shipping. Joseph Jones would prepare a draft of the President's message
for the White House. Everyone knew that the State Department
was facing its last clear chance to get a job done. The job of briefing
the press I took on myself, talking on the evening of February 27
off the record and with the greatest frankness to a group of twenty
men regularly assigned to the Department.

The next day with Lord Inverchapel I attempted to inject
some flexibility into the British position. We were moving with
incredible speed for so vast a country to assume a novel burden far
from our shores. The British should not set such short and arbitrary
deadlines, especially for the withdrawal of their troops. I quoted to
him our Air Force's motto, "The difficult we do at once; the impossible takes a little longer." London agreed to keep the troops on
for a while longer and to advance a little more cash for the Greek
army provided our aid was moving smartly along.

All this time Greece was in the position of a semiconscious
patient on the critical list whose relatives and physicians had
been discussing whether his life could be saved. The hour had

come for the patient to be heard from. On March 3, with the support of kind friends and their guidance of a feeble hand, the Greek Government wrote asking for the help—financial, economic, military, and administrative—which has already been mentioned. Of all this we kept General Marshall in Moscow fully informed, including a draft of the message to Congress that Joseph Jones had given to Clark Clifford, Counsel to the President. The General approved the message.

Like all presidential messages, this one stimulated controversy within the government. George Kennan thought it too strong, since it took the line I had taken with the legislative group, and feared that it might provoke the Soviet Union to aggressive action. Clark Clifford thought it too weak and added some points that I thought unwise. Using General Marshall's great prestige, I got Clark to withdraw his additions and recommend the message as the General had approved it. The President, back from a meeting with the Mexican President and a speech in Texas, met with me on March 7. Deciding that he had no alternative but to go ahead, and realizing that this was only a beginning, he approved a request for two hundred fifty million dollars for Greece and one hundred fifty million dollars for Turkey, and the message to Congress. We then moved into the Cabinet Room, where the President laid out the whole program, which got unanimous Cabinet support, and ordered a meeting with congressional leaders for March 10 and, depending on its outcome, a presidential appearance before Congress on March 12. I came back to the Department somewhat breathless. When President Truman had made a decision, he moved fast.

The large group of senators and congressmen who met in the President's office on March 10 gave us, despite Arthur Vandenberg's earlier assurance, a cool and silent reception. During the past three weeks the attitude of Congress toward Europe had been one of hardly suppressed skepticism. Its majority members had been elected after a campaign for economy and against the policies of President Truman. On the day (February 21) the British notes were given to me, and in ignorance of them, the President had asked Congress for three hundred fifty million dollars for relief, splitting both Republican and Democratic ranks. To add to the confusion, former President Hoover, who had returned from a tour of Europe to examine the food situation, urged Congress to "stop, look, and listen" before formulating a relief plan. He reported Europe to be on the verge of starvation, estimated its needs at a billion dollars, and, quite unrealistically, proposed that the British and we provide the funds equally on a loan basis. At this point the press brought news of the British notes and Congress dropped the whole matter until it could learn more, but not before the Democratic Congressional Conference in a long and secret meeting—fully reported in the press—warned the Administration against supporting British policies in the Mediterranean or the Greek monarchy. The Senate on March 4 had voted to cut the President's budget for the next fiscal year by four and a half billion dollars, the House earlier having voted a cut of six billion. Finally, Senator Taft had expressed opposition to the President's request for an extension of the War Powers Act and the Selective Service Act.

Such was the situation when we met with the legislative leaders who shared with us the responsibilities of government. The meeting did not materially change it. In his matter-of-fact way the President laid out the need for action and the action proposed, calling on me for detail from time to time. Vandenberg reiterated his insistence that the President put the crisis before Congress in its broadest setting. No one else said very much. No commitments were made. The meeting could be called a success only in the sense referred to by a colleague of Lester B. Pearson, later Prime Minister of Canada, for whom he made an election speech some years ago. To Pearson's surprise, the colleague was enthusiastic about the speech, while Pearson thought the audience wholly unresponsive. "That's just it," replied the colleague happily, "Not a boo! Not a boo!"

Two days later the Cabinet in a body went to the chamber of the House of Representatives to hear the President deliver his message. After describing the military and political pressures being applied to Greece and Turkey, their state of exhaustion, the consequences to ourselves and the free world should they collapse, and the absence of any other source of help, he said:

I believe that it must be the policy of the United States to support free peoples who are resisting attempted subjugation by armed minorities or by outside pressures.

I believe that we must assist free peoples to work out their own destinies in their own way.

I believe that our help should be primarily through economic and financial aid which is essential to economic stability and orderly political processes.

The world is not static, and the *status quo* is not sacred. But we cannot allow changes in the *status quo* in violation of the Charter of the United Nations by such methods as coercion, or by such subterfuges as political infiltration. In helping free and independent nations to maintain their freedom, the United States will be giving effect to the principles

President Truman proposes a new foreign policy to a joint session of
Congress, March 12, 1947, asking aid for Greece and Turkey. WIDE WORLD

of the Charter of the United Nations. . . .

Should we fail to aid Greece and Turkey in this fateful hour, the
effect will be far-reaching to the West as well as to the East.

We must take immediate and resolute action.

I therefore ask the Congress to provide authority for assistance to
Greece and Turkey in the amount of $400,000,000 for the period ending
June 30, 1948. In requesting these funds I have taken into consideration
the maximum amount of relief assistance which would be furnished to
Greece out of the $350,000,000 which I recently requested that the
Congress authorize for the prevention of starvation and suffering in
countries devastated by the war.

In addition to funds, I ask the Congress to authorize the detail of
American civilian and military personnel to Greece and Turkey, at the request of those countries, to assist in the tasks of reconstruction, and for
the purpose of supervising the use of such financial and material assistance
as may be furnished. I recommend that authority also be provided for
the instruction and training of selected Greek and Turkish personnel.

Finally, I ask that the Congress provide authority which will permit
the speediest and most effective use, in terms of needed commodities, supplies, and equipment, of such funds as may be authorized.[1]

When he finished, the President received a standing ovation
from both parties. This was a tribute to a brave man rather than
unanimous acceptance of his policy. As I cabled to General Mar-

1. *Public Papers of the Presidents of the United States: Harry S. Truman, 1947*
(Washington, D.C.: U.S. Government Printing Office, 1963), pp. 178–79.

shall in Moscow, the response to the message was not one of opposition, but it "did disclose the inevitable pain and anguish of
Congress in facing a difficult situation." For more than two months
it would undergo the anguish of its labor pains before an "Act to
Provide for Assistance to Greece and Turkey" would be delivered
to the President for approval.

Vandenberg and the Legislation

Arthur Vandenberg's part in the enactment of this proposal
into law was invaluable. He was born to lead a reluctant opposition
into support of governmental proposals that he came to believe
were in the national interest. A leader should be in advance of
his followers, but not so far in advance as to be out of touch. It
helps, also, if he can believe in his own little stratagems. One of
Vandenberg's stratagems was to enact publicly his conversion to a
proposal, his change of attitude, a kind of political transubstantia-
tion. The method was to go through a period of public doubt and
skepticism; then find a comparatively minor flaw in the proposal,
pounce upon it, and make much of it; in due course propose a
change, always the Vandenberg amendment. Then, and only then,
could it be given to his followers as true doctrine worthy of all men
to be received. He did it now with the Greek-Turkish proposal. He
would do it again with the Marshall Plan. Its strength lay in the
genuineness of his belief in each step. He was not engaged in
strategy; rather he was a prophet pointing out to more earthbound
rulers the errors and spiritual failings of their ways.

Within a few days of the message, Senator Vandenberg had
found, though he did not discover, his issue. The press and various
organized groups charged us with "bypassing the United Nations."
That ambivalent Jeremiah of the press, Walter Lippmann, although
he had advocated unilateral action in Greek-Turkish aid, found us
grievously at fault in not doing all the consulting with the United
Nations we should have done. We should expiate our sin by "a
full explanation and a willingness to consider objections." [2] This
fortunate error was mine. The President had made minimal obei-
sance to the United Nations, but since time was so short had not
been advised to go through the futility of appeal to an organization
in which the Soviet Union would veto action and where in any
event any help must come from the United States. If we had
proposed it, Vandenberg's task would only have been harder. We

2. *New York Herald Tribune*, March 18, 1947.

had made, he penciled in his private papers, "a colossal blunder in ignoring the U.N." [3] He proposed to correct it and, as corrected, to adopt our fumbling efforts.

Like Mr. Jorrocks' foxes, I lustily cried, *"Peccavi!"* and offered to make amends. But the Senator was going to make the amends and the amendments himself. These took two forms. First, Senators Vandenberg and Tom Connally drafted introductory "whereas" paragraphs to the bill, setting forth that Greece and Turkey had asked help from the United States and the United Kingdom as the United Nations Food and Agriculture Organization had advised them to do; the United Nations, the introduction continued, had recognized the seriousness of the border trouble in northern Greece and "if the present emergency is met" could "assume full responsibility for this phase of the problem," but it could "not now . . . furnish to Greece and Turkey the financial and economic assistance which is immediately required" and which "will contribute to the freedom and independence of all members of the United Nations." Second, Vandenberg introduced a curious amendment to section five directing the President to withdraw all aid if requested to do so by a government of either country "representing a majority of the people," or if the President found that the purposes of the aid had been accomplished by any intergovernmental body or could not be accomplished or if the Security Council (the United States waiving its veto) or the General Assembly found that United Nations action had made the aid undesirable.

This, of course, was window dressing and must have seemed either silly or cynical or both in London, Paris, and Moscow. Nevertheless, it was a cheap price for Vandenberg's patronage and warmly welcomed by Warren Austin, our representative at the United Nations. He had succeeded Edward Stettinius and, a former senator himself, could play legislative games with all the hyperbolic sincerity of Vandenberg himself. The amendment won over the bulk of doubters. Remaining objections—that the President's proposals put us on the road to imperialism, spheres of influence, and war, put forward by Senators Taft, Edwin C. Johnson, Democrat of Colorado, and Claude Pepper, Democrat of Florida, and that it was too "military," a favorite of some columnists and poll takers—soon received the kiss of death from Henry Wallace and a following from the extreme left and right. Public distrust of these views was accentuated when Wallace established a foreign base in England

3. Arthur H. Vandenberg, Jr., ed., *The Private Papers of Senator Vandenberg,* (Boston: Houghton Mifflin Company, 1952), p. 345.

from which to attack the Administration, and Andrei Gromyko, the Soviet Deputy Minister for Foreign Affairs, joined in from Moscow. We were fortunate in our enemies. Our friends were powerfully augmented on March 23 by Governor Thomas E. Dewey of New York.

Amid growing support for the policy, hearings in the House and Senate began and continued simultaneously from mid-March until the Senate committee unanimously reported its bill on April 23; the House committee, with only Representative Lawrence H. Smith of Wisconsin dissenting, reported its version on April 25. These hearings added to the heavy burden that had fallen on me since the last days of February. My colleague Will Clayton, Under Secretary of State for Economic Affairs, who had been ill in Texas, came back to testify before going off again to Geneva for the meetings on trade and tariff policies. The world outside Greece and Turkey did not stand still. General Marshall needed constant material for the Moscow conference, which, as might be expected, was going badly. We were engaged in futile protests to Moscow and General V. P. Sviridov in Budapest over the ousting of the popularly elected Smallholders government. State trials were going on in Rumania and Bulgaria. Finally, the Republican members of the Senate asked for immediate answers, which we gave, to one hundred and ten questions on the bill and its implications.

It fell to me to lead off both the executive and public hearings before both committees.[4] I appeared frequently and at length. The questions principally directed at me grew out of the general statements in the President's message in response to Senator Vandenberg's repeated request that the problems of the two small countries be put in the setting of the larger confrontation between the Soviet Union and ourselves. They were sharpened by the cross-examiners' desire to embarrass a witness by pushing statements to what has been called a "dryly logical extreme." Would we advocate doing the same thing everywhere under all conceivable circumstances? Obviously we were not doing the same thing almost next door in Hungary, because the circumstances, particularly for effective action, were wholly different. The China specialists, notably Representative Walter Judd of Minnesota, pressed me on what we should do in China. We were doing a great deal under radically different circumstances. He thought not enough. Senator Connally, a good friend in a free-for-all, summed up the position helpfully:

4. These hearings have been described most interestingly in Joseph M. Jones, *The Fifteen Weeks: February 21–June 5, 1947* (New York: Viking Press, 1955), pp. 189–98.

Senator Connally: This is not a pattern out of a tailor's shop to fit every-body in the world and every nation in the world, because the conditions in no two nations are identical. Is that not true?

Mr. Acheson: Yes, sir; that is true, and whether there are requests, of course, will be left to the future, but whatever they are, they have to be judged, as you say, according to the circumstances of each specific case.[5]

At length, the weary weeks came to an end, and as the event showed, not without having had a useful effect. The Greek-Turkish Aid Act passed the House by a vote of 287 to 107, and the Senate by 67 to 23. The President signed it on May 22.

The Department turned most effectively to administering the act. This fell largely to others. I faced another looming and even more menacing crisis about to engulf all Europe.

5. Senate Committee on Foreign Relations, 80th Congress, 1st Session, *Hearings on S. 938 to Provide for Assistance to Greece and Turkey,* p. 13.

II

THE CRISIS BROADENS:
BIRTH OF THE MARSHALL PLAN

First Stirrings

IT WILL BE RECALLED that when the State, War, and Navy departments were preparing material for the President on Greece and
Turkey, General Eisenhower had suggested that the request to
Congress should include funds for other countries resisting Communist penetration. We had feared that enlarging the proposal
would complicate and delay it. Other needs were great, but the
collapse of Greece, unless aid came, was only weeks away. By
March 5, however, it was plain that we should get work started in
the three departments on the suggestion and be ready to propose a
much larger program in Europe as soon as we knew the facts. Accordingly I wrote the two service secretaries saying that Assistant
Secretary of State Hilldring, the Chairman of the State, War, and
Navy Coordinating Committee, would get that group to work on
the problem with the aid of Treasury, and urging the Secretaries
to prod their people on. This they did. The work of the three departments would be put together by Colonel William A. Eddy,
Chief of Research and Intelligence in State, Brigadier General
George A. (Abe) Lincoln for War, and Rear Admiral E. T. Wool-
dridge, for Navy. They worked fast.

On the day these letters were written Will Clayton, ill and on
a plane to Tucson for a short rest before going to Europe, penned
an urgent memorandum on the same subject. He was deeply disturbed, he wrote, by the world situation and its implications for
our country. Only immediate assertion of leadership by the United

States could prevent war in the next decade. In every nation in the eastern hemisphere, and in some in the western, systematic campaigns were going on to destroy national integrity and independence. "Feeding on hunger, economic misery and frustration," he wrote, "these attacks have already been successful in some of the liberated countries." Prompt and effective aid for gravely threatened countries was essential to our own security. The President and the Secretary of State must shock the country into a realization of its peril by telling it the facts which daily poured in through our cables. He advocated a Council of National Defense of leading Cabinet officers and members of Congress and an emergency fund of five billion dollars.

In the interstices between appearances on Capitol Hill, meetings with the President, innumerable problems of organization, personnel, moving, and current work, I encouraged and harassed those assembling the facts. General Marshall would want these in intelligible form to know in detail the nature, location, and extent of the evil to be cured. His cables showed full awareness of dangers, both in Moscow and in Europe, and little hope of any desire in Moscow to cooperate in alleviating them.

My Speech in Mississippi

At this point the President intervened to stimulate my personal involvement in the larger crisis. On April 7 he said he was going to ask a favor of me, one he especially hoped that I could grant. Some time ago he had promised two warm friends, Mr. and Mrs. William T. Wynne, of Greenville, Mississippi, that he would speak at a meeting of the Delta Council to be held at the Delta State Teachers College at the neighboring town of Cleveland on May 8. The afternoon before he was to attend a gala reception in Greenville. It was a long-standing date; the Wynnes had gone to a great deal of trouble and had their hearts set on the occasion, and they had been devastated on learning that he contemplated asking to be excused. However, the fatal illness of Senator Theodore (The Man) Bilbo of Mississippi and the bitter fight that had broken out over the succession would make the President's presence in the state a serious embarrassment to him. The Wynnes had agreed to forgive him if he would provide me (in the absence of General Marshall) to make an "important foreign policy" speech.

Of course I agreed, and added that I had in mind a speech which very much needed to be made, but which must be very carefully considered. We could not afford a false start. The President had been kept in touch with the increasingly gloomy prospects in Europe and in Moscow as seen by the Secretary of State. He knew Will Clayton's views and the work on which I had started the State, War, and Navy committee. We could no longer postpone attention to this situation. Even if Congress passed the three-hundred-fifty-million-dollar relief bill, it would be pitifully inadequate. By the end of the fiscal year we would have no funds for Europe except for Greece and Turkey. Events were outrunning preparation. What I wanted to do was not to put forward a solution or a plan, but to state the problem and the facts. To do this would, as Clayton had pointed out, shock the country—and both the Administration and the Congress—into facing a growing crisis. Did the President agree to this being done? To my doing it? I was an eager volunteer and the time was short. If the Delta Council wanted an "important foreign policy" speech, here was one.

The President's answer to both questions was yes. Even so, I thought that between agreement and delivery of the speech there should be more talks with President and Secretary. However, galloping events and the attitudes of General Marshall and Will Clayton, when they both returned from Europe, eliminated any doubt that the shocking problem should be presented as soon as we could be ready. Joseph Jones and Francis Russell were deputized to start on the speech, which I outlined to them, with authority to commandeer help from anyone working on the problem. The committees were well along with their tasks when General Marshall got back from Moscow on April 28. Both the State Department group and the State-War-Navy group had filed reports—the latter ninety-three pages long—bristling with grisly facts. The General brought his own cargo of bad news. He could report no progress in his discussions with the Soviet Union. As for Europe, he reported to the country over the radio:

. . . We were faced with immediate issues which vitally concerned the impoverished and suffering people of Europe who are crying for help, for coal, for food, and for most of the necessities of life, and the majority of whom are bitterly disposed towards the Germany that brought about this disastrous situation. . . .

. . . The recovery of Europe has been far slower than had been expected. Disintegrating forces are becoming evident. The patient is sinking while the doctors deliberate . . . action cannot await compromise through exhaustion.[1]

He immediately put the Policy Planning Staff to work on suggestions for a plan of action to deal with facts already known. It

1. *Department of State Bulletin*, Vol. XVI, May 11, 1947, pp. 920, 924.

accomplished little more than reiteration that the crisis was immediate and desperate and called urgently for action. Not until a month later, when Clayton returned from Europe with a memorandum written on the plane, did a concrete outline for the Marshall Plan emerge.

Meanwhile my own speech, a speech to state the problem— "the prologue to the Marshall Plan," as the President was to call it —took form. On April 23 a first draft was produced. On May 1 my helpers came with me to an off-the-record luncheon with a group of League of Women Voters officers, where I gave it a "preliminary canter" to see how it would go. We thought it sound. It was finished on the sixth.

Before leaving Washington, I had had luncheon, as I often did, with three British newsmen, Leonard Miall of the British Broadcasting Corporation, Malcolm Muggeridge of the *Daily Telegraph*, and René MacColl of the *Daily Express*, and explained to them, off the record, what I was doing, why I was doing it, and under what authority. Europe was beginning to wonder whether the military and political aspects of the struggle in southeast Europe had blinded the United States to the imminent collapse of Western Europe. It was of the greatest importance that European opinion should be set right about this, and there was no better place to begin than London. Also, I was under no illusion as to the impact of an Under Secretary's remarks upon the American press and public. It would do no harm if whatever direct effect the speech might have could be reinforced by a returning wave of comment from abroad.

The speech [2] can be summarized as follows:

Europe and Asia were in a state of utter exhaustion and economic dislocation, resulting from (1) "planned, scientific destruction . . . carried out by both sides during the war"; (2) the fact that Germany and Japan, two of the greatest workshops of Europe and Asia, had not yet begun the process of reconstruction; and (3) the unprecedented natural disasters of the last two terrible winters.

The result had been that the world needed and should receive in 1947 exports from the United States—the only source—of sixteen billion dollars (four times our prewar exports), and could find imports to the United States with which to pay for them of only half that sum. The deficit would be made up by loans and grants from us and the remaining financial reserves of the stricken countries, leaving them bankrupt and hopeless. These means of meeting the deficit, after the current year, would no longer be available. We

2. *Ibid.*, May 18, 1947, pp. 991–94.

should therefore increase imports as much as possible to close the gap and find new methods of financing it.

In thinking about how to go about this, the speech continued, we must be acutely conscious of other facts of life. We could not greatly increase exports, since goods were urgently needed at home, too. Therefore we must export selectively to areas of special concern to us and our purposes.

Our objective was not relief, but to revive agriculture, industry, and trade so that stricken countries might be self-supporting. The countries of our immediate concern were those of the free world. The free areas of Europe and Asia could not function vigorously and healthily unless Germany and Japan could play a strong, productive role. General Marshall had concluded after weeks in Moscow that European recovery could not await "compromise through exhaustion" and must proceed without four-power agreement.

The conclusion, I said, was inescapable: new financing was needed from Congress in amounts and through methods beyond existing authorizations, and new powers also to allocate commodities and such services as shipping which might be in short supply. Finally, time was running out:

Not only do human beings and nations exist in narrow economic margins, but also human dignity, human freedom, and democratic institutions.

It is one of the principal aims of our foreign policy today to use our economic and financial resources to widen these margins. It is necessary if we are to preserve our own freedoms and our own democratic institutions. It is necessary for our national security. And it is our duty and our privilege as human beings.

I did not think at the time that my trumpet note from Cleveland, Mississippi, was the call to arms that would start the American people on one of the greatest and most honorable adventures in history. General Marshall sounded that a month later in Cambridge, Massachusetts. Perhaps it is not too much to say that it was reveille, which awoke them to the duties of that day of decision. At any rate the trumpet did not give an uncertain sound. On both sides of the Atlantic it stimulated a good deal of discussion, most of it encouraging to those preparing themselves for the battle. In one mind, however, it stirred disquiet. I had been discreet and vague about total amounts of money involved. Inferences could be drawn, but amounts, duration, and specific areas had purposefully been left undefined. Others, however, had not been so reticent. Henry Wallace, Harold Stassen, and, nearer to home, Ben Cohen,

Counselor to the State Department, in a speech in San Francisco, mentioned large amounts. This disquieted Arthur Vandenberg, who communicated his worries to General Marshall. The General invited him and me to a quiet and very private talk in the seclusion of Blair House, across Pennsylvania Avenue from Old State. There, away from inquiring reporters, telephones, and efficient secretaries, we had a long and useful talk.

Vandenberg began, as he had with UNRRA and the Greek-Turkish proposal, by viewing with alarm. What were we up to? Where was all this to end, with even Alben Barkley talking about opening the Treasury to every country in the world? General Marshall let him run on for a few minutes to reduce his steam pressure, and then told the Senator that the Administration had no intention of asking any further appropriation at the present session of Congress. If he had to change his mind, it would be only a small amount to carry over until the next session. Vandenberg visibly relaxed. The General went on to say that we wanted, in the meantime, to share our researches and our problem with congressional leaders and later with public groups. The situation called for wide national agreement on one of the greatest problems our people had ever faced. Now as never before national unity depended upon a truly nonpartisan policy in the year of a presidential election. Who would carry out an agreed policy no one was bold enough to predict —Vandenberg still had hopes that he might be the man. The security of the country itself was the supreme consideration. At the end of the meeting conversion had been accomplished and a search for the Vandenberg brand had begun. It was to turn up about a month later.

I shall not attempt to trace the genesis of the Harvard speech. It has been well done by Joseph Jones and will be further studied in Forrest Pogue's admirable biography of General Marshall.[3] A few recollections will suffice.

Clayton's Second Memorandum

The first of these concerns the powerful effect of a second memorandum [4] by Will Clayton, written on his flight home from Geneva, upon General Marshall's thinking and the framing of his proposal. The memorandum came to me on May 27 and went on

3. Jones, *The Fifteen Weeks*, pp. 239–56. Forrest C. Pogue, *George C. Marshall: Education of a General* and *George C. Marshall: Ordeal and Hope, 1939–1943*, ed. Gordon Harrison (New York: Viking, 1963, 1969). Additional volumes in preparation.
4. Ellen Clayton Garwood, *Will Clayton, A Short Biography* (Austin: University of Texas Press, 1958), pp. 119–21.

at once to the General. Clayton began by stating: "It is now obvious that we have grossly underestimated the destruction to the European economy by the war." We could see the physical destruction but the effect of vast economic disruption and political, social, and psychological destruction from five years of Hitler's remaking of Europe into a war machine completely escaped us.

Europe was steadily deteriorating, the memorandum continued, "The political situation reflects the economic. . . . Millions of people in the cities are slowly starving." French grain acreage was twenty-five per cent under prewar and grain was fed to cattle. The peasant had nothing to buy with the deteriorating currency. The current annual balance-of-payments deficit of four areas alone —the United Kingdom, France, Italy, and the U.S.-U.K. zones of Germany—was five billion dollars for this subminimum standard of living.

To survive, Clayton wrote, Europe must have two and a half billion dollars annually of coal, bread grains, and shipping services until her own shipping and production should be rebuilt. Further study was unnecessary. The facts were well known. The problem was to organize our fiscal services and our own consumption so that enough could be made available out of our own vast production. This should be paid for out of taxes and not "by addition to debt."

According to the memorandum, Europe should have from us a grant of "6 or 7 billion dollars' worth of goods a year for three years . . . principally of coal, food, cotton, tobacco, shipping services," largely in surplus. With this help, the International Bank should enable European reconstruction to get under way. (This calculation of the role of the Bank and Fund and the composition of the aid turned out to be unrealistic and erroneous.)

The three-year grant should be "based on a European plan which the principal European nations, headed by the UK, France and Italy, should work out." (Clayton also recommended a European economic federation in which he was nearly a decade ahead of the Treaty of Rome.)

Other nations might help with surplus food and raw materials, Clayton concluded, "but we must avoid getting into another UNRRA. *The United States must run this show.*"

When Clayton sent this memorandum to me, he asked that a meeting be arranged to discuss it with the General. This I did for the next day, giving him the memorandum to read. Meanwhile Kennan's study, requested by General Marshall had come in. It was more cautious than Clayton's, dwelling more on difficulties and dangers—which were certainly there—than on the imperative need for action. It agreed that European countries must produce a plan for recovery but pointed out how difficult a task this would be with the Soviet Union in its present mood. When we met on May 28 we had both papers before us.

Will Clayton was one of the most powerful and persuasive advocates to whom I have listened. Both qualities came from his command of the subject and the depth of his conviction. What he said at the meeting added to his paper principally corroborative detail to illustrate the headlong disintegration of the highly complex industrial society of Europe, through the breakdown of interrelations between the industrial cities and the food-producing countryside. Millions of people would soon die, creating a chaos of bloodshed and disorder in doing so. To organize the great effort needed to prevent this disaster would take time, but it had to begin here and now. Surely the plan should be a European plan and come—or, at any rate, appear to come—from Europe. *But the United States must run the show.* And it must start running it now.

On this main point there was no debate. It would be folly, the General said, "to sit back and do nothing." His principal concern was whether any proposal we might make should be addressed to all Europe or to Western Europe only. We were agreed—Clayton, Benjamin Cohen, Kennan, Charles Bohlen, at that time a Special Assistant to the Secretary of State, and myself—that the United States should not assume the responsibility of dividing Europe. I pointed out that Russian obstruction in developing a European plan could be overcome not by requiring her agreement; what might be fatal to congressional support would be Russian support and demands, as Henry Wallace had been advocating, of up to fifty per cent of the benefits. Kennan suggested that we might blandly treat the Soviet Union as, like ourselves, a donor of raw materials. The matter was left inconclusive. The General cautioned sternly against leaks. A hint of a new request for vast funds would cause immediate and adverse action; the manner of the first approach must be carefully considered. As one looks back on it, he left us with very little to leak.

His concern about congressional reaction was borne out a few hours later. Leslie Biffle, Secretary to the Minority, had invited me to lunch in his office with about a dozen senators. The talk there, as my memorandum to General Marshall reported, convinced me that some discussion with Congress in the near future was a necessity. With Senator Brien McMahon of Connecticut taking the lead, they insisted that they should be told what the Administration had in mind, or, at least, what the problem was as we saw it. If we attempted to confront them with a *fait accompli,* they would refuse to vote grants or credits. I was urged to talk to the policy committee of the Democratic minority—which would have been a fatal mistake. I was convinced that the General should begin talks very soon about the great seriousness of the problems and, later on, make a speech about them, before suggesting any solutions.

General Marshall's Harvard Speech

The next day he mentioned to me a Harvard invitation to receive an honorary degree, which had been pending for a long time, said he would probably be asked to make a short speech, and asked whether this would be a good time to say something about Europe. I advised against it on the ground that commencement speeches were a ritual to be endured without hearing. Undeterred,

George C. Marshall at the Harvard University commencement where he delivered the speech which outlined the "Marshall Plan," June 5, 1947.
WIDE WORLD

he accepted the invitation and agreed to speak. Bohlen was asked
to draft something from the Kennan and Clayton memoranda. A
few days later Clayton and I saw the drafts, contributed our own
suggestions, and heard no more. The most difficult portions of the
speech were, obviously, to whom should the proposal be addressed
and what should the proposal be. Whether the General discussed
the speech with the President and, if so, what they said, I do not
know. It is hard to believe that they did not discuss it. It will also
surprise many that the Secretary of State went off to deliver so
momentous a speech with an incomplete text and never informed
the Department of its final form. I had to pry it out of Colonel
Marshall Carter at almost the last moment over the telephone. We
had the release ready not too long before General Marshall began
to speak at midafternoon on June 5, but he knew that the attention
paid to what he would say that day would not be affected by the
techniques of publicity.

The speech was short, simple, and altogether brilliant in its
statement of a purpose and a proposal adapted to the necessities of
his position. A little more than half of the speech, just over a
printed page, set forth the condition of Europe and the causes for
it. This came straight from the two Clayton memoranda.[5]

The statement of purpose was designed to win over the critics
of the Truman Doctrine both at home and abroad, who deprecated
its stress on the confrontation with the Soviet Union strategically
and ideologically. Yet it did this without leaving doubt that along
with real understanding of the problem went determined will to
resolve it. Three notes composed this chord:

1. Our policy is directed not against any country or doctrine but
against hunger, poverty, desperation, and chaos. Its purpose should be the
revival of a working economy in the world so as to permit the emergence
of political and social conditions in which free institutions can exist.

2. Such assistance, I am convinced, must not be on a piecemeal
basis as various crises develop. Any assistance that this Government
may render in the future should provide a cure rather than a mere
palliative.

3. Any government that is willing to assist in the task of recovery
will find full cooperation, I am sure, on the part of the United States
Government. Any government which maneuvers to block the recovery
of other countries cannot expect help from us. Furthermore, governments,
political parties, or groups which seek to perpetuate human misery in
order to profit therefrom politically or otherwise will encounter the opposition of the United States.[6]

5. For the complete text of Marshall's speech see Appendix 1, pp. 205–207.
6. *Department of State Bulletin*, Vol. XVI, June 15, 1947, p. 1160.

If General Marshall believed, which I am sure he did not, that the American people would be moved to so great an effort as he contemplated by as Platonic a purpose as combating "hunger, poverty, desperation, and chaos," he was mistaken. But he was wholly right in stating this as the American *governmental* purpose. I have probably made as many speeches and answered as many questions about the Marshall Plan as any man alive, except possibly Paul Hoffman, and what citizens and the representatives in Congress alike always wanted to learn in the last analysis was how Marshall aid operated to block the extension of Soviet power and the acceptance of Communist economic and political organization and alignment. Columnists and commentators might play with bloodless words and conceptions like projectors of silent moving pictures, but the bulk of their fellow citizens were unimpressed.

It was in the formulation of the "proposal" that the genius of General Marshall's statement stands out. It comprised six sentences, only one of which concerned what this country might do:

It is already evident that, before the United States Government can proceed much further in its efforts to alleviate the situation and help start the European world on its way to recovery, there must be some agreement among the countries of Europe as to the requirements of the situation and the part those countries themselves will take in order to give proper effect to whatever action might be undertaken by this Government.

It would be neither fitting nor efficacious for this Government to undertake to draw up unilaterally a program designed to place Europe on its feet economically.

This is the business of the Europeans.

The initiative, I think, must come from Europe.

The program should be a joint one, agreed to by a number of, if not all, European nations.

The role of this country should consist of friendly aid in the drafting of a European program and of later support of such a program so far as it may be practical for us to do so.[7]

Surely no sensible man could object to a suggestion that if the Europeans, all or some of them, could get together on a plan of what was needed to get them out of the dreadful situation depicted and how they proposed to go about it, we would take a look at their plan and see what aid we might practically give. However, it was more than possible that an imaginative European could go far with such a start. I made sure that at least one should be given his chance. Getting hold of my British friends, Miall, MacColl, and

7. *Ibid.*

Muggeridge, with whom a month before I had discussed the purpose of my Delta Council speech, I explained the full import of the Harvard one, asking that they cable or telephone the full text and have their editors send a copy to Ernest Bevin, the British Foreign Minister, with my estimate of its importance. This they did while Miall broadcast the story to Britain from Washington.

Bevin was quick to seize the opportunity that General Marshall had offered him. Some years later Bevin told me that after reading the speech William Strang, then Permanent Under Secretary of the Foreign Office, suggested inquiring through the British Embassy in Washington what specifically the Secretary of State had in mind. Mr. Bevin vetoed the suggestion. He would not, he said, pry into what General Marshall was thinking about; what he had said was good enough for Bevin. He got in touch at once with Georges Bidault, Foreign Minister of France. In two weeks' time they met with Russian Foreign Minister Vyacheslav Molotov in Paris to discuss how Europeans might devise a European recovery plan, its requirements, and the parts they would play in it. The tripartite aspect of the talks soon blew up. I have described the scene as Bevin told it to me: "It seems that Molotov has a bump on his forehead which swells when he is under emotional strain. The matter was being debated and Molotov had raised relatively minor questions or objections at various points, when a telegram was handed to him. He turned pale and the bump on his forehead swelled. After that, his attitude changed and he became much more harsh. . . . I suspect that Molotov must have thought that the instruction sent him was stupid; in any case, the withdrawal of the Russians made operations much more simple." [8]

On the next day, July 3, Bevin and Bidault issued a joint communiqué inviting twenty-two other European nations to send representatives to Paris to consider a recovery plan. (Czechoslovakia, which had at first agreed to attend, withdrew its acceptance after a visit to Moscow by Premier Klement Gottwald and poor Jan Masaryk,[9] the Foreign Secretary.) Once again General Marshall's judgment and his luck combined to produce the desired result.

I was to make one more official contribution to the Marshall Plan before my days in the Under Secretary's office in "New State" expired. Although members of Congress were now assured that

8. Harry B. Price, *The Marshall Plan and Its Meaning*, published under the auspices of the Governmental Affairs Institute (Ithaca: Cornell University Press, 1955), p. 28.
9. Following the Communist coup in Czechoslovakia in February 1948, Jan Masaryk was killed in a fall from his office on March 10, 1948. Whether he was pushed to his death or committed suicide is still debated, but without doubt his death was the result of the purge that followed the coup.

they were not to be confronted by some sudden and unexpected demand, the conviction was growing that in time they would, if the Europeans should do their part, be confronted with a very sizable one. How could they participate in the preparation of some preliminary defenses? Arthur Vandenberg began to feel for a method. General Marshall in the Harvard speech had suggested that one part of this country's role might be "friendly aid in the drafting of a European program." On June 14 in *The New York Times* William S. White reported Vandenberg's idea of a non-partisan commission at the highest level to advise coordination of our resources with foreign needs. I feared a tripartite monstrosity such as the proposed Commission on Organization of the Executive Branch of the Government (the Hoover Commission) to be appointed by the House, the Senate, and the President. It seemed to me of the greatest importance for the President to anticipate this move by appointing as soon as possible a committee of his own choosing, after consultation with leaders of Congress, and I asked General Marshall to urge the President to do so, which he did. Within an hour I would have a list of suggested committeemen representing all branches of American life.

After consultation with Clayton, Averell Harriman—then Secretary of Commerce and the prospective chairman of our committee—and a few in the Department, we soon got together an eminent, knowledgeable, and representative committee. On the afternoon of June 22 everything, including a press release, was ready for the President when we met in his upstairs study in the White House with a nonpartisan group that included Senators Vandenberg, Connally, Wallace White, and Barkley, and Secretaries Marshall, John Snyder of the Treasury, Clinton Anderson of Agriculture, and Julius A. Krug of Interior. I acted as recording secretary.

The President gave Vandenberg full credit for the suggestion, read off the committee members and their qualifications (which were impressive), and asked for suggestions. Vandenberg suggested former Senator Robert M. LaFollette, Jr., of Wisconsin, whom the President added to the list. After a pause, he told me to go out and release the appointment of the committee and the membership to the press. The group then went on to discuss a second group to assist Secretary Krug in a study of available raw material and basic potential production of such necessities as coal and steel here and abroad, and another under Chairman Edwin G. Nourse of the Council of Economic Advisers, to study the effect of this amount of foreign aid on the economy of the United States. By the time the meeting broke up, the Harriman Committee [10] was an established fact.

When the Economic Cooperation Act had been passed in March 1948,[11] President Truman said, in signing the Act on April 3, 1948, that few presidents had "had the opportunity to sign legislation of such importance," and, after commending the Congress for its cooperation and promptness, he continued:

Its passage is a striking manifestation of the fact that a bipartisan foreign policy can lead to effective action. It is even more striking in its proof that swift and vigorous action for peace is not incompatible with the full operation of our democratic process of discussion and debate. . . .

Our program of foreign aid is perhaps the greatest venture in constructive statesmanship that any nation has undertaken. It is an outstanding example of cooperative endeavor for the common good.

The Foreign Assistance Act is the best answer that this country can make in reply to the vicious and distorted misrepresentations of our efforts for peace which have been spread abroad by those who do not wish our efforts to succeed. This measure is America's answer to the challenge facing the free world today.

It is a measure for reconstruction, stability, and peace. Its purpose is to assist in the preservation of conditions under which free institutions can survive in the world. I believe that the determination of the American people to work for conditions of enduring peace throughout the world, as demonstrated by this act, will encourage free men and women everywhere, and will give renewed hope to all mankind that there will one day be peace on earth, good will among men.[12]

My Successor Is Chosen

General Marshall went about choosing my successor as he did other decisions—no meetings, no lists of names, no papers on desired qualifications. He thought about the question and came to a conclusion. What would I think, he asked me, of Robert A. Lovett? He had been Assistant Secretary of War for Air during the war and had gone back to his banking business in New York. We had known each other since Yale days. He had all the necessary requirements of mind, character, and Washington experience. Most importantly, that experience included years of working with Gen-

10. For the membership of the Committee, see *Department of State Bulletin*, Vol. XVII, October 5, 1947, p. 696.

11. The Economic Cooperation Act of 1948 (Public Law 472, 80th Congress, 62 Stat. 137), passed by the Senate March 14, 1948, by a vote of 65 to 7 and by the House of Representatives on March 31 by a vote of 329 to 74, provided for $5.3 billion for European recovery.

12. *Public Papers of the Presidents, Harry S. Truman, 1948* (Washington, U.S. Government Printing Office, 1964), p. 203.

eral Marshall under the severe pressures of wartime. He knew Europe well. I thought it an excellent idea.

When Bob Lovett's nomination went to the Senate, he was confirmed, on May 28, unanimously. This gave him time for a period and method of preparation that so far as I know is without parallel before or since—though why, it is hard to understand. For a month before he took over the Under Secretary's duties Lovett went through what might be called "on-job training." First he learned the organization and functioning of the Department and met its principal officers in the course of doing so. Then he sat beside me in my office or in the Secretary's, hearing all conversations, reading all papers, attending all meetings, and participating in all decisions. More and more I pushed him forward and withdrew myself. On Tuesday, July 1, 1947, he merely moved to my desk, thoroughly familiar with what was going across it.

III

EUROPEAN RECOVERY PROCEEDS AND SOVIET HOSTILITY INCREASES

THE JOINT EUROPEAN-AMERICAN efforts in 1947–48, which put the Marshall Plan (the European Recovery Plan) into effect, marked a turning point in the postwar history of Europe. The health of the Western European countries—economic, social, and political —began to improve apace. Both within this area and between it and North America, conceptions and practices of joint action on common problems, almost of necessity, became the norm. At the same time, and in some part caused by these developments, Soviet hostility to the United States and Western Europe grew more marked and more bitter. Almost since the end of the war our efforts to find solutions for the international control of nuclear energy, conventional armaments, and the rehabilitation of the late enemy states had ended in frustration and bitter propaganda battles.

In this country, also, the domestic scene threatened to degenerate from bipartisan foreign policy to bitter political warfare, as the opposition looked forward with confidence to ending, in the election of 1948, sixteen years of Democratic control of the White House. General Marshall's health made it clear that upon release from the hospital following his major operation he must retire to recuperate. The President fought on bravely seeking re-election, but only a few believed that his political life expectancy exceeded his current term of office. The surprise of the year was his defeat of Governor Thomas E. Dewey. Only little less surprising was the

President's announcement, two months later, of my nomination to succeed General Marshall. I took the oath of office the day after the inauguration, January 21, 1949.

The Expectation

The last year of President Truman's first term and his inaugural address at the beginning of his second seemed to give a clear enough clue to my opening tasks. Mr. Lovett and Senator Vandenberg, working together, had produced a unique prologue to a major innovation in American foreign policy. Even more basic, however, than the Vandenberg Resolution in bringing about this innovation was the Communist *coup d'état* in Prague in February 1948, and the Soviet move against our position in Germany, culminating in the blockade of Berlin that summer. These capped the growing tension in Europe and underlined Europe's insecurity. Nowhere was this more clearly shown than in the pause in economic recovery after the first surge ahead accompanying the repair of physical damage and the replenishment of inventories. Real advance could not be expected until a sense of security made possible a repatriation of capital. This was the impetus that moved the Vandenberg Resolution, adopted on June 11, 1948, by a vote of 64 to 4. It informed the President that the sense of the Senate was that the United States Government should pursue:

Progressive development of regional and other collective arrangements for individual and collective self-defense in accordance with the purposes, principles, and provisions of the Charter [of the United Nations].

Association of the United States, by constitutional process, with such regional and other collective arrangements as are based on continuous and effective self-help and mutual aid, and as affect its national security.[1]

Senator Vandenberg, the Vandenberg-Lovett-Marshall collaboration, and its product, the Vandenberg Resolution, made possible the North Atlantic Treaty. All too often the Executive, having sweated through the compromises of a difficult negotiation, had laid the resulting treaty before a quite detached, uninformed, and unresponsive Senate in which a minority could reject the Executive's agreement. On this occasion Senator Vandenberg took seriously and responsibly the word "advice" in the constitutional phrase giving the President power to enter into treaties "with the advice and consent of the Senate." By getting the Senate to give advice in advance of negotiation he got it to accept responsibility in

1. 94 *Congressional Record*, 80th Congress, 2nd Session, p. 7801.

advance of giving its consent to ratification. Equally important, he got the Senate to give good advice. Senators are a prolific source of advice, but most of it is bad. To accomplish so great an achievement requires serious and responsible leadership by the chairman of the Foreign Relations Committee. Sporadic brilliance of an intellectual dilettante will not suffice. The man may be a prima donna, but he will need solid competence and power as well as temperament.

During the summer of 1948 Mr. Lovett met with the ambassadors of Canada and the Brussels Pact countries.[2] They agreed on the need to go forward and on the general nature of the desired commitment. Discussions then broke off for work on drafts and the outcome of the American election.

Along with the treaty, the Department had been working with our allies on a number of other developments to strengthen Europe. A military assistance program would help them develop some military muscle. The Humphrey Committee report (its chairman, George Humphrey, was later General Eisenhower's Treasury Secretary) on reducing the dismantling of German factories for reparations (mostly to the Soviet Union) recommended that this punitive program be brought more in line with the European Recovery Plan. Trizonal unification and currency reform had brought a new era in German-allied relations to the verge of achievement, with a new government by Germans in the western zones and a new relation between it and allied authority. Finally, the Defense Establishment pressed for a shift of responsibilities for this relation from its own shoulders to those of the State Department. All these seemed to be the fields in which I would be working.

The Unexpected

Hardly had we started on an orderly plan of work when the disorderly and uncontrollable world around us took over and moved us into it in an unexpected way. American ideas had changed greatly in the four years since the harsh occupation policy laid down in the April 1945 Joint Chiefs of Staff directive (JCS 1067) to General Eisenhower and his deputy for military government of the American zone, Major General Lucius D. Clay. This triune document had resulted from the uneasy blending of State, War, and Treasury (Morgenthau Plan) ideas. Its basic objectives were (1) to bring home to the Germans that they could not escape the

2. Britain, France, Belgium, the Netherlands, and Luxembourg.

suffering they had brought upon themselves; (2) to be firm, aloof, and discourage all fraternization; (3) to prevent Germany's ever becoming a threat to the peace—by eliminating nazism and militarism, apprehending and punishing war criminals, controlling Germany's capacity to make war, and preparing her for eventual democratic government; (4) to enforce reparations and restitution and the return of war prisoners; (5) to control German economy to achieve these objectives and prevent any higher standard of living than in neighboring nations. From the outset General Clay and his organization believed JCS 1067 to be unworkable.

Secretary of State James F. Byrnes had joined in this view as soon as Stalin's offensive against the West demonstrated the failure of the Potsdam program. A speech by Secretary Byrnes in Stuttgart on September 6, 1946, had marked a strong swing away from earlier policies. Germany, he said, should not be turned into an economic poorhouse; rather, we favored economic unification and, under proper safeguards, giving German people throughout Germany "primary responsibility for the running of their own affairs." [3] These ideas had gotten another push in December when Byrnes and Bevin announced the economic union of the British and American zones. "Bizonia" had gone into effect on May 29, 1947, when the new administration was set up in Bonn, allowing Germans to run their own economy subject to a bipartite control office. The French, in one of their noncooperative moods, had refused for the time being to join their zone with the others.

In the United States I had made my Cleveland, Mississippi, speech on May 8, 1947, pointing out that the world would need in that year goods from the United States to the extent of sixteen billion dollars, for half of which no means of payment was discernible, and adding: "The fourth thing we must do in the present situation is to push ahead with the reconstruction of those two great workshops of Europe and Asia—Germany and Japan—upon which the ultimate recovery of the two continents so largely depends." [4] On June 5 General Marshall made his speech at Harvard. Within a month a new and more liberal directive issued from Washington (JCS 1779 of July 11, 1947), aimed at the attainment of a self-sustaining German economy at the earliest practicable date. A U.K.-U.S. bizonal agreement in August had permitted industrial production in Germany at the 1936 rate, an increase of one-third. At this evidence of movement to a new policy toward our former enemy, France during late August had shown cautious

3. *Department of State Bulletin*, Vol. XV, September 15, 1946, p. 499.
4. *Ibid.*, Vol. XVI, May 8, 1947, p. 994.

willingness to add its zone to the other two in pursuit of it. By November the three allies were able to present a solid front to the Russians at the London meeting of the Council of Foreign Ministers.

From then on events moved swiftly to crisis.[5] Soviet action to divide Europe into hostile camps accelerated as Congress debated the European Recovery Program. By Communist coup in February 1948 Czechoslovakia was added to Soviet satellites. On March 17 the Western European allies—the United Kingdom, France, The Netherlands, Belgium, and Luxembourg—signed the Brussels Defense Pact. Three days later the Soviet representative walked out of the Allied Control Council in Berlin, and on April 1 Soviet authorities imposed restrictions on allied (but not German) rail and road traffic between the western zones and Berlin. The allies responded with the "little airlift" to supply, at this time, only their troops in Berlin.

In the meantime a six-nation negotiating group—the three occupying West Germany and the three Benelux governments—went to work on plans to strengthen Germany against developing Russian pressure. Preliminary recommendations in late March, as the Foreign Assistance Act of 1948 became law, provided for economic coordination of the three zones for association in the European Recovery Program, and broad agreement that a federal form of government was best adapted to eventual German unity. Final recommendations, announced in June from London, covered political institutions for the West Germans with "the minimum requirements of occupation and control." To reassure the French, provision was made for the control of the Ruhr and the continuance of supreme allied authority.

These recommendations and the much-needed currency reform for West Germany (though, at this time, not for Berlin, still regarded as under four-power control) triggered the final break with the Soviet Union in Germany. The calendar for June 1948 shows its precipitous course.

June 7 London recommendations announced.

June 11 Soviet Union stops rail traffic between Berlin and West for two days.

June 12 Soviets stop traffic on a highway bridge for "repairs."

June 16 Soviet representative leaves Kommandatura (four-power military control in Berlin).

5. For a first-hand account of the crisis in Germany in 1948, see Lucius D. Clay, *Decision in Germany* (New York: Doubleday & Company, 1950), Chapters 18–20.

June 18 Western powers announce currency reform in West Germany.

June 23 Soviet Union orders its own currency system for East Germany and all Berlin.

Western powers extend West German currency reform to West Berlin.

June 24 Soviet Union imposes full blockade on Berlin.

Western powers stop freight from combined zones to Soviet zone.

After a difficult and tense period in which General Clay's calm determination steadied our own government and held our allies together, the Western powers settled down to build up the airlift, tighten their own countermeasures against the Soviet Union, and fight the propaganda battle in the Paris sessions of the United Nations, which proved unable to ameliorate the situation. Soviet authorities, meanwhile, though belligerent in words, were careful to avoid physical interference with the airlift. The combined lift increased from seventy thousand tons in June and July 1948 to two hundred fifty thousand tons in May 1949.

General Clay and his Political Adviser, Ambassador Robert D. Murphy, believed and advised at the time that we should inform the Soviet authorities that on a specific date we would "move in an armed convoy which would be equipped with the engineering material to overcome the technical difficulties which the Soviet representatives appeared unable to solve. . . . In my [Clay's] view the chances of such a convoy being met by force with subsequent developments of hostilities were small. I was confident that it would get through to Berlin and that the highway blockade would be ended. . . . I shall always believe that the convoy would have reached Berlin." [6] The President is reported to have said that if the Joint Chiefs of Staff would approve this recommendation in writing, he would add his approval, too. However, neither they nor the Secretary of State nor the governments of Britain and France would approve. General Clay's confidence that an armed convoy on the ground would not be stopped was not based on belief that the Russians could not stop it but that they would not. "But," Murphy has written, "the National Security Council did not share our confidence that the Russians were bluffing." Clay, however, did not write that the Russians were bluffing, but that he believed that the "chances of such a convoy being met by force with subsequent

6. For sources of quotations in this paragraph, see Clay, *Decision in Germany*, pp. 374, 359; Robert D. Murphy, *Diplomat Among Warriors* (New York: Doubleday & Company, 1964), p. 317; Harry S. Truman, *Years of Trial and Hope*, Vol. II, *Memoirs* (New York: Doubleday & Company, 1956), p. 125.

developments of hostilities were small." President Truman reports asking him what "risks would be involved" if we tried armed road convoys and receiving the reply that "he thought the initial reaction of the Russians would be to set up road blocks. Our engineers would be able to clear such obstacles, provided there was no Russian interference, but the next step the Russians would take, General C' ·v thought, would be to meet the convoys with armed force." Indeed, when in April 1948 General Clay had tested a Russian order forbidding allied military trains to go to Berlin without Russian inspection, he had had a revealing experience. "The train," he tells us, "progressed some distance into the Soviet Zone but was finally shunted off the main line by electrical switching to a siding, where it remained for a few days until it withdrew rather ignominiously. *It was clear the Russians meant business.*" (Italics supplied.) The train crew would have been able to clear the obstacle by turning the switch, "provided there was no Russian interference." But since the Russians "meant business," there would have been interference. The question then would have been who would have shot first and what would have been the response to shooting. In April General Clay—I think wisely—did not attempt to find out.

Having had experience in counseling more than one President in problems about access to Berlin, I have never thought it wise to base our own action on a bluff or to assume that the Russians are doing so. Neither side wishes to be driven by miscalculation to general hostilities or humiliation. Therefore initial moves should not, if it is possible to avoid it, be equivocal—as a small ground probe would be—or reckless—as a massive one would be. So, although I was a mere observer in 1948, the choice of the airlift seemed to me the right one. It showed firm intention to insist upon a right, plain beyond question, and gave the Russians the choice of either not interfering or of initiating an air attack, which might have brought upon them a devastating response. To say, as Murphy has done, that the decision to use the "airlift was a surrender of our hard-won rights in Berlin," [7] seems to me silly. One can as well say that to put one's hands up at the command of an armed bandit is to surrender one's hard-won right to keep them down. One regains it, as we have regained and are now enjoying our hard-won rights to Berlin.

In January 1949, Kingsbury Smith, European General Manager of the International News Service (a Hearst organization), had filed with the Soviet Foreign Office four questions addressed to Stalin. This was common procedure. Sometimes questions were

7. Murphy, *Diplomat Among Warriors*, p. 321.

answered, if Stalin could see some advantage in doing so; more often they were ignored. Mr. Smith's, however, were answered within a few days, and the answers created a press sensation. On the day of this entirely unexpected development a small group discussed them with me in the Department and I took our conclusions to the President.

We judged the episode to be a cautious signal from Moscow. The significant fact was that in answering a question on ending the blockade, Stalin had not mentioned the stated Russian reason for it—the new West German currency. The signal, we thought, told us that Moscow was ready to raise the blockade for a price. The price would be too high if it required abandonment of tripartite plans for the allied zones of Germany, in which case the maneuver could be changed into a propaganda offensive against hard-won allied unity on German policy. I asked permission to signal back through a bland and relaxed press conference that we had gotten the message and then to follow this with a secret inquiry into just what Moscow was prepared to do. The President agreed, and agreed further that our purpose and operation should be kept close and secret.

The press conference took place on February 2,[8] on its regular day of the week, Wednesday, to rob it of any atmosphere of unusual significance. My remarks, though carefully thought out, were an "extemporaneous," patient examination of a press stunt built up out of all proportion to its intrinsic importance. No man of conscience, I said, should tamper with the world's hopes for peace by raising or lowering them as a move in any maneuver. In such an attitude we would examine what had been said.

I confessed myself puzzled by the first question Kingsbury Smith had put to Stalin—whether the Soviet Government would consider joining with the United States Government in declaring that neither had any intention of going to war with the other—and by Stalin's answer that "the Soviet Government would be prepared to consider the issuance of such a declaration." Both governments were already bound by the most explicit provisions of the United Nations treaty to "refrain . . . from the threat or use of force against" one another. Surely Stalin's willingness to consider saying it again was not news.

Then Stalin, when asked whether the Soviet Union would be willing to join with us in such measures as gradual disarmament to carry out such a declaration, had answered that "naturally" it would. "Now 'naturally,' " I said, meant " 'in the nature of things' "

8. *Department of State Bulletin,* Vol. XX, February 13, 1949, pp. 192–94

and the nature of things in the past three years would not have encouraged the expectation of much cooperation. Then I reviewed Russian obstruction in Europe since the war.

Would Stalin, he had next been asked by Mr. Smith, confer with President Truman about the declaration? His answer was ". . . there is no objection to a meeting." Clearly not. The President, I pointed out, had often invited Marshal Stalin to Washington but he would not come. Presidents Roosevelt and Truman had three times traveled halfway around the world to meet him. Was it worth doing again for so limited a purpose? We had repeatedly said that we could not discuss the affairs of others in their absence.

Finally we came to the only question Mr. Smith had asked relating to an issue between the Soviet Union and the allies: Would the USSR be willing to remove restrictions on traffic to Berlin if the United States, Britain, and France agreed not to establish a separate western German state pending a Council of Foreign Ministers meeting to discuss the German problem as a whole? Stalin answered that it would, upon acceptance by the allies of the condition stated in the question and upon their removing their counterrestrictions against traffic to the Soviet zone.

Stalin's second point, I said, raised no problem since the allies had "always stated that if the Soviet Government permits normal communications with and within Berlin their counter measures will, of course, be lifted." The important point, however, was that the very terms of the question made the answer unresponsive to the facts. The reasons given for the blockade had been technical transportation difficulties and the currency reform. At one time the question of postponing German governmental arrangements had been raised but had been abandoned by the Soviet Union as a condition to raising the blockade. The Western governments, I said, "have stressed, repeated again and again to the Soviet Union, that their agreements in regard to Western Germany do not in any sense preclude agreements on Germany as a whole . . . [and] are . . . purely provisional pending such agreement on Germany as a whole." For months, I continued, the "Western powers have tried patiently and persistently to solve the difficulties . . . put forward . . . as the reasons for the blockade," but Soviet authorities would not discuss them.

Then I signaled our message: "There are many ways in which a serious proposal by the Soviet Government . . . could be made. . . . I hope you [the press] will not take it amiss if I point out that if I on my part were seeking to give assurance of seriousness of purpose I would choose some other channel than the channel of a press interview."

This press conference aptly illustrates the difficulties faced by an open society in conducting diplomatic interchanges with a closed one through the press. Stalin need answer only such written questions as he chose to answer. He permitted no cross-examination. Whatever the correspondent cabled home went through a censor. The Secretary, however, spoke and was cross-examined *viva voce*. In this case I had two purposes—to play down Stalin's initiative in order to avoid premature hardening of the Russian position and to signal the Russians that if they wanted serious discussion they should use a more private channel. Continuation of a public one would be interpreted as an indication of propaganda purposes only. When I finished what I wanted to say for my purposes, able correspondents tried to push me further into saying what they wanted for their purposes, which unfortunately were incompatible with mine. They were entitled to try, but not to succeed.

What significance, they wanted to know, should be attached to Stalin's failure to mention the German-currency issue in his answers? If expressed, our view at the time would have been that it had quite possibly a good deal of significance, although it could have been a trap. The press could and would write their own ideas on the subject, but for me to disclose any of my own could only do harm. So I retreated behind the always reasonable refusal to speculate. The second question came more under the heading of having fun with the Secretary, trying to coax him onto the quicksand. Had my comment on the first question and answer been altogether ingenuous? Wasn't a joint declaration by the United States and the Soviet Union not to go to war with each other something different from the United Nations treaty? Suppose Kingsbury Smith had asked me that question—how would I have answered it? It was a good try, but irrelevant. Years later in response to a similar question, I recalled a politician from the Eastern Shore of Maryland who had got rid of a red-hot roast oyster in my partner's dining room with the ejaculation, "A damned fool would have swallowed that!" This time I merely refused to argue the merits of my remarks.

The Jessup-Malik Talks

A few days later we followed up on the press conference. Ambassador at Large Philip C. Jessup came to Washington from New York to talk with the Department's Counselor, Charles E. (Chip) Bohlen, and me rather than telephoning, telegraphing, or writing. We concluded that a highly secret, casual approach to the Russians could better be made by Jessup at the United Nations than through the embassy in Moscow or by the Department to the Russian Embassy. Fewer persons would be involved and those who were—Philip Jessup and Soviet Ambassador to the United Nations Jacob Malik—could act in purely personal and unofficial capacities. So it was agreed that Jessup when next he saw Malik should ask, as a matter of personal curiosity, whether the omission of any reference to the monetary reform in the Stalin answers was significant. An occasion to do so came as they walked into a Security Council meeting on February 15. Malik did not know the answer. Jessup suggested that if Malik learned anything about the matter, Jessup would be interested to know.

A month later Malik asked Jessup to call at his New York office, and told him that the omission was not accidental. The currency question was important, he said, but it could be discussed at a meeting of the Council of Foreign Ministers. Did that mean, asked Jessup, after the lifting of the blockade? Malik had not been asked to ask that question, he said, to which Jessup replied, "Why don't you ask it now?" Less than a week later, on March 21, the answer came back that if a definite date for the foreign ministers' meetings could be set the blockade could be lifted before the meetings took place. It was now Malik's turn to ask a question. Would we hold up preparations for a West German government until after the meetings? As instructed, Jessup answered that we expected to continue preparations, but since they could not be completed for some time they would be of no moment—that is, if the Russians really wanted to get on with the Council of Foreign Ministers meetings. This caused a great deal of talk, but Jessup refused to waver from our simple logic.

The time had come to tell the British and French what was going on. Foreign Ministers Ernest Bevin and Robert Schuman were due in Washington in two weeks for the signing of the North Atlantic Treaty and important talks about Germany. The President, who had been kept closely in touch and was delighted at his Administration's ability to conduct a professional diplomatic maneuver, authorized Jessup to inform his British and French colleagues at the United Nations—Sir Alexander Cadogan and Jean Michel Henri Chauvel, both experienced diplomats—of his private and personal explorations with Malik. Although the Quai d'Orsay's insecurity continued to be proverbial, its leaks were usually to the Russians. In this case these leaks might only give added assurance in Moscow of our seriousness as evidenced by our secrecy. The President also authorized me to continue to hold within our small group all knowledge of our feeler. Secrecy was of the utmost importance.

Meeting with Bevin and Schuman

Bevin and Schuman, neither of whom I had met before, arrived in Washington on March 31 and stayed a week. In that week began warm friendships, which grew through the all too few years left to both of them and, I believe, benefited far more than the individuals who shared them. Never were two men more different than these in appearance, temperament, and background. Bevin, short and stout, with broad nose and thick lips, looked more suited for the roles he had played earlier in life than for diplomacy. The child of a servant girl from western England and an unknown father, he had gone to work as a trucker after a few years of schooling. Moving on to a career as a labor leader and then to the top of the labor movement, on the way he organized the giant Transport and General Workers' Union and, with others, led the general strike of 1926. When Churchill became the hard-pressed wartime Prime Minister he drafted Bevin, whose steel he had felt from the government side in the general strike, into the War Cabinet for the heavy task of Minister of Labour. Bevin never became, like his two immediate successors, Herbert Morrison and Anthony Eden, "a House of Commons man"; he was more at home in the tougher atmosphere of the Trades Union Congress. When the Labour Party came to power in 1945, Bevin hoped for the Exchequer, but Prime Minister Clement R. Attlee, husbanding his assets, chose Hugh Dalton and put Bevin in the Foreign Office.

Never has a Foreign Secretary been more beloved by his often formidable staff. Bevin knew his mind and his limitations. He could lead and learn at the same time, qualities much appreciated by a disciplined and professional Foreign Service. Soon he became absorbed in his work and often seemed to commune with the spirits of his predecessors with an informality that might have surprised them. One day he said to me, "Last night I was readin' some papers of old Salisbury. 'E had a lot of sense." He used to chuckle admiringly over "old Palmerston," too. George III, that much-painted monarch who gazed down from a panel behind Bevin's desk, might not have appreciated the Foreign Secretary's view that if the monarch had not been so stupid the United States might not have been so strong and, hence, so able to come to Britain's rescue in the war and after it.

Schuman, slender, stooped, bald, with long nose, surprised and shy eyes and smile, might have been a painter, musician, or scholar rather than a lawyer, member of parliament, former Premier of France who had put the Communists out of the Government. He had grown up and been educated for the law in Metz under German rule, was an intellectual, and broadly read in both French and German literature. His humor was quick, gentle, and ironic; Bevin's, broad and hearty. The Quai d'Orsay did not give Schuman the support that Bevin got from the Foreign Office. It was deeply divided by strong personalities—Hervé Alphand, Maurice Couve de Murville, Alexandre Parodi, Maurice Schumann—and the victim of conspiratorial habits left over from the war and the resistance. This made for delays in negotiation with Schuman, who continually had to watch his flanks and rear and his communications with Paris.

Schuman's knowledge of English was always a source of amusement to me and often of confusion to him in our meetings. He spoke it haltingly and preferred to speak in French and use an interpreter. However, he could understand English if the words came through in recognizable sounds. Bevin's West Country speech, Morrison's cockney, and Anthony Eden's Eton-Oxford quite baffled him. However, to my embarrassment he not only understood me but explained that this was due to my speaking slowly and clearly. One evening in New York we put his English to the test at Cole Porter's *Kiss Me Kate*. He recognized the plot of *The Taming of the Shrew* and loved the music, but the intrusion of the gangster theme threw him off the trail, as well it might.

Both Bevin and Schuman held firm political convictions growing out of the tragic experience of Europe in this century; both saw the menace of communism and of the imperialism of the Soviet state; both believed unshakably in the essential nexus of Western Europe and North America to maintain a balance of power and, with it, peace. Schuman, however, went further, and as a man of the border country between France and Germany, believed like Lincoln in reconciliation after strife and in unity.

My affection for both of these men became very great, but my relations with each developed differently. Bevin soon became "Ernie," while I became to him "me lad." Life with Ernie was gay and turbulent, for his temper could build up as suddenly as a summer storm, and could flash and thunder as noisily, then disappear as the sun broke through it. Schuman always remained "M. Schuman" or "M. le Président"—since a Premier was President of the Council of Ministers—while with me he always used formal address. Our terms of office almost coincided, his beginning in July 1948 and ending in January 1953. Bevin came earlier to the Foreign Office, but resigned, and subsequently died, in 1951.

It was my good fortune during my time in office to work with colleagues from other countries who inspired both respect and affection—Sir Winston Churchill, Anthony Eden, later Lord Avon, and Oliver Franks, later Lord Franks, of Britain; Jean Monnet of France; Alcide de Gasperi of Italy; Dirk Stikker of the Netherlands; Halvard Lange of Norway; Konrad Adenauer of Germany; Lester Pearson and Hume Wrong of Canada; Sir Owen Dixon and Richard Casey of Australia; Antonio Espinosa de los Monteros of Mexico; Walther Moreira Salles of Brazil; Shigeru Yoshida of Japan. Since the best environment for diplomacy is found where mutual confidence between governments exists, relationships of respect and affection between the individuals who represent them furnish a vitally important aid to it.

Our first week with Bevin and Schuman in April 1949 was one of rarely equaled achievement. Its announced purpose was the final approval and signing of the North Atlantic Treaty. We three also agreed on our governments' positions for ending the Berlin blockade, on the Military Assistance Program operation, and on a plan for a German government in the western zones and its relations to the allied occupation authorities, which will be gone into later. First we went over in detail with Schuman and Bevin the Jessup-Malik talks and discussed whether, and if so how, to push the Russians farther. We all three saw the danger in allowing Stalin to edge his way into the incomplete and delicate negotiations among us regarding our relations among ourselves and with the Germans in our zones, which could lead to disunity among us and no progress in lifting the blockade. The greatest danger of disunity lay in any postponement of our tripartite preparations together and with the Germans. If the blockade was lifted and the Council of Foreign Ministers promptly convened, it would soon be apparent whether the Russians were serious about any plans for Germany as a whole acceptable to the three. My own view was that, if the council meeting failed, the blockade would not be reimposed. Stalin was lifting it because as a means to his end—allied withdrawal from Berlin—it had failed and was hurting him. He would not walk back into the trap.

We agreed that the Jessup-Malik exploration was the best method to pursue and that the support of the three ministers should now be thrown behind Jessup's position. He was given a short statement, which he read to Malik on April 5, to the effect that the three ministers understood that only two points were under discussion—simultaneously lifting the blockade and counter-blockade, and fixing a date for a meeting of the Council of Foreign Ministers. They wished to be sure that these two points were not conditioned upon any other point. If this was clear, Jessup pointed out, no question of "postponement" of any preparations for a German government in the western zones arose. Malik insisted that the currency problem must appear on any agenda. Since it had been a matter of discussion for nearly a year, Jessup saw no problem.

While Malik was awaiting instructions from Moscow, the week with Schuman and Bevin saw almost prodigies of agreement on Germany (to which we shall return) and the signing of the North Atlantic Treaty. These events impressed Moscow that Western Europe, from which the Russians had withdrawn, was getting along well without them. Before the French and British ministers left Washington, we arranged that liaison among us on the blockade could be maintained through our representatives at the United Nations.

Agreement to Lift the Blockade

On April 10 the Russians were still trying to maneuver a cessation of preparations for a West German government. Malik told Jessup that Andrei Y. Vishinsky, the Soviet Minister of Foreign Affairs, understood that no such government would be established before or during the sessions of the Council of Foreign Ministers. Jessup had, of course, said nothing of the sort and made this clear.

The difficult of multiparty diplomacy now appeared. The President approved a strong message to Malik in which the three ministers backed Jessup's position, but we could not get clearance from London. I urged upon Bevin the importance of pressing the Russians and, if necessary, taking some public action before they did. What we got was a leak out of London about the talks. This required an account of our own, which ended with this sentence: "If the present position of the Soviet Government is as stated in the Tass Agency release as published in the American press, the way appears clear for a lifting of the blockade and a meeting of the Council of Foreign Ministers." A few more weeks of jockeying among Washington, London, and Moscow were necessary to convince the Russians that there was no use delaying further.

While waiting for Vishinsky's unconditional agreement, we worked out with our allies important points of procedure. The Conference of Foreign Ministers should meet in Paris on May 23, the blockade having been lifted not less than ten days before. Preliminary talks with British and French representatives on a joint position would begin on May 9 and be completed by the three ministers on May 21 and 22 in Paris. The agenda should not fix the order in which items must be discussed *and* disposed of; agreement would be reached on individual points only after discussion of all. Details of lifting restrictions would be reached locally after discussion with General Clay. After the blockade had been lifted we would apply to the United Nations to have this item dropped from the Security Council agenda.

On May 4 unconditional agreement was reached, and it was announced the next day in a four-power communiqué.[9] All restrictions imposed since March 1, 1948, would be removed on May 12, 1949. Eleven days afterward, on May 23, 1949, a meeting of the Council of Foreign Ministers would be convened in Paris to consider questions relating to Germany and problems arising out of the situation in Berlin, including also the question of currency in Berlin. The day was proclaimed a legal holiday and a day of rejoicing in Berlin. I paid grateful tribute to all those who through operation of the airlift had made this achievement possible. Great as it was, however, it had not solved the German problem. It put us, I warned, "again in the situation in which we were before the blockade was imposed." Whether a solution could be reached in Paris would depend upon Russian willingness not to retard the progress the Western powers had made in their efforts to make West Germany a peaceful and constructive member of the community of free nations in Europe.

My own view was that the airlift had been a success, but had not ended the Russian campaign. That would be continued at the foreign ministers' meetings. With the blockade a demonstrated failure, Stalin had raised it to carry on the war against a West German government by political means. Until the council session was over we could not judge the net effect of the attempt at coercion by the use of force and the threat to use more. I did not expect the Council of Foreign Ministers to accomplish more than an uneasy *modus vivendi* with the Russians.

Reflections on Soviet Diplomacy

The history of the Berlin blockade is so typical a demonstration of Soviet political values and diplomatic method that it has been worth more than usual attention to detail. It shows the extreme sensitivity of Soviet authorities to developments in Germany and an almost equal lack of judgment in reacting to them. We were to see this again in 1952 when further steps would be taken

9. *Department of State Bulletin*, Vol. XX, May 15, 1949, p. 631.

by the West toward ending the occupation and toward a new association of Germany with NATO; again in 1955 when the actual admission of Germany was proposed; and once again in 1963 when closer association in nuclear planning was under consideration.

On all these occasions the same clumsy diplomacy resulted: an offer to abandon a long and bitterly held Soviet position was made on condition of allied abandonment of its proposed innovations. When this was firmly refused, the Soviet Union abandoned its own long-held position in the hope of dividing the allies or seducing the Germans. In 1952 this took the form of threats to Bonn if it should sign the 1952 agreements and offers if it should not; in 1955, of signing the long-delayed Austrian State Treaty and the reunification of Austria as an earnest of what Germany might get by declining to join NATO; in 1963, the nuclear-test ban as a means of staving off a multilateral force. What one may learn from these experiences is that the Soviet authorities are not moved to agreement by negotiation—that is, by a series of mutual concessions calculated to move parties desiring agreement closer to an acceptable one. Theirs is a more primitive form of political method. They cling stubbornly to a position, hoping to force an opponent to accept it. When and if action by the opponent demonstrates the Soviet position to be untenable, they hastily abandon it —after asking and having been refused an unwarranted price—and hastily take up a new position, which may or may not represent a move toward greater mutual stability.

Sir William Hayter has admirably summed up the Russian idea of negotiating:

Negotiation with the Russians does occur, from time to time, but it requires no particular skill. The Russians are not to be persuaded by eloquence or convinced by reasoned arguments. They rely on what Stalin used to call the proper basis of international policy, the calculation of forces. So no case, however skilfully deployed, however clearly demonstrated as irrefutable, will move them from doing what they have previously decided to do; the only way of changing their purpose is to demonstrate that they have no advantageous alternative, that what they want to do is not possible. Negotiations with the Russians are therefore very mechanical; and they are probably better conducted on paper than by word of mouth.[10]

10. *London Observer,* October 2, 1960.

IV

THE NORTH ATLANTIC TREATY:
AN OPEN COVENANT OPENLY
ARRIVED AT

On January 24, 1949, the President received me for the first of
the two, and sometimes three, meetings that for the next four
years we usually had alone each week. The two subjects discussed
were the current ambassadorial negotiations on the North Atlantic
Treaty text and his views about the Point Four (technical assistance) program. In the light of his guidance my first two press
conferences took up these two subjects.

Problems of Negotiation

1. *The Press* · What I tried to do in the press conferences was
give the men who covered the State Department a somewhat
broader view of the purpose and significance of these great policy
decisions than most of them had. With some distinguished excep-
tions, such as Paul Ward of the *Baltimore Sun* and John Hightower
of the Associated Press, they were inclined to bring to the reporting
of foreign affairs the same nose for controversial spot news that they
had learned to look for on the City Hall and police-court beats.
This did the country and their readers a disservice. In reporting
news about the North Atlantic Treaty they tended to speculate on
what countries might or might not be invited to sign it, what
territory it might cover, what commitments might be made. None
of these matters was ripe for decision. What I hoped to get them
to discuss were the dangers the treaty was aimed to meet, how

they could be met or avoided, the relation of the treaty to other measures contemplated—in other words, the place of the treaty in the developing strategy of the West. I made the same effort to enlighten reporting on the Point Four program. What most of my hearers would have much preferred would have been comments on the attacks made on these measures by their opponents. That would be news!

2. *The Parties* · My education on past discussions about the treaty text was taken in hand by those of Mr. Lovett's assistants who had participated in them—Charles Bohlen, John Hickerson, Theodore Achilles, Dean Rusk, and Ernest Gross. When the sessions resumed in February, I found myself working with a group of ambassadors whom I had known well for so long that we were truly—and not spuriously—on a first-name basis. The original group was small—Oliver Franks of Britain, Hume Wrong of Canada, Henri Bonnet of France, Eelco van Kleffens of the Netherlands, Robert Silvercruys of Belgium, and Minister Hugues Le Gallais of Luxembourg. Wilhelm Morgenstierne of Norway joined us on March 4. The Wrong-Acheson friendship went back over two generations. His father had been at the University of Toronto with mine, and Mrs. Wrong's father, Professor Hutton, had taught them both. Wilhelm Morgenstierne and I had first worked together twenty-eight years before; all the others had been colleagues of mine for many years. We talked easily and frankly. To preserve secrecy and the integrity of communications systems, reports of meetings were transmitted through our embassies to the various foreign offices.

3. *The Congress* · At our first meeting on February 8 I pointed out the unwisdom of our trying to move any faster with a text than I could move in my discussions with Senators Connally and Vandenberg, since agreement would mean little unless it carried senatorial opinion with it. In fact, I had already started with the senators on February 3 and had three more meetings with them during the month, and one with a group from the House Committee on Foreign Affairs. Three issues engaged both the ambassadors and the legislators: Should the treaty deal with more than military security? What nations should be signatories of it? What commitments should it contain? In general, the ambassadors wished to push further than the senators were prepared to follow. It was therefore most important to keep meetings with both groups moving along concurrently. I was like a circus performer riding two

horses—for one to move ahead of the other would mean a nasty fall. Safety required use of the ambassadors to urge on the senators, and the senators to hold back the ambassadors.

The early drafts, the senators thought, went too far on all three issues. The first was the Canadian proposal of Article 2, which got us into cultural, economic, and social cooperation. The senators were strongly opposed. We had all just been through a punishing experience. On February 2 I had been before the Senate committee doing my best to support agreements that came out of the Bogotá Conference attended by General Marshall. The Senate would have none of them. The agreements announced sweeping alleged human rights to education, the good life, welfare, and so on, reminiscent of a good many UN resolutions but which to Senator Walter George and others posed serious constitutional complications in federal-state relationships. Our senators saw Article 2 threatening our treaty with the same danger for no important benefit. I agreed, and proceeded to redraft the article toward the expression of desired goals. Even so defused, Article 2 has continued to bedevil NATO. Lester Pearson continually urged the council to set up committees of "wise men" to find a use for it, which the "wise men" continually failed to do.

4. *New Members* · Regarding membership, the original intention of the negotiating group (Belgium, Canada, France, Luxembourg, the Netherlands, the United Kingdom, and the United States) was to work out a text and then consider what other countries might be asked to join with us in signing it. Before the text was completed, however, other countries became interested and made inquiries. The first of these was Norway; soon afterward came two other Scandinavian countries, Denmark and Iceland, and then Italy from the Mediterranean. On February 7 Halvard Lange, the Norwegian Foreign Minister, arrived in Washington on a voyage of discovery. He came neither to apply for membership nor to ask for other help, but to learn what we were planning to do and to discuss Norway's problems. His visit set off a barrage of bluster and threats from Moscow that did not disturb him in the least. From our first meeting I found him a most delightful and impressive man. A member of the Norwegian resistance during the war, he had been caught—due to his own carelessness, he told me—and imprisoned under death sentence. For months he never knew whether footsteps approaching his cell were those of a guard bringing the inevitable vegetable soup and bread or a summons to face a firing squad. Eventually he was transferred to Dachau. This

substitution, he said, of the grave risk of death for the near certainty of it was a change from hell to heaven. He emerged broken in health, but with his courage, high intelligence, and gift of humor unimpaired.

In Lange's view, experience had taught Norway that neutrality was an illusion. She must find security in association with others. Association in the United Nations, once so hopeful, had in recent years lost its promise. The Swedish proposal of a Scandinavian security treaty had much to be said for it, but Swedish insistence that its members must not seek other association would leave the group too weak to afford its members much protection. He asked both specific and general questions about our proposed treaty, for the purpose of advising his Government upon his return. Would the territorial integrity of signatories be guaranteed? Would they have priority in military assistance over nonsignatories? The answer in both cases was no. The purpose was to establish a system of individual and collective self-defense against attack. No guarantees could be given, no system of priorities assigned. What Norway chose to do was for Norway to decide. We urged no course upon her people. If her Government wished to join the rest of us, the United States would support it. My clear impression was that both Lange and Wilhelm Morgenstierne, Norwegian Ambassador in Washington, favored that course, and that the lack of any pressure increased their desire to do so.

At the end of February the Norwegian Government made application to join. At once the French attempted to condition Norwegian membership upon acceptance of Italy also, Bonnet suggesting that "French public opinion" would not understand acceptance of Norway ahead of Italy. At the same time General Charles de Gaulle, then in retirement, was reported as opposing both the North Atlantic Treaty, on the ground that it had been devised by the United States for its—not Europe's—security, and the Brussels Pact because it was meant to secure Britain, not Europe. The President and the two senators lost patience with this haggling. I reported to the ambassadors at our meeting on March 1 that our Government, while open-minded about Italy, was united in requesting that we accept Norway at that meeting. We would also agree to extend the treaty to cover Algeria. Norway was accepted. A few days later Wilhelm Morgenstierne joined our group. He was a solemn man, wholly lacking in humor, with an expression of having been weaned on Ibsen. In welcoming him I recalled a minister in my home town who welcomed new members of his church "to all our joys and all our sorrows," adding, "so far there haven't been many joys." I suggested that we were counting on Wilhelm to furnish joys for us.

Our next caller was Gustav Rasmussen, the Danish Foreign Minister. He brought irresistibly to mind a phrase in a letter from Abbé Bernard to Louis VII of France during the second crusade: "Like a sparrow with careful watchfulness, avoid the snares of the fowler." Rasmussen moved "like a sparrow with careful watchfulness"; he had to, dependent as he was on a coalition government at home and an unstable environment abroad. In the end he would probably do what the Norwegians did; and so he did. So did Foreign Minister Bjarni Benediktsson of Iceland.

5. *The Problem of Italy* · Italy presented a perplexing problem. She was most decidedly not a North Atlantic state in any geography. Both European and American military opinion held that Italy would make little military contribution to Western Europe's security against attack and might be a considerable drain on available military assets. Yet from a political point of view an unattached Italy was a source of danger. A former enemy state, without the connection with the United States such as Greece and Turkey had had since 1947 through our economic and military programs, without connections to Western Europe, except for the late, unlamented one made between Mussolini and Franco, Italy might suffer from an isolation complex and, with its large Communist party, fall victim to seduction from the East. We had expressed these ideas to Bevin at the end of January, stressing the importance of strengthening Italian resistance to Russian domination and our intention to continue the supply of arms whether or not Italy became a party to the treaty. Although the senators were reluctant and Henri Bonnet's clumsy advocacy came near to defeating his purpose, we eventually joined in asking Italy to become an original signatory. The importance of Portugal, the possessor of the Azores, to Western European defense was clear enough. Here the difficulty was the other way around, in reconciling the Portuguese Premier, Dr. Antonio de Oliveira Salazar, to an alliance from which Spain, because of strong objection from many members, was excluded. At length my close friend Pedro Pereira, the Portuguese Ambassador, was able to report that consultation between Portugal and Spain had convinced them that the North Atlantic Treaty was not incompatible with the nonaggression and friendship treaty between them.

On March 17 invitations went out from the eight states conferring in Washington to Italy, Denmark, Iceland, and Portugal to join them as original signatories of the treaty. Both before and after these invitations, representatives of Turkey had talked with me in considerable agitation over our failure to invite them, once the Atlantic character of the alliance had been breached by the invitation to Italy. No assurances, explanations, or other forms of words eased their painful sense of abandonment, soon shared in Greece. Their joint lamentations continued until, two years later, both countries were received into membership.

6. *The Issue of Automatic Involvement* · The most difficult issue both with the ambassadors and with the senators arose in the drafting of Article 5. The Vandenberg Resolution in broad generality supported "regional and other collective arrangements for individual and collective self-defense" and our "association" with such of them as might "affect [our] national security." Since individual and collective self-defense was expected to take place in Europe against Soviet (and possibly—as Henri Bonnet kept reminding us—German) attack, the Europeans were naturally the most fervent advocates of strong and unequivocal commitments for aid in case of attack. The British characteristically wished an opportunity to appraise an emergency before plunging in, and the Americans and Canadians were most wary of what came to be known as automatic involvement. All joined in the doubtful dogma that in two world wars Germany had picked off her victims one by one and that if her rulers had known from the start that such conduct would have brought in Britain and America (presumably at the start) neither war would have occurred. Therefore a collective-security agreement should make it clear to potential aggressors that to attack one member of the collectivity was to attack all. This was very resonant and rotund, but when one took pencil to draft, one was immediately reminded that "clear as day" must not mean "automatic involvement."

De Tocqueville has told us that in America every political question is soon transformed into a judicial one. Nowhere is this more true than in treaty making. According to the Constitution a treaty is the "supreme law of the land" and its provisions are drafted as if for the construction of a court, with our constitutional provisions not only in mind but often, as here, specifically preserved. So when Article 11 declared that "this Treaty shall be ratified *and its provisions carried out* by the Parties *in accordance with their respective constitutional processes*," these words, insisted upon by the senators, meant to them that while the President by constitutional provision was Commander in Chief of the Army and Navy of the United States, the power to declare war was given to the Congress.[1] Against this background the negotiation of Article 5 became a contest between our allies, seeking to impale the Senate on the specific, and the senators attempting to wriggle free. The struggle brought Vandenberg to an anguishing consciousness of his dilemma. He understood clearly that the more specifically the commitment was defined the more nearly the opposition might approach that one-third-plus-one of the senators present that could defeat it, while the more vaguely it was stated the less would it achieve his purpose. The dilemma seemed inherent in the Constitution: What was this sovereign—the United States of America— and how could it insure faith in promised future conduct? In reality, the problem was general and insoluble, lying in inescapable change of circumstances and of national leadership and in the weakness of words to bind, especially when the juice of continued purpose is squeezed out of them and their husks analyzed to a dryly logical extreme.

In our drafting we started out with two ideas familiar to the senators and previously approved. The idea of an attack on one considered as an attack on all came from the Treaty of Rio de Janeiro [2] and the idea of allies jointly and severally taking measures to restore peace and security came from Article 51 of the United Nations Treaty, in both of which both Vandenberg and Connally had collaborated. To apply these ideas to Europe was new, but that hurdle had been passed in the Vandenberg Resolution. Then the question arose whether we should say that the action to be taken to restore peace and maintain security should be "such action as each deems necessary." It seemed to me clear that no power existed to force any other action upon any signatory, and that to appear to do so would only raise the outcry that General de Gaulle later raised against transferring the sovereign power to declare war to some supranational organization. The senators, of course, agreed. The ambassadors believed this weakened the article.

However, they agreed that the net impact of the article would be strengthened if another phrase was added—such action as each deems necessary, *"including the use of armed force."* Logically the

---

1. Except for the War of 1812, Congress has never "declared war." Beginning with the Declaration of Independence, it has found that some foreign power has made war on the United States and that a state of war exists with that power.
2. Article 3 of the Inter-American Treaty of Reciprocal Assistance provides: "The High Contracting Parties agree that an armed attack by any State against an American State shall be considered as an attack against all the American States and, consequently, each one of the said Contracting Parties undertakes to assist in meeting the attack in the exercise of the inherent right of individual or collective self-defense recognized by Article 51 of the Charter of the United Nations" (*Department of State Bulletin*, Vol. XVII, September 21, 1947, p. 565).

first clause included the second, but to leave no doubt that armed force was contemplated helped greatly.

A Cat Among the Pigeons

In our private talks Senator Connally was still worried about "automatic involvement," but Vandenberg argued strongly for "the concept of making our position clear as a preventive measure." At this point Senator Forrest C. Donnell, Republican of Missouri, set off a land mine under our discussions. It all came from an irresponsible senator reading the gossip of an irresponsible reporter. He read to the Senate a report from the *Kansas City Times* of a secret meeting between Lange of Norway and me at which I was said to have said that the treaty would contain "the strongest possible commitment to give prompt and effective aid if any one of the countries in the alliance is attacked, but only Congress can declare war. Military action, therefore, cannot be committed in advance. But in joining the Alliance, the American Government would subscribe to the principle that an attack on one member nation was an attack on all, and this would be interpreted as a moral commitment to fight." [3] Donnell, in protesting against any moral commitment to go to war, was in fact attacking the treaty language "including the use of armed force."

Vandenberg jumped to his feet, referred to the Rio treaty and the ideas that each signer must decide what action was required, that the whole matter was being worked out, that both world wars would have been prevented if the attitude of the United States had been made clear in advance. Tom Connally followed, asserting that there was no difference between a moral commitment and a legal one and the treaty would contain neither. William Knowland of California quite sensibly observed that the purpose was to make clear in advance our full commitment against aggression and any treaty which did not do that was useless. Henry Cabot Lodge, Jr., of Massachusetts said that what the signatories would do would be more important than the words they used; if they united to make themselves strong enough to resist aggression and did resist it, then they would have accomplished something. Connally, returning to the fray, spread total confusion by declaring that the Senate was quite as patriotic and able as the State Department to protect the United States, adding: "We cannot, however, be Sir Galahads, and every time we hear a gun fired plunge into war and

3. For remarks of Senators Donnell, Vandenberg, Lodge, and Connally, see 95 *Congressional Record*, 81st Congress, 1st Session, pp. 1163–67.

take sides without knowing what we are doing and without knowing the issues involved. That is my attitude." Senator Donnell insisted that he was still not satisfied and did not want anything in the treaty "which constitutes 'the moral commitment to fight' referred to by the writer . . . [as] covered by Secretary Acheson." The next day Tom Connally in an effort to "clarify his position" stated that "we could not legally sign a treaty providing for automatic entrance into war," and gave his own version of a satisfactory Article 5.[4]

The press, having had a field day with the Senate, turned to the State Department and the White House to continue the fun. I opened my press conference[5] on February 16 with a statement that had been mimeographed for my questioners to prevent any possibility of misquotation. It pointed out that the treaty was still under negotiation; that there was no difference within the United Sates Government between the purposes stated in the Vandenberg Resolution, the President's inaugural address, and the unanimous report of the House Committee on Foreign Affairs on H.R. 6802 of the Eightieth Congress; that I was working in close consultation with senior members of the Senate committee; and that soon we hoped to have a draft treaty ready for discussion in all countries. In the meantime no further public discussion would be helpful. All efforts to draw me out failed. Similar efforts the following day with the President were equally unsuccessful. He adopted a procedure that we often used later in similar situations. My statement would lead off. When asked about the same subject the President would say merely that my statement had been made after consultation with him and that he had nothing to add to it. This smothered the fire.

At Length a Treaty Emerges

I have reported this ridiculous episode at far greater length than its importance justifies because it illustrates the difficulty of negotiating when one is operating through an executive-legislative soviet. The tempest had the salutary result of convincing the negotiators that the time had come to conclude their work before it became impossible through what Brooks Adams described as the "degradation of the democratic dogma." On March 18, after much debate within the international and senatorial groups, we succeeded in releasing a treaty text for public discussion before final accept-

4. *The New York Times*, February 16, 1949.
5. *Department of State Bulletin*, Vol. XX, February 27, 1949, p. 263.

ance of it by governments (but, in reality, to force it). Never has a debutante been presented with more fanfare, appearing simultaneously in twelve capitals. In Washington I presented it with a detailed explanation of each paragraph at an early-morning press conference and again that evening in a radio address to the nation.[6]

On these two occasions I tried especially to give reality to the political commitment which as a nation it was proposed we make to our allies, and they to us. The confusion in people's minds was well brought out by a reporter's request to explain the "moral obligation as distinct from specific, written-out obligation to use armed force."

Decent people, I said, kept their contract obligations. If they could not, or if they differed over what they meant, then—and then only—they went to court. We were decent people, we could keep our promises, and our promises were written out and clear enough. They were to regard an attack on any of our allies as an attack on ourselves and to assist the victim ourselves and with the others, with force if necessary, to restore and maintain peace and security. Twice in twenty-five years there had been armed attacks in the area involved in this treaty and it was abundantly clear what measures had been necessary to restore peace and security. This did not mean that we would be automatically at war if one of our allies was attacked. We should and would act as a nation in accordance with our promises—not in repudiation of them— and, as a nation, "that decision will rest where the Constitution has placed it."

In press conference, speech, report to the President on the treaty, and testimony before the Senate committee I hammered away at this vital point, that the necessity of acting as a nation in the manner the Constitution provided did not mean either that in some undefined way the nation would act "automatically" or that legislators could act properly under "the law of the land"—in this case, the treaty—by going contrary to its provisions. No power but their own sense of right could force them to do their part in enabling the nation to keep its lawful promise, but that did not affect either the lawfulness or the meaning of the promise.

At the hearing before the Senate committee I applied this reasoning to Article 3 of the treaty, to the annoyance of the senators. This article bound the parties to develop their individual and collective capacity to resist armed attack by self-help and mutual assistance. If the treaty should be ratified, the United States, I

6. *The New York Times,* March 19, 1949; *Department of State Bulletin,* Vol. XX, March 27, 1949, pp. 384–88.

said, was under obligation to do its part to assist others to develop a capacity to resist armed attack. A senator who opposed military assistance (as did Senator Taft) in any and all forms was, as part of the United States Government, repudiating that obligation. So far as I could prevent it, I would oppose attempting to win votes for the treaty by denigrating its commitments.

On the morning of March 19 a long telegram came in from

The author signing the North Atlantic Treaty while President Truman and Vice President Barkley look on, April 4, 1949. WIDE WORLD

President Truman, who had escaped from the Washington winter to the naval station at Key West, Florida, to clear up a bronchial trouble from which he often suffered. He and his party had listened to my speech; he was most generous in praise of it and, he said, approved every word. Another telegram gave his approval to my publishing his message if I wished to do so, which, of course, I did.[7] This was typical of the President's thoughtfulness in letting no opportunity pass to support and encourage me.

All the North Atlantic Treaty ministers met in Washington on April 2 to approve the draft treaty and arrange for its signature at a ceremony set for April 4. Here President Truman again showed his consideration for me. I had told him that it would be appropriate and fitting for him to sign the treaty on behalf of the United States, but this he refused to do. He would attend the ceremony and stand beside me as I signed, but the treaty should bear my name. The meeting decided that before the signing each of the foreign ministers would make a statement. When I inquired about the languages they would use, so that appropriate interpreters would be present, Lester Pearson of Canada replied that he would speak "North American English with a French accent."

The signing ceremony was dignified and colorful, with the President and Vice President of the United States standing on either side of me as I signed the treaty. The Marine Band added a note of unexpected realism as we waited for the ceremony to begin by playing two songs from the currently popular musical play *Porgy and Bess*—"I've Got Plenty of Nothin'" and "It Ain't Necessarily So."

The Senate Advises and Consents to Ratification

The Senate hearings covered well-explored territory. Only two new ideas cropped up. Vandenberg asked me how the agreement of the United States to the accession of new signatories to the treaty would be expressed—that is, whether by the President alone or by the President acting by and with the advice and consent of the Senate. Fortunately we had thought of this point and I had asked the President to reflect upon our recommendation as it affected his prerogatives. After thinking the matter over, he gave me my answer. "I am authorized by the President of the United States," I said, "to say that in his judgment the accession of new members to this treaty creates in regard to each new member coming in in effect a new treaty between the United

7. *Ibid.*, p. 388.

States and that nation, and that therefore the President would consider it necessary to ask for the advice and consent of the Senate before himself agreeing to the admission of a new member." To this Senator Vandenberg replied, "I do not know how you could make a more totally persuasive or righteous answer." [8]

A question from Senator Bourke Hickenlooper of Iowa evoked from me a less felicitous answer and a charge, later on, that I had misled the Senate. The question was whether under Article 3, which related to mutual assistance in developing capacity to resist armed attack, we were "going to be expected to send substantial numbers of troops over there as a more or less permanent contribution to the development of these countries' capacity to resist?"

"The answer to that question, Senator," I replied, "is a clear and absolute 'No.'" Even as a short-range prediction this answer was deplorably wrong. It was almost equally stupid. But it was not intended to deceive. This exchange occurred a year before the united command was thought of, at a time when our troops were regarded as occupation forces for Germany and not part of a defense force for Europe, which at that time was composed of Field Marshal Viscount Montgomery's Brussels Pact command. At the moment we had presented to Congress as fulfillment of our Article 3 obligation a Military Assistance Program consisting wholly of military hardware. I thought he was asking whether Article 3 would also obligate us to keep an army in Europe, and replied that it would not. When two years later in the "troops for Europe" debate Senator Hickenlooper threw this answer back at me, I could see that he had a point but was unwilling to cry *"Peccavi!"*

The debate in the Senate was long, often noisy and not a little ridiculous, and forecast some of our troubles in the next few years. Senators Connally and Vandenberg led off on successive days to keep their press coverage undiluted. To Connally the treaty was "a flaming sign to any aggressor . . . —'Do not enter,'" but it did not commit us to automatic involvement or an arms program. To Vandenberg it was a "warrant for . . . doom" for any aggressor; earlier he had hailed it as the "most important step in American foreign policy since the promulgation of the Monroe Doctrine." [9]

Donnell spoke against it, asking whether Portugal was a democracy. Taft "with great regret" had to oppose it-because he found it inseparably linked to the arms program. Ralph Flanders of Ver-

8. Senate Committee on Foreign Relations, 81st Congress, 1st Session, *Hearings on the North Atlantic Treaty*, p. 26; Senator Hickenlooper's question and the reply are found on page 47 of same.
9. *The New York Times*, March 23, 1949.

mont came out for a strong United Nations and intensified propaganda, which wrung from William Langer of North Dakota the heartfelt ejaculation, "By God, absolutely unanswerable!" John Foster Dulles, appointed to the Senate on July 7 by Governor Dewey of New York to fill a vacancy, in a maiden speech a few days later supported the treaty and lashed out at "preposterous and dangerous interpretation[s]." This brought shouted and angry interruptions from Senator Taft. William Jenner of Indiana found the treaty shrouded in secrecy and wanted to know the whole truth, though about what remained vague. After ten days of such statesmanlike deliberation the vote was taken on July 25 and the treaty approved by 82 to 13.[10]

10. See 95 *Congressional Record*, 81st Congress, 1st Session, for the speeches of the senators: Connally, pp. 8812 ff; Vandenberg, 8891 ff; Donnell, pp. 9023 ff; Taft, pp. 9205 ff; Flanders, pp. 9011 ff; Dulles, pp. 8275 ff; Jenner, pp. 9552 ff.

V

ALLIED POLICY TOWARD GERMANY MOVES FORWARD ANOTHER STEP

Tripartite Agreement on Germany

THE FORMAL SIGNING of the North Atlantic Treaty on April 4, 1949, made possible quiet meetings with Bevin and Schuman to begin another equally far-reaching move in Europe. Even before Stalin's answers to Kingsbury Smith's questions in January 1949, developments in Germany had made a meeting of the Western occupying powers a necessity. The imminent possibility of the foreign ministers' meetings lent urgency to it. Our view in the Department was that the purpose of the Russian move was to stop or delay formation of a West German government, either as a condition to lifting the blockade or by dividing the Western powers on the subject during the council meetings. Therefore, agreement among the three powers on a plan was essential before we got into four-power talks. I found both Bevin and Schuman wholly agreed on this in our first meeting. Indeed, both thought the chances high that the Moscow move was a trap, Bevin even suggesting that it might be better to let things stay as they were in Berlin while we worked out an agreement on Germany and ratified the North Atlantic Treaty. Contributing to this view was an apprehension that a merely temporary lifting of the blockade might seriously disorganize the airlift. I believed that the spur of an approaching four-power meeting was the best inducement to agreement.

My first impression on going over the material prepared in

London by British, French, and American "experts" in anticipation of the April meetings was one of despair. The papers were long, tremendously complex, and totally incomprehensible. Nearly two hundred questions had been "reserved" for decision by the ministers because of disagreement among the experts. The draft of the occupation statute was fifty pages long, almost all of it subject to dissents. The chances of the three ministers even understanding, to say nothing of disentangling, this mess seemed small. The uncharitable conclusion came to me that "experts" were expert because only they understood the makeshift complexities created as the zones began to operate together and rough divisions of function were made between German and occupation administrators. It was literally "unthinkable" to them to discard the whole substance of their expertise. But this had to be done.

Two weeks before the April meetings I did it, telling them to take their papers away and start over again. George Kennan had talked with Schuman in Paris and got from him the suggestion that we might find guidance in the simpler arrangements which had been followed in Austria, a liberated, not an enemy, country. This had the advantage of being sensible and of being attributable to Schuman. I asked for two papers, neither to exceed two or three pages. The first should be a draft occupation statute specifying those governmental powers which it was proposed to turn over to a German federal government and those to be given to German Laender (state) governments. These powers would be exercised in accordance with a federal basic law and Laender constitutions that the Germans were drafting, and subject to powers reserved to the three occupying powers. The other paper should state how, among themselves, the occupying states should exercise their reserved powers. These papers could be and must be as clear and simple as they were short, even though getting agreement, especially on the second, might be difficult. I told my department colleagues to read the Constitution of the United States as a model of declaratory statement.

My first talks with Bevin and Schuman delighted me by their broad approach to European and German problems. Bevin told me of his hopes that arrangements under the Brussels treaty could include a cabinet for Western Europe. They must get used, he said, to dealing with matters of common concern and to reaching common judgments. He would like to see Germany brought in, and believed that the North Atlantic Treaty could give needed confidence in action of this kind. I agreed that the Council and Defense Committee proposed under the treaty should not "derogate from the effectiveness of Western Union." A year later, however, when Schuman moved, with the Coal and Steel Plan, to give real substance to the vague views that Bevin had voiced to me, the latter drew back. Unhappily, his health was then failing and his judgment with it. In April 1949 Schuman saw that the time had come in Germany to move from direct allied responsibility to maximum German responsibility under allied control and from military to civilian relations. These attitudes held high promise of an agreed plan for Germany, though there remained some rapids to shoot before we reached the calm of agreement.

More than twenty years later what remains interesting in those talks is not what we agreed upon but how, through all the complexity and confusion, we found a path to agreement. The task was to fix on the broad line along which we wanted to move, and then by increasingly specific development find what was common ground and what was not. Disagreements could be dealt with last, and would then appear not as isolated points of principle but as items in an otherwise acceptable and workable scheme. We did not begin with papers, which so often divert readers to trivia, but with dialogue. To aid in it we had colleagues of high quality. With me were Philip Jessup and Robert Murphy, who had come back from Germany to head our German office. Bevin had Sir Oliver Franks, one of the most creative minds I have worked with, and Bevin's secretary, Roderick Barclay (later Sir Roderick). With Schuman were Couve de Murville, from the Foreign Office, and Ambassador Henri Bonnet.

I began by saying that our preliminary talks had left me with the impression that all of us wished to reduce the responsibilities for government in Germany that our occupation authorities had been carrying and increase the responsibilities of the Germans. Schuman in his earlier talks with Kennan had pointed to our experience in Austria as a guide. Such a plan would lighten our present task, since we could concentrate on what we wanted to reserve and how to exercise our reserved powers, leaving to the Germans how to manage all that was turned over to them. They were already at work on a federal basic law and constitutions for the Laender. Broadly speaking, what we would wish to reserve was supreme power to resume all authority, should that eventuality be necessary, but, more specifically, power to act directly in certain defined areas, such as disarmament, security, denazification, decartelization, foreign affairs, reparations, and so on. For the rest, the Germans should be free to govern themselves, subject to the power of the occupation to review and veto if they should wander outside their basic laws or run counter to occupation policy. All this met with approval and we undertook to begin broad drafts for discussion.

Coming to our handling of reserved powers, I suggested that we might be preparing a model for the treatment of Germany as a whole, dim as that prospect might seem. We should keep to a minimum the power of one occupying government to paralyze action by the others or by the Germans and devise a system into which we would be willing to receive the Soviet zone and government. This proved to be a sobering and useful thought.

Letting these ideas simmer over the weekend, we came back to them on Monday after the treaty was signed, moving from dialogue to broad instructions for the ultimate drafters and still trying to avoid those meticulous pedants referred to by Mayor Fiorello La Guardia as "the semicolon boys." As anticipated, the occupation statute moved along without much trouble, but discussion of tripartite controls flushed some real problems, chiefly for the French. At the outset Bevin had fulminated that the power over financial matters which the United States claimed in the Trizonal Fusion Agreement went too far, giving the United States Military Governor a veto over state legislation and making him a tyrant over his colleagues. Proposed authority for the German Government to participate in European economic-recovery activities and to deal directly with the United States greatly eased this problem. But Schuman's worries were still acute, relating in one form or another to the extent to which France alone could block action upon which German, British, and American authorities were agreed.

One of our earliest agreements in principle had an important bearing upon this delicate and vital negotiation. We had decided that in all fields, even in those "reserved" to the occupying powers, decisions of German governing bodies would not require positive approval to be valid. They would be valid unless positively disapproved. This raised the question—disapproved by whom? Clearly, if all three occupying powers disapproved, the German action would be invalid. The same could be strongly argued if two disapproved. But it would require special provision to allow one to disapprove over the opposition of the other two. From the point of view of negotiating position, Schuman found himself at a disadvantage. It would not have bothered Vishinsky, but Schuman was an intellectually honest man and a very fair man. A solution was possible if we abandoned abstractions and began to analyze categories of specific issues that might arise from the point of view of France's special position and experience.

As we discussed, we began to get imaginative and helpful ideas. One was to break down the conception of the occupying state into two separate realities: the individuals on the spot, and the government at home. The degree of involvement in an issue and the resulting stubbornness were different. So final decision should move from those scuffling at the front to the comparative calm and broader considerations affecting foreign offices. Then came the idea of the suspensive appeal and the possibility of different periods for different issues; in labor disputes a "cooling-off period" gave time for second thoughts and compromises. Again, the number of issues warranting a departure from majority rule on the spot ought to be rigorously cut down by the decent trust and comity among allies, for which I made an eloquent plea. Finally, I introduced an idea from American constitutional practice that proved helpful. A decision to repeal or amend a tripartite agreement would require tripartite agreement, but an action said by a dissenter to violate one could be only temporarily suspended.

At first, Schuman asked too much, but, as I have said, he was eminently reasonable and fair. Also he followed the discussion remarkably closely, always speaking in French translated by Couve de Murville, but understanding most of the English. Final agreement, reached within a week of our first meeting, was completely realistic and workable. Allied controls would be in the hands of an Allied High Commission made up of three High Commissioners. Approval of amendments to the German federal constitution would require unanimous action, and approval of requests for financial assistance from the United States would be by weighted voting, which in practice left the United States in control. Approval of all other matters required only a majority vote, with important qualifications. Where the proposed action would alter a tripartite agreement on specified matters of great importance to France an appeal would suspend action indefinitely, pending tripartite agreement. This gave a veto in a narrow section and raised the discussion to the intergovernmental level—a compromise by all three parties. In the case of other appeals suspension would continue, depending on the issue, from twenty-one to thirty days unless a majority voted to prolong it.

Within this same week seven important agreements were made about Germany, going beyond occupation matters to the Ruhr, reparations, state boundaries, the federal constitution, and our future policy to bring about the closest integration of the German people under a democratic federal state within the framework of a European association. The first week of April 1949 was one for which none of us ever needed to feel apologetic. The basic agreements were all made public within a month, before our representatives met in Paris to begin preparations for the meetings of the Council of Foreign Ministers scheduled to open May 23.

A Progress Report to the Nation

Before plunging into these preparations myself, I took advantage of a meeting of the American Society of Newspaper Publishers on April 28 to broadcast a report to the nation not only on what we had just done but on our approach to the forthcoming talks with the Russians about Germany. Our recent agreements on West Germany did not mean, I said, that we had abandoned hope of a solution that would be applicable to Germany as a whole. It did mean that we were not prepared to wait indefinitely for four-power agreement before making a start on creating healthy and hopeful conditions in those parts of Germany where it could be done. We would do our best in the four-power discussions to help solve what was plainly one of the most crucial problems in world affairs. But certain principles we would not compromise:

The people of Western Germany may rest assured that this Government will agree to no general solution for Germany into which the basic safeguards and benefits of the existing Western German arrangements would not be absorbed. They may rest assured that until such a solution can be achieved, this Government will continue to lend vigorous support to the development of the Western German program.

The people of Europe may rest assured that this Government will agree to no arrangements concerning Germany which do not protect the security interests of the European community.

The people of the United States may rest assured that in any discussions relating to the future of Germany, this Government will have foremost in mind their deep desire for a peaceful and orderly solution of these weighty problems which have been the heart of so many of our difficulties in the postwar period.[1]

1. *Department of State Bulletin,* Vol. XX, May 8, 1949, p. 588.

VI

THE RUSSIANS REJECT ANY
AGREEMENT ON GERMANY

ALL THE EFFORTS OF APRIL, 1949—the conclusion of the North Atlantic Treaty and the agreements on a government for West Germany—had been preparatory to the meeting so clearly foreshadowed by Stalin's answers in January to Kingsbury Smith's questions. Even before April work had been going on in the Department, and between it and the Pentagon, which I had been discussing with the President in order to infuse his thoughts into its guidance.

Our Objective Clarified

As our analysis of the German problem deepened, our conception of the principal objective changed. At first we had discussed the relative merits of placing primary importance either on the reunification of all Germany or on the unification and strengthening of West Germany. However, we soon came to believe that our chief concern should be the future of Europe, and that the reunification of Germany should not be regarded as the chief end in itself. It was plain that this would require the cooperation of the Soviet Union, which occupied a third of German territory. If reunification ranked first in importance, the price which might properly be paid for Soviet cooperation could be very high indeed. If, however, one attached first importance to the future of Europe and if the Soviet price for reunification of Germany imperiled or destroyed prospects for the future of Europe, then that price should not be paid.

The meeting of the Council of Foreign Ministers would probably disclose what price the Russians were demanding. European recovery was only at its beginning. It would not go far without both a sense of security and full German participation in the economic renaissance of Europe. A reunited Germany bought at the price of military insecurity in Europe, or milked by reparations, or paraly d politically and economically by Soviet veto power or stultifying Soviet control over East German economy, would fatally prejudice the future of Europe. These ideas were embodied in a paper called "An approach to the CFM," which was approved by the President and cabled to Bevin and Schuman as an indication of how our thoughts were running.

At the beginning of its work the Policy Planning Staff had been much interested in various plans by which Soviet and allied troops might be withdrawn from their respective zones to enclaves on the eastern and western borders of Germany. However, General Bradley, then Chairman of the Joint Chiefs of Staff and a worthy pupil of General Marshall, pointed out that the result of such an effort would be to back British and American forces into indefensible positions in port areas, while Russian forces would not be moved far enough eastward to make much difference. Interest in this approach waned. Other conclusions of our preparatory studies and my talks with the President were that the council meeting would probably not produce more than a *modus vivendi* on Berlin and an easing of the dangerous tension brought on by the open hostility of the blockade and our response. We could accept this without alarm, but we would like more. A good opportunity to get more should not be rejected on the theory that a better opportunity would surely come. Our reading of the future held no such assurance.

Our requirements for a "good opportunity" were severe but not impossible:

Any plan for four-power control over an all-German government must operate as automatically as possible, leaving no room for Russian opposition to stop the machinery. Russian assurances of good will and cooperation were worth nothing. Therefore, as in our tripartite agreement, the principle should be majority rule with a veto only as an exception from it in matters of truly basic importance to the security of one of the supervising powers.

The creation of an all-German government should be based on the reception of the eastern zone into the trizonal government already in process of creation. We could not set the clock back.

Discussion and settlement of the terms of union could be

carried on by representatives of the East and West German regimes, provided that in properly supervised elections, in which all German parties might participate, East German representatives were given some real basis of popular representation, as in West Germany, and were not mere stooges of the Communist Party and hence of Moscow. A West German government could not be expected to negotiate with Moscow.

Another provision was that the eastern zone be freed of Russian reparation claims and that industrial enterprises partly or wholly owned by Soviet Government agencies be returned to private German interests. We did not propose to have Marshall Plan aid given to West Germany siphoned into Russia via East Germany.

We also put down as an objective to be sought in the council meetings obtaining some clear allied jurisdiction and exclusive control over the autobahn from the western zones to Berlin and much clearer rights than we had to a rail line also. The blockade and airlift had left us with a political stake in Berlin and moral obligation to its people, both of which we were ill equipped to sustain.

Liturgy and Tactics in the Council

From broad strategy we turned to tactics. The Council of Foreign Ministers over the years had developed a liturgy and tradition of its own. The ministers sat at a circular table covered by a green baize cloth. Each minister had three assistants with him at the table and others seated behind him. The sixteen people at the table completely filled it without crowding. The seating was rigidly formalistic. To the left of the French sat the British, then the Russians, and to their left the Americans. Speaking went in similar clockwise order. At the first meeting the host minister presided. The chairmanship moved each day to the left. Whether intended or not this arrangement gave both the laboring oar and the leadership to the American Secretary of State, since he always followed the Russian and set the tone for the next round. The meetings were unduly prolonged by two translations of each speech so that all three languages were covered. This was an excruciating bore except on those occasions when Vishinsky introduced a new gambit; then it gave us plenty of time—usually far too much—to prepare our reply.

In the light of this procedure, opening tactics seemed to be pretty clear. We obviously wanted Vishinsky to disclose his hand as fully as possible as early as possible. This could best be done by Schuman opening the session with a welcome, a review of the unhappy past, and a plea for a brighter future. Bevin could then follow by goading the Russian. The Soviet Union had broken up four-power control of Germany, brought us perilously close to trouble of major proportions, and now insisted upon this meeting. Where did Vishinsky propose that we go from here?

With these ideas of strategy and tactics Jessup, Murphy, and Bohlen went to Paris to concert plans with British and French colleagues.

We Move to Paris

On my last day in Washington, May 19, 1949, after a closed session with the Senate Committee on Foreign Relations, I urged that no one indulge extravagant hopes of our meeting. After reviewing earlier council failures to reach agreement with the Soviet Union, I concluded:

It is not our intention, no matter how much we may desire agreement, to accept anything which would tend to undo what has been accomplished . . . toward the revival of health and strength for the free nations of the world. . . .

There is perhaps nothing more important in the world today than the steadiness and consistency of the foreign policy of this Republic. Too much depends on the United States for us to indulge in the luxury of either undue pessimism or premature optimism. . . .

It remains to be seen whether the present favorable developments have brought about a situation in which workable and effective agreements can be reached with the Soviet Union on the central problem of Germany. . . .

I cannot, therefore, honestly state whether or not this new attempt will end in success.[1]

In Paris Ambassador and Mrs. David Bruce most hospitably took in the Achesons and Lucius Battle, then my young and invaluable Special Assistant, who was to have a distinguished career as twice an Assistant Secretary of State and as Ambassador to Egypt. In the next three years, until David Bruce came back to Washington to be Under Secretary of State, we imposed unconscionably on the Bruces' kindness. It is no exaggeration to say that not since Benjamin Franklin had anyone been closer to or more understanding of the French situation than David Bruce. After 1953 he went on to a diplomatic career very probably unique in American

1. *Department of State Bulletin*, Vol. XX, May 29, 1949, pp. 675–76.

history, adding to his service in Washington and Paris the representation of his country in Bonn and London.

Our advance party had done a good job of working out agreement with Quai d'Orsay and Foreign Office officials, but as Schuman, Bevin, and I went over it for two days, I had no conviction that it would withstand very heavy pressure from Vishinsky if Moscow had given him discretion for broad forays into our lines. Schuman's support of majority voting in four-power control of Germany would be weak. Bevin's support of the return of West German industry to German control would be the same. Both were nervous about advocating an armed German gendarmerie to maintain internal security, and yet this would be necessary if in all zones we wished occupation troops to withdraw as soon as possible from this controlling role.

The Paris meeting brought my introduction to Andrei Vishinsky, the Soviet Minister of Foreign Affairs. Short and slim, with quick, abrupt gestures and rapid speech, he gave an impression of nervous tension. His close-cropped gray mustache, mercilessly cold blue eyes, and sharply, if not finely, cut features set him apart from the stocky, peasant-faced Soviet officials and secret-police agents around him. Vishinsky had been born a Pole and educated for the law, entering the Communist faith as a menshevik, not a bolshevik. As public prosecutor during Stalin's bloody purges of the party, officialdom, and army in the 1930s, he had hounded former friends and colleagues to breakdown and death. Yet Vishinsky was never accepted into the hierarchy. He was an instrument, not a source of power. I was braced for a dangerous and adroit antagonist, but neither then nor later did I find him so. Instead he proved to be a long-winded and boring speaker, as so many Russians are. His debate held no surprises or subtleties; his instructions evidently left him little latitude.

The Setting of the Conference

The council meetings were held in the Palais Rose, so called because of what *The New York Times* described as the "acute sunburn" color of the marble pilasters set into its walls. Built by Count Boni de Castellane for his American bride, Anna Gould, the entrance hall and double marble staircase, on which the Garde Républicaine saluted the ministers with ruffles and flourishes on the opening day, embody its Edwardian elegance. My own office had been a bedroom suite, the original furnishings of which had given way to hotel sitting-room and office equipment, except that it lacked a filing cabinet. A bathtub with what appeared to be gold-plated fixtures served that purpose, although classified documents had to be returned each evening to the Chancery. Council meetings were held in the Grand Salon, upon the frescoed ceiling of which satyrs pursued nymphs through clouds without gaining on them even through the double translation of Vishinsky's longest speeches. French windows looked out on a garden. One day I got a smile out of Vishinsky by passing him a note drawing his attention to two pigeons building a nest and suggesting that they were Picasso's peace doves come to inspire him.

The Meetings Begin

In the first few minutes of the first day's meeting on May 23, Vishinsky caught us off guard by a proposal that we should now decide when we would take up, with China present, discussion of a peace treaty with Japan. He claimed that it had been decided at Potsdam by the four heads of government that the Council of Foreign Ministers, with China added, should be the forum in which a Japanese treaty would be worked out, and this decision was binding on us. What he wanted us to do then and there was to acknowledge this binding decision and to set a date for beginning work on the treaty. This was a frightening and impossible idea. Having gotten a German peace treaty hopelessly entangled in the council with its Soviet veto, Vishinsky now wanted to do the same with a Japanese treaty.[2] I was not familiar with what, if anything, had been decided at Potsdam on this subject, but what Vishinsky now proposed simply could not be permitted to happen. If it had been, we would still have no Japanese treaty.

The tiresome process of double translation now proved to be of value. By some fast work we got hold of the Potsdam Declaration and had worked out a position by the time translations were completed. Potsdam, I said, gave the council as such no jurisdiction over Asian questions, only over European settlements. It did say that the four powers would consider how to go about a Japanese treaty and so they would, but not in the council, not until other members of the Far Eastern Council could be consulted, and not now. Schuman and Bevin took the cue, the latter stressing the

---

2. The negotiations leading to the Japanese Peace Conference in San Francisco from September 4 to 8, 1951, and the signing of the treaty on September 8 are related in Chapter 56 of Dean Acheson, *Present at the Creation* (New York: W. W. Norton & Co., 1969). The Russians attended the Conference sessions through September 7 but were not present at the signing ceremony on September 8, and the Soviet Union is not a party to the treaty.

particular necessity for him of Commonwealth consultation. After that we just refused to discuss the subject. Vishinsky had made a good try and failed.

It seemed to take the heart out of him for the day, for he made only token resistance to the agenda as presented by Schuman. The Russians in the past had attached importance amounting almost to mystique to the agenda, insisting that the council could not proceed from one item to another without reaching agreement on the item under discussion, a procedure that was eminently adaptable to blackmail, and distorting what had seemed to be merely clumsy English translation of agenda items into admissions and concessions. So great was the importance attached to the formulation of the agenda by Andrei Gromyko, Vishinsky's deputy, in preliminary conferences with Jessup and Bohlen in the same Palais Rose for a proposed session of the council in 1951 that after fifteen weeks no agenda was agreed upon and no council was held. In 1949 we dealt with the matter brutally. The agenda as put forward by Schuman was what we proposed to discuss; and when we found that, temporarily at least, the utility of discussing a subject had ended, we would pass on to the next. Even with that stern view, the spring 1949 session of the council went on for four weeks without reaching any agreement beyond maintaining the *modus vivendi* in Berlin.

A Bleak Exchange about Germany

The real business of the meeting began on May 24 with Vishinsky's presentation of the Soviet position on Germany. Though the discussion was conducted courteously and without polemics, the first week showed that the Russians had nothing to propose for Germany as a whole and sought only to recover the power to block progress in West Germany. One can trace the discussion from my daily cables to the President. Vishinsky led off with a plea to the Western powers to restore the Soviet Union (which had walked out) to the Allied Control Council for all Germany. Potsdam required it; it was a logical step following the tripartite agreement. On the next day we asked what the Soviet Union offered in return. There was no surplus in West German economy to be skimmed off for reparations. East Germany had a deficit economy. It had no vestige of free political institutions. What gain to the West could come from joint economic operation with the East under these conditions? I challenged him to discuss reparations and Soviet-held property in East Germany. His proposal, I said, was like asking a victim of paralysis who was three-quarters recovered to return to total paralysis. "Today's session," I cabled the President, "was completely sterile." Vishinsky was continuing to call for four-power control under the old system to perpetuate a split Germany with maximum East-West trade to Soviet advantage. We felt that Soviet intentions were sufficiently clear so that we could with confidence take positive initiative in the council.

This we did on the twenty-eighth, Bevin acting as our spokesman. We would extend the Bonn constitution to the whole country, making it one political and economic unity with one currency and free trade throughout. Reparations should end and Soviet-controlled stock companies (*Aktien Gesellschaften*) would end also. Elections would follow throughout Germany for a national federal government under four-power supervision everywhere and with all German parties, except Nazi ones, freely participating. Four-power supervision should act only on majority vote, except as specifically agreed otherwise. Vishinsky rejected this. Later he proposed that we receive a delegation from the Third Congress of the German people then meeting in Berlin. We declined and suggested that we go on to discuss Berlin.

On May 30 at the end of our first full week of discussion Schuman and I reviewed the situation after dinner at the Bruces'. It seemed to us plain that Vishinsky had no proposals acceptable to us nor authority to accept, or even consider, any which we might make. The time had come to push on with the agenda in the hope of finding something, even though small, in our discussions of Berlin and Austria that would help ease our relations in either place. Perhaps I should have a brief talk with Vishinsky urging that we get on with the work, minimize the propaganda brawls, and find a way to end the council session without aggravating the situation. We decided to sound out Bevin. This we did, gaining his agreement and the valuable suggestion that we propose to Vishinsky an initial exploration of each subject in small meetings with minimum press briefing afterward. If any area for agreement existed this would permit us to find it before each attempted to place the blame for failure on the other side.

We Try Private Ministerial Meetings

I saw Vishinsky in his room in the Palais Rose and gained his agreement. On June 3, after a final flurry of propaganda exchanges on our respective proposals for unifying Germany under four-power control, we turned without fuss to Berlin. I outlined our proposals in a secret session, described in a cable to the President as "the first businesslike session we have had so far," trying to inject some relaxed common sense into the discussion. A city was not a nation and it ought to be possible to let a unified municipal authority operate without four nations having to supervise everything down to and including street cleaning. The city charter and amendments to it would require approval, but other municipal decisions should stand unless within twenty-one days a majority of the Kommandatura (the four-power organization supervising the four zones of Berlin) disapproved. For a couple of days we went into details, including currency matters, and then heard Vishinsky's proposal, which, I cabled the President later, involved more extensive controls than before 1948. Under the Soviet plan "everything the Berliners might do except die required unanimous four-power permission." Soviet advisers made it plain to some of our delegation that the Russians would run no risk of having a German administration in Berlin adopt "anti-Soviet attitudes." When Vishinsky dined at the embassy on June 4 every attempt to draw him out brought the reply that "the dinner was too good to be spoiled by business talk."

The tone of the discussions as well as their content declined. We were getting tired and exasperated. Bevin suggested that the council meet twice a day, in the morning as well as the afternoon. Vishinsky agreed but insisted on afternoon and evening meetings. Bevin said that the length of Vishinsky's speeches would put him to sleep in the evening, to which Vishinsky replied that something put Bevin to sleep in the afternoon. Bevin recommended the practice; it was restful and helped one through the meetings. The result of the evening meetings was a long day. Each of us had a meeting with our own delegation in the morning, then a tripartite meeting to go over the afternoon and evening programs. By the time the meetings were over and our cables sent, it was often two in the morning. As one of my colleagues remarked, "There must be an easier way of earning a living than this."

The Conference Faces a Crisis

By the end of the next week the situation in Berlin had become acute. By the Jessup-Malik agreement the council had been called upon condition of the mutual lifting of restrictions on traffic to Berlin and the eastern zone. But traffic was not flowing freely because of a railroad strike in Berlin. The railroad yards lay in

East Berlin; the workers lived in West Berlin. The East German railway company paid them in eastmarks, which were worth little in West Berlin. With the support of the western commandants the railway workers struck; the Russians refused to attend any further meetings to work out this tangle. We had succeeded in blockading ourselves. The situation became serious when the Russians found an excuse to impose impediments to barge traffic. I proposed to the French and British ministers a demand on Vishinsky that the four commandants find and report not later than the following Monday, June 13, a solution to all impediments to traffic with Berlin.

The other ministers agreed and together we privately made the demand on Vishinsky. He wished to consider it overnight (obviously to get instructions). The next day at the beginning of the council meeting he rejected the proposal. This led to a rather heated discussion of whether in view of the failure of the New York agreements and of the council meetings there was any point in continuing the session. As we were about to recess the meeting, Vishinsky said that he had received new instructions from Moscow and would now accept our proposal. Traffic with Berlin was resumed.

The council meeting, however, did not improve. On June 11, it being my turn to dine at the Soviet Embassy, I tried a new gambit with a little, but very little, success. After dinner I asked Vishinsky whether it would be abusing the privileges of a guest to discuss some business matters. With alacrity he pulled his chair over so that we might talk apart from our colleagues. I said that from the general tenor of our meetings, I concluded that no agreement would be possible on the underlying questions. But everyone expected some result from the council; let us try the small matters. Vishinsky agreed that it was clear to him, too, that we were not ready to settle the main questions.

I outlined four "small matters" and one larger one. It might prove possible to improve trade between the eastern and western zones, and even with Eastern Europe. Meetings of East and West Germans might discuss this. Secondly, we might pick out some matters of Berlin city administration, nothing elaborate, and give authority to our representatives in Berlin to work out citywide cooperation. Thirdly, the French, British, and we ourselves wanted to improve our means of access to Berlin. The New York agreement did not go far enough and left too much room for minor officials on the spot to get us all involved in major friction. Fourth, we both needed an arrangement for continuing contact on German problems through a less cumbersome apparatus than the council. Finally, there was Austria. Its problems had been dragging on too long. These questions should, in all common sense, be settled before we broke up.

Perhaps, I concluded, the most useful thing the four ministers could do would be to meet absolutely alone after the scheduled meeting tomorrow, with only one interpreter, and discuss my suggestion. Vishinsky's immediate reaction indicated the nature of his personal problem. Would it not be possible, he asked, for each minister to have one adviser with him? I agreed, explaining that the purpose was to have very frank talk with no papers, nothing to accept or reject, no press briefing. If we could agree, we would work out a joint paper. If not, we would go back to plenary sessions and fight it out vigorously.

Vishinsky wanted to add to our list of topics procedures for a German peace treaty. I refused, saying that I was unprepared on the subject. Privately, it seemed to me a silly idea to get involved in procedures for discussing a matter on the substance of which we were light-years apart. The council was to last ten days more. When it adjourned, our only agreements fell within the meager list I had outlined to Vishinsky. It was plain that on the only "small matter" of consequence, improvement of our access to Berlin, the Russians were unwilling to yield an inch, though on the Austrian treaty several small but sticky points were agreed on and sent back to the deputies for incorporation into the treaty. The other "small matters" padded out the communiqué, but are not worth recalling here. Finally, and wearily, on June 20 we signed and released the communiqué, adjourned the council *sine die*, drank a last glass of champagne and parted about six o'clock hoping not to meet soon again.

Then a curious development occurred. About eight o'clock Vishinsky telephoned Schuman, then holding a press conference, and demanded that the council reconvene. We learned through French friends that Gromyko, Vishinsky's deputy, had telephoned him *en clair* from Moscow and told him in brutal language that the Austrian agreements were unsatisfactory and must be reopened. Vishinsky wanted a change, the significance of which he could not explain, in the wording of a financial clause of the Austrian agreement. "Bevin," as I have written, "congratulated him on a new record. Soviet agreements were fragile things but today's was the frailest yet. It had not even survived the day. However, he saw no reason to reconsider our adjournment, or change our words. Schuman and I briefly agreed. The meeting adjourned. By midnight the lights of Paris and then London disappeared behind us as the *Independence* gained altitude on her northerly course back to Washington." [3]

The President met us next day as we stepped out of the plane. In my report to him and later to the Senate and House foreign affairs committees and in a released press conference,[4] I explained the significance of the council meeting as marking the changed positions of the United States and the Soviet Union in Europe over the past two years. In 1947 General Marshall had said that the great issue in Western Europe was whether or not it would recover and regain its strength. He had predicted that it would, the Soviet Union that it would not. Two years of intensive effort now showed General Marshall's prediction being fulfilled. The council meeting had been a clear indication of it, of a Soviet move from an offensive attitude in 1947 to a defensive one in 1949. They dared not relax in any degree such hold as they had on any part of Germany or Berlin. Since the essence of Western policy was to return responsibility in Germany to Germans, under a system that guaranteed the basic freedoms and contained the safeguards necessary for the security of Europe and the world, agreement between the two attitudes was not now possible. We wished to bring Germany into the life of a free and strong Europe as an equal. We would not retreat from our purpose. Its obvious and growing success was the most impressive fact in Europe. The Russians could not bring themselves to accept it.

I doubt whether, had I foreseen what the next twelve months had in store for us—the Soviet nuclear explosion and the Korean War—I would have been so calmly optimistic.

3. Dean Acheson, *Sketches from Life* (New York: Harper & Brothers, 1961), pp. 15–16.
4. *Department of State Bulletin,* Vol. XXI, July 4, 1949, pp. 860–61.

VII

THE MILITARY AID
CONTROVERSY OF 1949

The Nature of the Political Issue

THE HEAT GENERATED by the Military Assistance Program, which first obtained legislative authorization in 1949, came from subterranean fires far deeper than any issues contained in the legislation itself—desire for economy and a balanced budget at a low level, an unwillingness to face and accept the responsibilities of power, the China bloc's belief that our interest and funds were excessively concentrated in Europe, and, perhaps most of all, bitter resentment of the Republicans over the President's wholly unexpected victory in 1948. These were all present in the military aid controversy of 1949. They were all to grow in the next three years, until they at last reached the nearly nihilist proportions of a desire to destroy the very government the party wished to capture. Out of it sprang separate themes of distrust of the President and the State Department, the hysteria over Communists in government, education, and the church, and even a tinge of neo-xenophobic isolationism.

Discussion of a Military Aid Program, as of the North Atlantic Treaty, began early in 1948, motivated by fear in Europe of Stalin's increasingly minatory attitude. On March 17, 1948, five Western European states—Britain, France, and the Benelux countries—signed the Brussels Pact with American support and approval. In July decisions were made in Washington to have talks with these countries, some of which led to the North Atlantic Treaty and others to the Mutual Defense Assistance Program. Both, though separately developed, flowed from a common source. American officers, including a future Supreme Allied Commander, General Lyman L. Lemnitzer, were sent to Field Marshal Lord Montgomery's Western Union headquarters staff at Fontainebleau, where plans for defense of Western Europe were considered and lists of needed military equipment and supplies prepared. While this work went forward, the coup in Czechoslovakia and the blockade of Berlin exposed the shocking military weakness of Western Europe and the unpreparedness of the United States (we had at the time total ground reserves in the United States of two and a third divisions).[1]

From the earliest discussions both European defense planning and military assistance programs have been bedeviled by the conflict between the desirable and the attainable, or—putting it another way—by the attempt to clothe the attainable in respectable strategic theory. It was still going on three years later (as it is today). At this time we did not have the vast number of strategists —military, semimilitary, and journalistic—who later did so much to confuse themselves and the rest of us.

The Nature of the Military Issue

The problem faced by the soldiers at Fontainebleau was a formidable one. The Soviet Union had present in Eastern Europe some thirty divisions. Facing them were three and a half American and two and a half British divisions scattered throughout Germany, performing occupation and police duty. The entire French establishment in Europe consisted of less than half a dozen ill-armed divisions. The Benelux countries could, perhaps, assemble as many more. The conception of a collective-security treaty in early 1948 was of a political commitment to go to war to aid any signatory allies attacked. It might also contain obligations on each and all to prepare the necessary forces and plans. In Washington and Europe the United States monopoly of nuclear weapons encouraged the hope that political commitment to fight would be enough to deter an attack upon or subversive overthrow of an allied state, but allied weakness in the face of the Russian-managed Communist takeover in Czechoslovakia and the blockade of Berlin gravely impaired confidence in this theory. The Russian nuclear explosion in 1949 and the attack on South Korea in June 1950 would destroy the myth that "making our intention clear" would provide security.

1. Walter Millis, ed., *The Forrestal Diaries* (New York: Viking Press, 1951), p. 459.

The soldiers properly began by considering what would be required to stop a Russian attack from overrunning Europe while American strength of all sorts was being brought to bear. The answer appeared to be an impossible initial investment of between thirty and forty billion dollars and annual burdens far beyond practical capabilities. Paul Nitze of the Policy Planning Staff, after a tour of inquiry, suggested reversing the process and working backward from attainable figures to an appraisal of the military results they would produce. Accepting the principle that the first task of the European economies was recovery, the amounts available for defense could be fairly accurately judged. Amounts of United States aid varying between one and two billion dollars per annum were assumed. The result attainable would be a force in Europe that would preclude a quick victory by sudden marches, backed up by an American capability for punishing blows against an aggressor's home territory. This placed the emphasis on deterrence. Later in the year I described the effort as one to put a hard shell on the soft European community painfully exposed to predators. Even that was an exaggeration; it was only a start.

By the time the ministers met in Washington during April 1949 we were able to get an estimate from our allies for military aid on a basis which at least approached practicality. The Brussels group made a joint request; Denmark, Norway, and Italy separate ones. Original principles were simple and sensible. The Mutual Defense Assistance Program must not impede the European Recovery Program. Needs should be jointly considered and equipment jointly allocated. Forces should be developed on a coordinated and integrated basis to operate under a common strategic plan. Unnecessary duplication should be eliminated and maximum defense derived from available manpower, money, and materials. Agreement on these simple principles seemed to us adequate for a start on raising forces in Europe, a task that would take long enough to permit the development of strategic plans for their ultimate deployment and organization.

Vandenberg Leads a Revolt

Accordingly, within a few hours of signing the ratification of the North Atlantic Treaty on July 25, 1949, the President sent to Congress a request for military aid authorization in the amount of one billion four hundred million dollars, and with wide executive discretion regarding its use. Congress, particularly the Senate, was most unsympathetic. Senator Connally would later observe that the Military Assistance Program had been the most difficult major foreign policy legislation to enact since the Lend-Lease Act.[2] To be sure, trouble over military assistance had been forecast when I testified before the Senate committee on the North Atlantic Treaty in April and Senator Taft had voted against it because he foresaw an arms race ensuing. When now the arms bill itself came up, he returned to the fray with strengthened Republican cohorts and the formidable addition of Democratic Senators Byrd, George, and Russell on grounds of economy. Senator Vandenberg, going through the familiar gambit of opposing and obtaining amendment before he could support it, was also arrayed against us. Vandenberg hyperbole pointed to the horrendous fault of the dictatorial powers sought by the President. He wrote his wife: "It's almost unbelievable in its grant of unlimited power to the Chief Executive. It would permit the President to sell, lease or give away anything we've got at any time to any country in any way he wishes. It would virtually make him the number one war lord of the earth. In today's . . . Committee meeting, Walter George, Cabot Lodge, Bill Fulbright and Alex Wiley backed me up one hundred per cent. . . . The old bipartisan business is certainly 'out of the window' on this one. . . . So it's a pretty tight 'poker game' between Acheson and me." [3]

However, Senators Tom Connally, Elbert Thomas of Utah, Scott W. Lucas (the Majority Leader), Millard E. Tydings, Theodore F. Green, and Brien McMahon joined in introducing the bill. The fact that Vandenberg was now in the minority and Connally chairman of the committee, and very conscious of it as well as resentful of Vandenberg's recently acquired prestige as an "internationalist," made the "old bipartisan business" somewhat difficult to recapture.

On July 28 I opened the hearings before the House Committee on Foreign Affairs,[4] being supported in the next few days by Secretary of Defense Louis Johnson, General Bradley, General Marshall, and Ambassador Averell Harriman. We anticipated most of the objections that had been discussed publicly, and answered a rather steady stream of new ones from Republican members, largely centering on the desirability of postponing military assistance until strategic and organizational plans had been worked out and accepted by all the allies in the North Atlantic Treaty

2. *The New York Times*, September 29, 1949.
3. Vandenberg, *The Private Papers of Senator Vandenberg*, pp. 503–4.
4. House Committee on Foreign Affairs, 81st Congress, 1st Session, *Hearings on a Bill to Promote the Foreign Policy and Provide for the Defense and General Welfare of the United States by Furnishing Military Assistance to Foreign Nations*, pp. 9–43.

Council. These suggestions would have postponed a start on provision of the most elementary military formation until the Greek kalends.

On August 2, Louis Johnson and I attended an executive session of the combined Senate committees on foreign and military affairs, where we found that Arthur Vandenberg had stirred up such a revolution that, with the aid of important Democratic defections, at the moment he had the support of a majority of the two committees. With his usual dramatic flair the Senator has recorded his part in what he called "our telltale showdown on the arms program": "I bluntly laid the 'facts of life' before Secretary of State Acheson and Secretary of Defense Johnson. I gave 'em an ultimatum—write a new and reasonable bill or you will get no bill and it will be your fault! Both Committees backed me up—and at the end of a rather dramatic session, they went downtown to write a new bill." [5]

We Try a New Lure

In fact, we went downtown to see the President, who took the typically sensible position that he did not care about the section granting him powers, inserted to provide for unpredictable—and hence unlikely—developments, such as an Austrian peace treaty. What he wanted, and quickly, was the money. But August 5 we gave the Senate a new bill. Vandenberg metaphorically rubbed his hands. "The State Department," he wrote, "came up with a new bill today in re arms. They have totally surrendered on eighty per cent of my criticisms. The new bill is really pretty good. But it still has too much money." In fact, it authorized only ninety dollars less, but the total amount was divided into three categories: North Atlantic Treaty countries; Greece and Turkey; and Iran, Korea, and the Philippines. Vandenberg's concern over the President's broad powers to transfer was assuaged by forbidding any transfer out of U.S. military stocks if the Secretary of Defense after consultation with the Joint Chiefs of Staff should determine it detrimental to the national interest. Transfers of funds out of any category to other categories might not exceed in the aggregate five per cent of the amount out of which the transfer might be made. Generally speaking, the bill was shorter and its purposes more closely linked to the North Atlantic Treaty and other military purposes already authorized by Congress.

Senator Connally, who loyally took the laboring oar in getting

5. For this quotation and the one in the next paragraph, see Vandenberg, *The Private Papers of Senator Vandenberg*, p. 508.

the bill through the Senate and had not been overly pleased by the prominent position his colleague Vandenberg had taken in criticizing it, opened the hearings on August 8 with an attempt to give me a leg up in the new draft. As was well known, he said, it was a new edition of the earlier bill seeking to remove certain controversial points, and he added: "The Secretary of State rewrote the bill, and I want to pay him a high compliment on the magnificent job which he did in redrafting the measure. It elicited praise from some of those who had been opposing the original measure." [6]

In my statement,[7] in addition to explaining the limited purposes of the bill, I followed Senator Connally's cue by pointing out how it eliminated the major objections that had been advanced. It was not intended to put into effect a definitive plan for defending Europe against major attack. The immediate need for Atlantic security and world peace was to make plain that easy victory could not be gained by quick marches, and this could not brook delay. Vandenberg, however, now joined by John Foster Dulles, appointed to the Senate from New York to fill an unexpired term, returned to earlier demands for a mere interim measure to tide over until the North Atlantic Treaty Council had worked out a strategic plan which Congress could appraise. My rejection of so hesitant an approach with its possibilities of delay resulted in what the press called a "heated exchange," though the heat was largely forensic.

From then on for a month Washington enjoyed a ding-dong battle in which everyone, including the President, joined, where the advantage shifted from time to time as dramatically as at Gettysburg, and which proved that the Administration as well as the President could and would fight. Bipartisanship was not abandoned, but tempered by a little political bloodletting.

And Catch a Fish

The main engagement centered on the appropriation-authorization provisions. Here we had two groups of opponents: those who wanted to cut the amount authorized for economy reasons, led by Senators Harry F. Byrd, Walter George, and Richard Russell and Representatives James P. Richards and John Vorys, and those who wanted to delay funds as much for ideological reasons as for econ-

6. Senate Committees on Foreign Relations and Armed Services, 81st Congress, 1st Session, *Joint Hearings on a Bill to Promote the Foreign Policy and Provide for the Defense and General Welfare of the United States by Furnishing Military Assistance to Foreign Nations*, p. 5.
7. *Ibid.*,pp. 5–15.

omy, led by Vandenberg and Dulles. The two latter on August 15
made public their proposal to cut the treaty assistance authorization to one billion dollars (a cut of almost a hundred sixty-one
million dollars) and insure that this amount would be available
only to assist common defense plans made by the treaty council.
To accomplish this a small amount would be authorized at once,
more when the President approved the treaty defense plans, and
five hundred million dollars authorized to be charged to the fiscal
year ending June 30, 1951. This, as they put it, would give Congress "a second look" during the next session. The idea was wholly
without merit, since it did not, as its proposers claimed, underline
the supremacy of the council and its common-defense plan, which,
in the absence of commander or staff, would exist only as provided by Washington. However, the tide of battle moved in such a
sudden and unexpected direction that the Administration rose
above ideology to the best compromise possible. This was to split
our opponents and restore nonpartisanship by adopting Vandenberg's proposal.

On August 16 the House committee, having beaten back one
attempt by Richards and another by Vorys to cut the bill drasti-
cally, sent it on to the House for action. There it met disaster.
Richards and Vorys joined in offering an amendment on the floor
to cut the appropriation in half. The House was in one of its berserk
moods. In spite of Speaker Sam Rayburn's deserting the rostrum
and making an impassioned plea for the bill from the well of the
House, the amendment carried 238 to 122. This blow was as surprising as it was stunning. On the twenty-second the President
rallied our forces in a speech in Miami to the Veterans of Foreign
Wars; the whips got to work; and the House awoke from its spree
a trifle ashamed of such public irresponsibility.

The two Senate committees approved the Senate bill except
for the big issue of the amount, which they passed over. August
ended in a flurry of rumors, proposals, and counterproposals. During this time Washington was also racked by the Air Force debate
over the B-36, the British monetary crisis, Yugoslav-Russian tension, the imminent arrival of Schuman and Bevin, and a hurricane
in Florida. The congressional tempest was reduced to its true di-
mensions of one in a teapot. Happily, it was soon over. After
Senators Connally and Knowland had exchanged high words over
Chiang Kai-shek's appropriation of China's monetary reserves, we
let it be known that if Congress chose to add seventy-five million
dollars to the Military Assistance Program for the purposes and
policies of the act "in the general area" of China, we would accept

but not necessarily expend the sum. This was done. The two committees, first defeating Senator George's amendment to reduce the appropriation by more than two-thirds, approved it substantially as amended by Vandenberg. A hot fight had been expected in the Senate, but did not materialize. Connally opened the debate. Vandenberg acclaimed the bill as "bargain insurance for peace." Dulles joined in support. All attempts to reduce the amount were beaten down and on September 22 the Military Assistance Program passed the Senate by a vote of 55 to 24.

An Ill Wind Blows Some Good

At this time I was in New York attending the annual meeting of the General Assembly of the United Nations. Under Secretary James Webb telephoned to tell me that a most important matter had arisen requiring urgent action on which the President wanted my advice. The Air Force would fly Carlisle Humelsine, Director of the Executive Secretariat, to New York with some papers and an explanation of a matter that could not be discussed over the telephone. We arranged an hour for meeting at our apartment at the Waldorf. Carl soon arrived to tell me of the first Russian atomic explosion and to discuss what action the United States Government should take. First he explained to me how we knew what we knew, and then gave me the President's thoughts on the subject, which were for him to make a short and calm statement, a draft of which Carl had, and for me to accompany it with one relating current actions to the explosion. This statement Humelsine and I worked out together and gave out in New York on September 23.[8]

This action of the President in keeping me fully informed and in consulting with me even though we were separated was typical of his consideration and of the innate orderliness of his procedure as head of government. It made my discussion of the Russian atomic explosion with other delegates to the General Assembly infinitely more effective; it gave us in New York an assurance that we were in close touch with our own Government; and it enabled me to point out the urgent importance of the military assistance bill.

Once again the Russians had come to the aid of an imperiled nonpartisan foreign policy, binding its wounds and rallying the divided Congress into accepting the Senate version of the Mutual Defense Assistance Program. On October 6, 1949, the President signed the bill into law.

8. *Department of State Bulletin*, Vol. XXI, October 3, 1949, p. 487.

VIII

EVENTS MOVE ALLIED POLICIES TOWARD ONE ANOTHER AND TOWARD GERMANY

IN THE FIVE YEARS since the end of the European war the ideas of the Western allies regarding the reality of their relations toward one another and toward Germany had greatly changed as the true power situation in Europe and the intentions of the Soviet Union were driven home to them. In two important respects, however, they lagged behind the facts. Some of them still believed in the conception of the Potsdam conference that reparations in kind could continue to be exacted from Germany; and most of them believed that the political commitment of Article 5 of the North Atlantic Treaty to treat an armed attack on any one of the allies as an attack upon all had made the intentions of all so clear as to effectively prevent any such attack. The Communist coup in Czechoslovakia and the Soviet blockade of Berlin, both in 1948, had shaken faith in this bit of political folklore. It was further shaken when examination of the state of military preparedness in Europe and the United States revealed deplorable weakness. The Military Aid Program was designed to help our allies in remedying that weakness, but Senator Vandenberg had succeeded in having inserted into the legislation a provision that the bulk of the funds should be withheld until "the President of the United States approves recommendations for an integrated defense of the North Atlantic area which may be made by the Council and the Defense Committee to be established under the North Atlantic Treaty."

The Strategic Concept

At a meeting of December 1 the defense ministers of the treaty states agreed on an ingenious recommendation, called a strategic concept, and passed it on to be considered by the NATO Council. The concept was not a plan but a collection of principles for devising an integrated defense. No European nation was to attempt a complete military establishment, but rather each was to make its most effective contribution in the light of its geographic position, economic capability, and population. The United States would be responsible primarily for naval and air forces with a supporting role on the ground; the British would concentrate on sea and air control of the western approaches, the Channel and the North Sea, with an Army of the Rhine; the French, largely on ground and air defenses in Europe and naval forces in the Mediterranean; and so on.

The paper went on to inventory what was presently available and included in defense budgets, what was most urgently needed over and beyond that for the assigned role of each. The "strategic concept" was admittedly a sketchy recommendation. It could hardly have been otherwise. A meeting of the Council, convened in Washington on January 6, 1950, and attended by the signatories' diplomatic representatives in Washington, approved the "strategic concept." The President approved it on January 27, after I had signed agreements, as required by the Act, with each of the signatory states asking defense aid, and by executive order set the administration of the Act in motion. It had been a long, hard struggle. I felt that the Norwegian Ambassador, Wilhelm Morgenstierne, was quite justified in paying on behalf of his treaty colleagues, "a warm tribute to the initiative, the vision, and the constructive statesmanship of America ever since the inception of the idea of an integrated defense of the North Atlantic Area." [1] No one deserved it more than Senator Tom Connally of Texas.

Germany—Enemy on Parole or Potential Ally?

Allied attitude also moved when the three foreign ministers met in Paris in November 1949 to reconsider dismantling of German plants to provide reparations in kind. Schuman introduced the subject by asking how the allies should treat Germany while the occupation continued—as an enemy on parole, as a security problem, or in some other way? In Britain, said Bevin, Germany was regarded with bitter hostility.

To me, one conclusion seemed plain beyond doubt. Western

1. *Department of State Bulletin*, Vol. **XXII**, February 6, 1950, p. 199.

Europe and the United States could not contain the Soviet Union and suppress Germany and Japan at the same time. Our best hope was to make these former enemies willing and strong supporters of a free-world structure. Germany should be welcomed into Western Europe, not kept in limbo outside, as had been the case after the war of 1914–18, relegated to maneuvering between the Soviet Union and the allies. If the former was to be done, "Western Europe" must become more than a phrase. American policy had been strongly directed to this end through the European Recovery Program, the North Atlantic Treaty, and military assistance. Both Bevin and Schuman had done the same in the Council of Europe, the Western Union, and their response to General Marshall's proposal.

To begin the task, I continued, the High Commissioners should speak with one voice in dealing with the German Government. Accordingly, when we had hammered out both what we wanted it to do and the concessions we were willing to make, we should leave to the High Commissioners the use of concessions on dismantling and on limited and prohibited industries in order to obtain German agreement to join the International Ruhr Authority, cooperate with the Military Security Board, and carry out the denazification and decartelization programs. The others agreed and we turned to specific problems.

With a brief rest the first night, we remained in practically continuous session until ending at two o'clock in the morning of November 11. Our session in many ways resembled those which often precede the deadline for a strike in industry. Couches were set up in anterooms on which the exhausted might rest—a facility found most helpful by Ernest Bevin. Tables at the side of the large meeting room were continuously provided with tea, coffee, and sandwiches. Little groups of assistants charged with special problems would retire to work them out. At one time our meeting was interrupted so that the French Cabinet could give Schuman new instructions; at another to consult on matters of importance to them with the foreign ministers of the Benelux countries, who had come to Paris for the purpose. Issues moved from broad questions of policy to disposition of particular plants or products, to the weight to be given to competitive as against purely security considerations, and so on. The success of the sessions lay in their reaching a great many specific and clear decisions. It was a process in which time, immense good will, and tolerance were indispensable.

Bevin helped greatly by his frank, common-sense view. Dismantling needed immediate review. Plants useful only for war materials should be quickly dismantled and the rest kept, if only in reserve for future trade expansion and for negotiations with the Germans. He was already thinking of allowing an increase of steel capacity from eleven million to sixteen or seventeen million tons a year, even though this would cause "heartburn" in some countries (already one could see Schuman begin to suffer). Bevin was tired of the issue of German steel capacity, which had already dragged on far longer than had been contemplated at Potsdam.

Schuman's approach uncovered a novel gambit. Dismantling, he said, was less interesting as an end in itself than it had been as a means for providing reparations, but involved considerations of security in a new sense. Excess steel capacity in Germany would jeopardize the success of integration in Europe. Steel capacity must be looked at from the point of view of Europe as a whole, reconciling security interests, trade positions, and respect for international agreements, as well as our common interest in not subjecting the new German Government to undue strain. This seemed to me both too obscure and too smooth. I rather bluntly said that beyond purely war-use plants, some fifteen or twenty of which we were all agreed on, the choice was between destroying or leaving the rest. Leaving them seemed to me more sensible and less dangerous. The United States, I added, would not provide facilities to replace dismantled plants. The level of permitted steel production need not be presently raised because of a theoretical, but not actually operable, increased capacity. General Sir Brian Robertson, in command of the British zone, foresaw riots there if dismantling continued at Hamborn and Salzgitter. After many hours of talk the High Commissioners were asked to bring us back specific recommendations on each of the various plants. During our last meeting, the French Cabinet authorized limiting the dismantling as Bevin and I had suggested, provided that there should be no present increase in authorized steel production and that the Germans should accept the positions we had authorized the High Commissioners to take. Agreement on this most difficult subject marked a considerable step forward.

Another matter of some significance was settled before we adjourned, an authorized beginning of a German foreign office through a Bureau of Consular Affairs under the Chancellor and a consular service to care for a reviving German foreign trade.

First Meeting with Adenauer

From Paris the American group flew to Frankfurt on November 11 to stay with High Commissioner John J. McCloy and

Mrs. McCloy in Bad Homburg, around which security precautions were still extensive and severe. Germany was an only recently defeated enemy. Impressions of the scenes about me remain vivid —from the people, the troops, the bomb damage, to the high personalities, both German and allied. During our first day we motored to Heidelberg, the headquarters of General Thomas T. Handy, our Commander in Chief in Europe, to lunch with him and his staff and learn his views. The old university town was much as it had been forty years before' when I had been there with my father. In the evening André François-Poncet and Sir Ivone Kirkpatrick, the French and British High Commissioners, dined with us at the McCloys' house, and later the senior members of the High Commission staff came in for a reception. Then on Sunday, McCloy's diesel train took us down the Rhine to Bonn to pay my respects to the President of the new republic, Theodor Heuss, and to have the first of many talks with the Bundeskanzler, Dr. Konrad Adenauer, the beginning of a warm friendship.

At this time Adenauer was not at all the well-known, patriarchal figure he later became. Seventy-three years of age, he had spent most of his mature years in the almost civil service position of a Bürgermeister in Cologne, becoming chief Bürgermeister, sometimes translated "lord mayor," of that city in 1917. There he continued, directing municipal affairs until the Nazis dismissed him in 1933 and imprisoned him twice in the next ten years. After the fall of Hitler, he became one of the founders of the Christian Democratic Union and, as political activity was permitted to Germans in the British zone, took an active part in Laender (state) and zonal affairs. The British, however, were suspicious of Adenauer's conservative and strongly Catholic orientation, and it was not until he became active in interzonal affairs that Americans began to recognize his very considerable abilities.

One's first impression of the Chancellor was as the human embodiment of the doctrine of the conservation of energy. He moved and spoke slowly, gestured sparingly, smiled briefly, chuckled rather than laughed, was given to irony. Sir Ivone Kirkpatrick recalls his observing that God made a great mistake to limit the intelligence of man but not his stupidity. Adenauer's inscrutability was enhanced by wide-set eyes and a flatness of the bridge of his nose that gave him an oriental look, caused—so wags insisted—by having been kicked by a horse in childhood.

Members of his Cabinet and the President of the Bundestag joined us for luncheon, at which the Chancellor talked learnedly and lovingly of the distinguished German white wines he had provided. Then he and Dr. Herbert Blankenhorn, his assistant, took McCloy, Assistant Secretary of State for European Affairs George Perkins, and me to his office. Beginning slowly and pausing every few minutes for translation, he talked about his broad hopes and policies for Germany, saying that he had been told that the results of our recent meetings in Paris would be taken up with him by the High Commissioners.

I was struck by the imagination and wisdom of his approach. His great concern was to integrate Germany completely into Western Europe. Indeed, he gave this end priority over the reunification of unhappily divided Germany, and could see why her neighbors might look upon it as almost a precondition to reunification. All peoples to some extent, but Germans more than most, he thought, took on the color of their environment. Germans undiluted were different from Germans diluted; Germans in St. Louis, for instance, were different from Germans in Berlin, particularly prewar Berlin. He wanted Germans to be citizens of Europe, to cooperate, with France especially, in developing common interests and outlook and in burying the rivalries of the past few centuries. Their common heritage had come to them down the Rhine, as the successors of Charlemagne, who guarded European civilization when human sacrifice was still practiced in eastern Germany. They must lead in the rebirth of Europe. He had no interest, Adenauer concluded, in the rearmament of Germany. Too much blood had been shed; it was too dangerous at this stage to provide Germany with arms, menacing as was the recent appointment of Marshal Konstantin Rokossovsky to command the reorganized Polish army. Even McCloy's high praise of Adenauer had not prepared me for views from the head of the German Government which raised such hope for a new day in Europe. His words took on added authority from the patriarchal impression he gave. Although some years younger than I am now, he was even then called *"Der Alte"* ("the Old Man"), perhaps because, as I suggested earlier, of his conservation and prudent use of energy.

I was soon to learn that not all Germans shared his views or his calm. His chief opponent was Kurt Schumacher, whose years of resistance to the Nazis had left him harshly nationalistic and aggressive, as well as physically handicapped by the loss of the use of a leg and an arm, due, it was said, to Nazi torture. Shortly after talking with Adenauer, I met his adversary with two of his less abrasive lieutenants, Erich Ollenhauer and Dr. Carlo Schmid. Hardly had we exchanged greetings before Schumacher violently attacked Adenauer for collaboration with the occupation. His idea of sound policy for Germany was neutrality between East and

West and evacuation of all foreign troops from German soil, thus winning Soviet agreement to the reunification of Germany. When I pointed out that Russian attitudes at the May foreign ministers' meeting in Paris left little ground for belief that such a policy would produce such a result, he turned his attack on me. I told him frankly that an attempt by the Social Democratic Party to curry favor with the voters or the Russians by baiting the occupation would be given short shrift. We had all made great sacrifices to remove Hitler and nazism from Germany and bring about her admission to the community of Europe. If he believed that the occupation would tolerate an attempt to play the Western allies and the Russians off against one another, he would find himself mistaken. Not long after this meeting Schumacher accused Adenauer in the Bundestag of being not the Chancellor of Germany but the Chancellor of the Occupation, for which he was suspended for three weeks. With his death, the Social Democrats rapidly assumed a constructive role in German political life.

After a large public reception the Chancellor drove us to our train at the Bonn railway station for the return journey. It was dark as we drove through the station square, packed with people, through the station itself and onto the platform beside our train. To the people waiting outside this must have been disappointing. It seemed to be unwise, too. Adenauer was not then the well-known figure he later became; he needed building up. To the horror of his security guards I persuaded him to walk out to the middle of the square with me alone, and there shake hands. The result was an instantaneous population explosion through the police lines and triumphal escort to our train by the cheering mob. What both Adenauer and the German people needed in 1949 was some good-natured disorder.

First Visit to Berlin

From Bad Homburg we flew the next day to Berlin. From first to last our visit there was a thrilling experience. The spirit of that exposed outpost was tremendous, from General Maxwell Taylor, Commandant of the American Sector, and the honor guard that awaited me, to Mayor Ernst Reuter and the Berliners themselves. In those days West Berlin was not the resplendent city it became later, but still the scene of grim destruction, with heaps of rubble and burned-out, roofless buildings. The moment one passed through the entrance to East Berlin at the Brandenburg Gate (this was more than ten years before the Wall), one passed from bustle and energy to a sort of furtiveness, a stillness without silence.

Almost the first subject of discussion during luncheon at the High Commissioner's Berlin residence was whether I should go to East Berlin. Some thought that it might be provocative and lead to an incident, even a dangerous one, in the Soviet sector. General Taylor became impatient with this talk.

"Come on," he said. "You have a right to be there. Let's exercise it." He and I went off in his car with a small national standard flying on the right mudguard and a red one with the three stars of his rank on the left. These did not make it inconspicuous. At the Brandenburg Gate our military-police escort pulled off to the side and we passed through, I feeling very much alone. At the first intersection we were stopped by a red light and traffic closed in around us. The General turned to me cheerfully. "If it doesn't happen now," he said, "I think we're all right."

And we were. However, no one, I noticed, stopped to watch the car go by, despite its flags. To do so, explained the General, would attract undesirable attention to whoever did so. After a short drive along the Stalinallée, with its presentable shop fronts, we explored the streets on either side a block back. This disclosed the avenue to be a Potemkin façade for a drab wreck of a city.

Back in the western sectors, Mayor Reuter received us at the City Hall and presented his council. He was a truly impressive man of immense courage, representing the very essence of the Berlin spirit. Any idea, he told us, that the Soviet Union could be persuaded to withdraw its troops from East Germany was utterly absurd. The moment they were withdrawn, the local Communist collaborators would be swept aside in a bloody purge. The reception that the crowd gave us when the Mayor and I came out on the steps was tumultuous and moving. The Russian occupation of the city, the blockade, and the airlift were recent experiences. The Siberian soldiery had given them a demonstration of the nature of Soviet power more vivid than the analyses of more remote press pundits and the Schumacher school of disengagement. Their welcome to me carried the conviction that to the Berliners hope resided in the United States.

Ten days later on November 24 the Petersberg Protocol was released. This was a broad and highly satisfactory agreement worked out with the Chancellor by the High Commissioners (and named after their headquarters on a hilltop outside Bonn). It covered and largely put to rest most of the troublesome matters we had so exhaustively discussed in Paris. In 1949 we had advanced far along the road toward the rehabilitation of Germany.

IX

THE PRESIDENT MAKES TWO MAJOR DECISIONS

SEVERAL DAYS after our return from Europe in November 1949, the President asked for advice on two pressing matters: whether or not to attempt development of a hydrogen bomb, and for a review of our foreign and military policy in view of Moscow's atomic explosion and aggressive behavior since the end of the war. To deal with the first matter, the Secretaries of State and Defense with the Chairman of the Atomic Energy Commission would act as a special committee of the National Security Council. The two Secretaries would do the same on the second matter.

The international situation we were about to review not only resulted in intensified policies on the part of the Administration, but also led to intensified action by the opposition. The bipartisan foreign policy of the 1947–49 period gave way, from 1950 to 1952, to partisan in-fighting as bloody as any in our history. The essential difference in the two periods was that during most of the first the Republicans had looked forward confidently to a return to power, while in the second they looked back with bitter frustration to a fifth straight failure to retain or regain it. The success of the Chinese Communists and of Russian nuclear scientists at home and their subversive agents abroad, combined with the Administration's advocacy of political and military involvement in Europe and economic aid in undeveloped countries, produced in the pressure cooker of this frustration a veritable witches' brew. Sometimes it seethed; sometimes, under the influence of international crises, it simmered down. At the hands of one of the most unlovely characters in our political history since Aaron Burr, it was about to seethe.

The Soviet explosion and Communist successes in the Far East led the Administration directly to the United Command in Europe and the strengthening of our own and allied forces there. The Taft-Hoover neo-isolationist opposition drew the opposite lesson that we should rely on atomic weapons (later known as "massive retaliation") and move toward withdrawal of ground forces from abroad. Thus, while the Administration was moving energetically to devise new scientific, diplomatic, and military means and policies to meet new dangers, the opposition was charging that administration fumbling and worse had been a main cause of these dangers. This conclusion was confirmed for opposition critics by the trials of the leaders of the Communist Party and of Judith Coplon in New York, the conviction of Alger Hiss for perjury in early 1950, and the arrest of Klaus Fuchs in London for passing secret information to the Soviet Union. These and other accusations were used to fuse in the public mind criticisms of American foreign policy toward Europe and Asia with fears of disloyalty. All this occurred just as the Department was serving as the President's chief instrument for developing the foreign policy, to be followed by the United States for the next twenty years.

The Hydrogen Bomb Decision

While the immediate cause of the review of our military and foreign policies was the Russian atomic explosion, we had been unhappy in the Department since, in the summer of 1949, the President had fixed the limit of the military budget at thirteen and a half billion dollars. In fairness to Secretary Louis Johnson, the zeal with which he undertook to impose this decision upon the uniformed services came more from loyalty to the President and the zest of battle than from belief in it on the merits. However, he soon convinced himself on that score so completely that when reversal of the decision became necessary later on, he presented a major obstacle. Collapse of the Nationalist regime in China and the Soviet explosion made it clear that changes in power relationships were imminent. By October the Policy Planning Staff had started to work on a reappraisal of our position, inquiring initially whether the situation did not require a renewed attempt on our part to get international control of atomic energy. October also saw ferment in another agency. Commissioner Lewis Strauss of the Atomic Energy Commission had filed a memorandum proposing intensive work on the possibility of cracking the hydrogen atom and producing a hydrogen bomb. This led to a strong difference of opinión within the commission. On November 1 Senator Edwin Johnson of Colorado announced over television what he called the "top-secret" fact that the United States was at work upon a "super-bomb" that might develop "1,000 times" the power of the Nagasaki bomb.[1]

In this situation Atomic Energy Commission Chairman David E. Lilienthal came to see me on November 1. My education in nuclear physics had ended in 1946 with the impression gained from Dr. J. Robert Oppenheimer and other colleagues in the Acheson-Lilienthal group that the hydrogen atom could not be cracked. Lilienthal now told me that the chances seemed about even for doing it and that the commission's General Advisory Committee unanimously opposed Commissioner Strauss's proposal, while a majority of the commissioners tended in that direction. The reasons for this view varied: some believed the use of limited materials for experimentation would dangerously delay the production of atomic weapons, others that the chances of success were not so good as represented and that valuable time, effort, and material might be wasted.

A broader issue also evoked a great deal of moral fervor. This was that research should not be undertaken at all—the position Lilienthal has described as "forswearing development along this line." Enough evil had been brought into human life, it was argued by men of the highest standing in science, education, and government, through development of atomic weapons without adding the superhorror of thermonuclear ones. If the United States with its vast resources proved that such an explosion was possible, others would be bound to press on to find the way for themselves. If no one knew that a way existed, research would be less stimulated. Those who shared this view were, I believed, not so much moved by the power of its logic (which I was never able to perceive— neither the maintenance of ignorance nor the reliance on perpetual good will seemed to me a tenable policy) as by an immense distaste for what one of them, the purity of whose motive could not be doubted, described as "the whole rotten business."

The Pentagon was strongly pushing a crash program. Lilienthal believed that the decisions involved were essentially foreign policy decisions, and, indeed, required a thorough review of our whole foreign policy. He left with me the memorandum of the General Advisory Committee and a list of persons whose views I might find helpful. By letter of November 10, 1949, the President

1. *Current Developments in United States Foreign Policy* (Washington, D.C.: Brookings Institution), Vol. II, No. 4, November 1949, pp. 4–5.

David Lilienthal, Louis Johnson, and the author meet to discuss matters relating to atomic weapons. WIDE WORLD

designated Louis Johnson, David Lilienthal, and myself, acting as the Special Committee of the National Security Council, to advise him regarding "whether and in what manner the United States should undertake the development and possible production of 'super' atomic weapons [and] . . . whether and when any publicity should be given this matter." [2]

Meanwhile, the Policy Planning Staff, and George Kennan in particular, had been at work on an approach to international control of the atomic race, a study which George completed after he left the Planning Staff to devote himself to the duties of Counselor to the Department on the first of the year. Immediately after my talk with David Lilienthal, I met with the whole Policy Planning Staff, all of whom recognized the far-reaching consequences of the even broader decision that now faced the President. The National Security Council also considered the need of a broad appraisal of the nation's foreign commitments, capabilities, and the existing strategic situation, and on January 5, 1950, began one. While Paul Nitze, Atomic Energy Adviser Gordon Arneson, and Legal Adviser

2. Truman, *Years of Trial and Hope*, p. 309.

Adrian Fisher were to work with me on the immediate problem of the H-bomb decision, Nitze, who succeeded to the post of head of the Planning Staff, supported in this effort by the whole Planning Staff, would prepare for the broader inquiry being gestated by the National Security Council.

Nitze was doubtful of the line of argument George Kennan had taken in his paper—a thesis Kennan summarizes in his memoirs[3]—that if we wished to secure nuclear disarmament we should renounce first use of atomic weapons; rely on other weaponry for deterrence and defense against all threats short of atomic attack—threats he regarded as unlikely and probably even impractical; and make every effort to reach international agreement on control, even at a certain risk. I could only join Nitze in measuring the risks on a different scale, the one on which NSC-68 was to be based.

From the outset, in trying to outline with these groups the field of inquiry relevant to the decisions, I became aware, without full comprehension, that our colleagues Kennan and Bohlen approached the problem of policy definition with a very different attitude and from a different angle from the rest of us. At the time, impatient with obscure argument, I had to push through it to do what the President had asked of me. Now, understanding better what they were driving at and why, it seems to me rather more important and interesting than its application to the particular issues involved. Their viewpoint, clearly and sympathetically put by Professor Paul Y. Hammond,[4] deserves reading in full. It may be summarized, with some damage, in two points:

1. The attempt to compress into a manageable paper, "cleared" by superiors, the vast and infinitely complex considerations upon which such decisions as those involved here should rest, would so distort the issues presented as to affect the decisions.

2. The creation of such a document not only affects the immediate decision but also introduces into policy-making a new rigidity that limits flexible response to unexpected developments and thus affects future decisions as well.

In short, concluded Professor Hammond, "at the extreme, the foreign service officer would . . . rely emphatically upon the personal skills and noncommunicable wisdom of the experienced career

3. George F. Kennan, *Memoirs: 1925–1950* (Boston: Little, Brown and Company, 1967), pp. 471–76.

4. Warner R. Schilling, Paul Y. Hammond, and Glenn H. Snyder, *Strategy, Politics, and Defense Budgets* (New York: Columbia University Press, 1962), pp. 307–18.

official and would view the requirements of large-scale organizations (such as the armed forces with their demands for forward planning), as a direct threat to the practice of this diplomatic art." On the other hand, the rest of us accepted "the necessity in the administration of large-scale operations of forward planning with all its rigidities, simplifications, and artificialities." [5] At the time I recognized and highly appreciated the personal and esoteric skill of our Foreign Service officers, but believed that insofar as their wisdom was "noncommunicable," its value, though great in operations abroad, was limited in Washington. There major foreign policies must be made by the man charged with that responsibility in the Constitution, the President. He rarely came to his task trained in foreign affairs, nor did his personal entourage. What he needed was communicable wisdom, not mere conclusions, however soundly based in experience or intuition, what the man in the street called "educated hunches." I saw my duty as gathering all the wisdom available and communicating it amid considerable competition. The alternative we have seen in doubtful operation in the Roosevelt, Kennedy, and Johnson administrations, when the President has used the White House staff as the agency for collection and evaluation of wisdom.

Due to the acerbity of Louis Johnson's nature, the Special Committee held only two meetings: one on December 22, the other on January 31. The first meeting turned into a head-on confrontation between Louis Johnson and David Lilienthal on the basic issue referred to us and produced nothing either new or helpful to the President. The issue as to whether the use of fissionable material in the experimentation on the H-bomb would be detrimental to A-bomb production would, it seemed to me, yield to further analysis; the "moral argument" appeared less persuasive as one examined it critically. Perseverance was necessary but not through meetings, so we examined one another's views and narrowed our differences by my shuttling among my colleagues.

As December wore on, Lilienthal and I seemed close to a recommendation to investigate the H-bomb, defer decision on production pending investigation, and immediately inaugurate a review of foreign and military policies, including the possibility of reopening discussion of international control of atomic energy. (Indeed, such a review was already under discussion in the National Security Council, which approved it on January 5, 1950.) The Defense Department's Scientific Adviser, Robert LeBaron, did not rule out such a program.

At this point Louis Johnson, becoming impatient with us,

5. *Ibid.*, pp. 317–18.

sent a memorandum from General Bradley directly to the President. Admiral Sidney W. Souers, Executive Secretary of the NSC, told me on January 19 of this unilateral approach, adding that communication could be held within the orderly Special Committee procedure if the committee would move soon. The President wished to do this, since he was being pushed by growing press and congressional speculation on conflicting views within the committee and on post-H-bomb policies. I too was very much aware of this pressure, having recently engaged in a vigorous exchange of views with a group of senators which drew from me the remark that if their views should develop into governmental policies I would not want to remain Secretary of State—perhaps not the best argument to induce a change in their views. Reporting the committee close to—I hoped—unanimous agreement, I enlisted the Admiral's sympathetic interest in Lilienthal's desire for a thorough review of our foreign and military policies.

After Lilienthal and I had had another talk, the Special Committee met on January 31 in Admiral Souers' office, my former room in the old State Department. Having proposed that our report be restricted to recommendations and a statement to be made by the President, I had given my colleagues drafts based on the recommendations previously discussed with Lilienthal. He thought they did not go far enough and was further depressed when Louis Johnson objected to any statement that a decision on production should be postponed until after research was completed. Both Lilienthal and I foresaw correctly that the purpose was to open the way for renewed pressure for a decision on production.[6] However, nothing we recommended could prevent this, and I agreed.

Lilienthal then stated eloquently and forcefully his objection to authorizing investigation and research while a review of our policies was going on, since this, he believed, would extinguish whatever faint hope there might be of finding a way to prevent development of the weapon.[7] Equally or even more important, to

6. Thus on February 24, 1950, the Secretary of Defense and the Joint Chiefs of Staff recommended that our program be stepped up by "immediate implementation of all-out development of hydrogen bombs and means for their production and delivery." The Special Committee of the National Security Council, to which this recommendation was referred, reported on March 9, 1950, that "there are no known additional steps which might be taken for further acceleration of the test program." President Truman decided to assume that the test would be successful and on March 10 directed the Atomic Energy Commission to begin planning at once for production in quantity so that there should be no delay in getting under way if the bomb proved feasible. See Truman, *Years of Trial and Hope*, pp. 309–11.

7. David E. Lilienthal's own account of the H-bomb controversy, the work of the National Security Council Special Committee, and the meeting with the President is well worth reading. It is found, interlarded with other reflections, in *The Atomic Energy Years, 1945–1950*, Vol. II, *The Journals of David E. Lilienthal* (New York: Harper & Row, 1964), pp. 580–636.

launch out on the path toward the H-bomb with so much haste would tend to prejudge defense budgets and strategy and their relation to foreign policy. He believed other weapon systems were needed more. Much that he said was appealing, and in our later review we were strongly persuaded toward increased conventional capability. But I could not overcome two stubborn facts: that our delaying research would not delay Soviet research, contrary to an initial hope I had briefly entertained; and that the American people simply would not tolerate a policy of delaying nuclear research in so vital a matter while we sought for further ways of reaching accommodation with the Russians after the experiences of the years since the war.

The paper was retyped after editorial changes agreed on by Johnson and me. To my considerable surprise Lilienthal signed it, although insisting that he wished to express his views to the President. The three of us with Admiral Souers crossed the street to the White House to present it. After the President had read the short recommendation and proposed statement, I asked him to hear some additional views from Lilienthal. David began an outline similar to the one he had given us but was soon interrupted by the President, who signed the recommendations and the statement, saying that he felt further delay would be unwise. Later the same day, acting on our recommendation, he instructed the Secretaries of State and Defense "to undertake a re-examination of our objectives in peace and war and of the effect of these objectives on our strategic plans, in the light of the probable fission bomb capability and possible thermonuclear bomb capability of the Soviet Union." [8]

Reappraisal of Objectives in War and Peace

After nearly three months of work by the State and Defense planners, with which I had kept in close touch—and kept the President in close touch—Nitze, Major General James H. Burns—who had returned to active duty as the Secretary of Defense's liaison officer with the State Department—and I thought that the two groups should meet with Secretary Johnson and me to go over a preliminary draft report for such guidance as we might give before it was put into form for departmental review in both places. I was not sure to what extent General Burns had kept Johnson abreast of his own department's work. Because in our building at that time the Secretary did not have adequate conference facilities,

8. *Ibid.*, p. 624.

Johnson and his people were invited to meet us on March 22, 1950, in Nitze's Planning Staff room, next door to my own. Copies of the draft paper had been given to him a week before.

After apparently friendly greetings all around, I asked Nitze to outline the paper and its conclusions. Nitze, who was a joy to work with because of his clear, incisive mind, began to do so. Johnson listened, chair tilted back, gazing at the ceiling, seemingly calm and attentive. Suddenly he lunged forward with a crash of chair legs on the floor and fist on the table, scaring me out of my shoes. No one, he shouted, was going to make arrangements for him to meet with another Cabinet officer and a roomful of people and be told what he was going to report to the President. Who authorized these meetings contrary to his orders? What was this paper, which he had never seen? Trying to calm him down, I told him that we were working under the President's orders to him and me and through his designated channel, General Burns. As for the paper, he had had it for a week. But he would have none of it and, gathering General Bradley and other Defense people, stalked out of the room. The rest of us were left in shocked disbelief. General Burns, who had stayed behind, put his head in his hands and wept in shame. I was then summoned into my own office, where Louis Johnson began again to storm at me that he had been insulted. This was too much. I told him since he had started to leave, to get on with it and the State Department would complete the report alone and explain why.

Rejoining the still shell-shocked group, I reported the latest episode to Admiral Souers and James Lay, who left, in turn, to inform the President. Within the hour the President telephoned me, expressing his outrage and telling me to carry on exactly as we had been doing. At the slightest sign of obstruction or foot-dragging in the Pentagon I was to report to him.

Nitze and his group pressed on with their work, getting complete cooperation from their Pentagon associates. We had no more meetings with the Secretary of Defense. When the paper was completed early in April, I had it submitted to him so that he might sign it, if he chose to do so. To my surprise he did, and it went to the President on April 7, 1950, as a Joint Report. Johnson's signature, I learned later, did not surprise my colleagues as much as it did me, for they had submitted the report to him bearing not only my signature but the concurrences of the Chiefs of Staff, the Joint Strategic Survey Committee, the Liaison Committee, and the secretaries of the three services. Johnson was not left in a strong offensive position.

The Threat Stated

Discussing the paper some years later with a group of veterans of this campaign, one who had entered it toward its end remarked that when he first read NSC-68 he thought that it was "the most ponderous expression of elementary ideas" he had ever come across. Allowing for the natural exaggeration and tartness of a bon mot, this was so. As Oliver Wendell Holmes, Jr., has wisely said, there are times when "we need education in the obvious more than investigation of the obscure." The purpose of NSC-68 was to so bludgeon the mass mind of "top government" that not only could the President make a decision but the decision could be carried out. Even so, it is doubtful whether anything like what happened in the next few years could have been done had not the Russians been stupid enough to have instigated the attack against South Korea and opened the "hate America" campaign.[9]

NSC-68, a formidable document, presents more than a clinic in political science's latest, most fashionable, and most boring study, the "decision-making process," for it carries us beyond decisions to what should be their fruits, action. If it is helpful to think of societies as entities, it is equally so to consider their direction centers as groups of cells, thinking cells, action cells, emotion cells, and so on. The society operates best, improves its chances of survival most, in which the thinking cells work out a fairly long-range course of conduct before the others take over—provided it has also a little bit better than average luck. We had an excellent group of thought cells. They supported the facts of the paper by tables and tables of figures. Less than one per cent of these figures drew upon classified sources, but they put these "facts" beyond argument—facts about ourselves, our allies, and the Soviet Union. Conclusions on unmeasurable matters were painstakingly checked against past performance. Upon the resulting analysis rested judgment, answers to the question: What should be done about it?

NSC-68 has not been declassified and may not be quoted, but its contents have been widely discussed in print.[10] Many of my own public statements were properly based upon the fundamental conclusions stated in this leading embodiment of government policy.

9. See Schilling, Hammond, and Snyder, *Strategy, Politics, and Defense Budgets,* for Paul Y. Hammond's discussion, entitled "NSC-68: Prologue for Rearmament," pp. 271–378.

10. See Samuel P. Huntington, *The Common Defense,* (New York: Columbia University Press, 1961), pp. 50–51.

The paper began with a statement of the conflicting aims and purposes of the two superpowers: the priority given by the Soviet rulers to the Kremlin design, world domination,[11] contrasted with the American aim, an environment in which free societies could exist and flourish. Throughout 1950, the year my immolation in the Senate began, I went about the country preaching this premise of NSC-68.

The task of a public officer seeking to explain and gain support for a major policy is not that of the writer of a doctoral thesis. Qualification must give way to simplicity of statement, nicety and nuance to bluntness, almost brutality, in carrying home a point. If we made our points clearer than truth, we did not differ from most other educators and could hardly do otherwise.

So our analysis of the threat combined the ideology of communist doctrine and the power of the Russian state into an aggressive expansionist drive, which found its chief opponent and, therefore, target in the antithetic ideas and power of our own country. It was true and understandable to describe the Russian motivating concept as being that "no state is friendly which is not subservient," and ours that "no state is unfriendly which, in return for respect for its rights, respects the rights of other states." [12] While our own society felt no compulsion to bring all societies into conformity with it, the Kremlin hierarchy was not content merely to entrench its regime but wished to expand its control directly and indirectly over other people within its reach. "It takes more," I said, "than bare hands and a desire for peace to turn back this threat." [13]

Such an analysis was decried by some liberals and some Krem-

11. In the State Department itself we ran into a stultifying and, so I thought, sterile argument between the Planning Staff and the Soviet experts. The latter challenged the belief which I shared with the planners that the Kremlin gave top priority to world domination in their scheme of things. They contended that we attributed more of a Trotskyite than Leninist view to Stalin and that he placed the survival of the regime and "communism in one country" far ahead of world revolution. We did not dissent from this, but pointed out that, assuming the proper semantic adjustment, the effect of their point bore on the degree of risk of all-out war which the Soviet Government would run in probing a weak spot for concessions. Granted that they might not go as recklessly far as the Japanese had gone at Pearl Harbor—where they really did give the East Asia co-prosperity sphere priority over the certainty of war and the gravest risk to the regime—the difference seemed to me more theoretical than real in devising courses necessary to eliminate the weak spots which so tempted Moscow to probe our resolution and that of our allies. Khrushchev's conduct in the 1962 missile crisis seems to have borne us out.

A decade and a half later a school of academic criticism has concluded that we overreacted to Stalin, which in turn caused him to overreact to policies of the United States. This may be true. Fortunately, perhaps, these authors were not called upon to analyze a situation in which the United States had not taken the action which it did take. The literature of this period is listed and analyzed by Hans J. Morgenthau in "Arguing About the Cold War," *Encounter*, May 1967, p. 37 ff.

12. *Department of State Bulletin*, Vol. XXII, March 13, 1950, p. 403.

13. *Ibid.*, Vol. XXIII, October 16, 1950, p. 613.

linologists. The real threat, they said, lay in the weakness of the Western European social, economic, and political structure. Correct that and the Russian danger would disappear. This I did not believe. The threat to Western Europe seemed to me singularly like that which Islam had posed centuries before, with its combination of ideological zeal and fighting power. Then it had taken the same combination to meet it: Germanic power in the east and Frankish in Spain, both energized by a great outburst of military power and social organization in Europe. This time it would need the added power and energy of America, for the drama was now played on a world stage.

If these were the intentions of the Kremlin, what were its capabilities for realizing and ours for frustrating them? Ours was demonstrably the potentially stronger society, but did it have the strength now, and would it have it in the future, to frustrate the Kremlin design? At the end of the war we were the most powerful nation on earth, with the greatest army, navy, and air force, a monopoly of the most destructive weapon, and all supported by the most productive industry and agriculture. But now our army had been demobilized, our navy put in mothballs, and our air force no longer had a monopoly of atomic weapons. In three or four years at the most we could be threatened with devastating damage, against which no sure protection appeared. Surely we produced far more aluminum, for instance, than the Soviet Union; but while we splashed it over the front of automobiles, in Russia more went into military aircraft than here. On the other hand, our almost minute army cost many times what theirs did. A brief comparison of the pay, care, and equipment of private soldiers showed why. Half the total effort of their rival society went into creating military power, which in a short time at present rates could top ours. What relation did these facts have to foreign policy, national security, the existence of a spacious environment for free societies? How much of our national product would we need to divert, as sensible insurance, to an arms effort we loathed? The paper recommended specific measures for a large and immediate improvement of military forces and weapons, and of the economic and morale factors which underlay our own and our allies' ability to influence the conduct of other societies.

The Response Recommended

In explaining to the nation the course it recommended, I made clear, also—in an address in Dallas on June 13, 1950—those it would not recommend.[14] We should not pull down the blinds, I said, and sit in the parlor with a loaded shotgun, waiting. Isolation was not a realistic course of action. It did not work and it had not been cheap. Appeasement of Soviet ambitions was, in fact, only an alternative form of isolation. It would lead to a final struggle for survival with both our moral and military positions weakened. A third course, euphemistically called preventive war, adopted with disastrous results in other times by other types of people and governments than ours, would take the form of nuclear attack on the Soviet Union. It would not solve problems; it would multiply them. Then as now nothing seemed to me more depressing in the history of our own country than the speeches of the 1850s about "the irrepressible conflict." War is not inevitable. But talk of war's inevitability had, in the past, helped to make it occur.

While NSC-68 did not contain cost estimates, that did not mean we had not discussed them. To carry through the sort of rearmament and rehabilitation-of-forces program that we recommended, at the rate we thought necessary, for ourselves and with help for our allies, would require, our group estimated, a military budget of the magnitude of about fifty billion dollars per annum. This was a very rough guess, but, as the existing ceiling was thirteen and a half billion, the proposal—or rather the situation out of which it grew—required considerable readjustment of thinking. It seemed better to begin this process by facing the broad facts, trends, and probabilities before getting lost in budgetary intricacies. If that begins before an administration has decided what it *wants* to do, or made what diplomats used to call a decision "in principle"—in essence—the mice in the Budget Bureau will nibble to death the will to decide.

Furthermore, whatever the cost might be, some such program was essential and well within national economic capacity. It obviously would raise some difficult choices between this and other uses of production, but the national product was not static and might be increased—as, indeed, it was. Our duty was not to make these decisions but to press for decisions, combining persuasion with the most powerful statement of the case. We also had a duty to explain and persuade.

The need to tell the country how we saw the situation created by the Soviet Union and the necessary response to it came soon after the President's announcement of his hydrogen bomb decision. Two friendly Democratic senators, Brien McMahon and Millard Tydings,

14. *Ibid.*, Vol. XXII, June 26, 1950, pp. 1037–41.

made dramatic speeches in the Senate during February 1950.[15] They reflected liberal criticism of administration policy and a sort of guilt complex common among atomic scientists about the atomic bomb. McMahon urged the end of atomic armaments and an era of "world-wide atomic peace" and "atomic-created abundance for all men." This was to be achieved by a "moral crusade for peace" and a fifty-billion-dollar "global Marshall Plan" financed by the United States and augmented by an undertaking by all nations to put two-thirds of their armament expenditures to "constructive ends." Tydings, Chairman of the Armed Services Committee, proposed that the President convoke a world-disarmament committee to deal with all weapons.

My long press conference on February 8, 1950, immediately after the two Senate speeches, began a continued discussion of our response to the Soviet threat.[16] Four themes ran through it, beginning with the different conception in Soviet and Western thought of the purpose and role of negotiation in international relations and the consequences of this difference. In Western tradition negotiation was bargaining to achieve a mutually desired agreement. In communist doctrine it was war by political means to achieve an end unacceptable to the other side. In both cases it was a means to an end, but in the latter case the ends were, if understood, mutually exclusive. The second, related theme was that in dealing with the Soviet Union the most useful negotiation was by acts rather than words, and stability was better and more reliable than verbal agreement. From all this came insistence upon repairing weaknesses and creating "situations of strength" and, as a means to them, the NSC-68 program. Third came the transformation of our two former enemies into allies and their attachment by firm bonds of security and economic interest to the free nations in Europe and Asia. The fourth point was doubtless a futile one to make in view of existing political passions, but it had the small merit of being true. It was that continued quarreling within our own country regarding the proper mix of negotiation and strength in dealing with the Soviet threat created a major source of both weakness and the appearance of weakness.

I pointed out to the press that the speeches of the two senators dealt more with the goal toward which we were striving than with the way to get there; more with ends than means. If we could reach the ends on which we all agreed—peace, stability, and

15. 96 *Congressional Record*, 81st Congress, 2nd Session, pp. 1338–40 (McMahon), and pp. 1473–78 (Tydings).
16. *Department of State Bulletin*, Vol. XXII, February 20, 1950, pp. 272–74.

progress—by agreement on the means, that would be the simplest, easiest, and most desirable way to do it. Four years of trial had convinced us that agreement with the Kremlin was not then possible. Certain obstacles stood in the way that had to be removed. Among them was the existence in the non-Communist world of large areas of weakness, which by its very nature the Soviet system had to exploit. They presented irresistible invitations to fish in troubled waters. To urge them not to fish, to try to agree not to fish, was as futile as talking to a force of nature. One cannot argue with a river; it is going to flow. One can dam it or deflect it, but not argue with it. Therefore, we had been at work to create strength where there had been weakness, to turn our former enemies into allies, to replace the dams that once contained Russia to the east and to the west, to aid growth and progress in the undeveloped areas in the world.

The Need for National Unity

The next week I was talking to a group in the White House about the impediments to national unity that came from those who insisted upon the rightness and righteousness of their own paths to peace.[17] There were those, I said, who believed that good will and negotiation would solve all problems, that if only the President and Stalin would "get their feet under the same table" they could iron out any and all international difficulties. The problem lay not in where the leaders' feet were but where their minds were. We had tried most earnestly to get Kremlin minds running toward cooperation and failed. Then there were those who frightened themselves and their fellow citizens into paralysis by apocalyptic warnings of the end to come through nuclear weapons. The dangers were great enough in all conscience, but the fact that war could be even more terrible in the future than in the past should increase rather than diminish action to eliminate situations that might lead to it.

Other fomenters of disunity declared that the time had come to "call the bluff" of our opponents and "have a showdown" with them. These resorts to the language of poker showed the recklessness of the gamble inherent in them. Finally, I said in concluding my talk, there were purists who would have no dealings with any but the fairest of democratic states, going from state to state with political litmus paper testing them for true-blue democracy. They were repelled by some of the practices reported in Greece, Tur-

17. *Ibid.*, March 20, 1950, pp. 427–30.

key, and North and South Africa, among other places, but curiously hopeful about the Russian future. All these points of view represented escapism in dealing with the world as it was and escape from building with the materials at hand a strong, safer, and more stable position for free communities of which we were one.

My constant appeal to American liberals was to face the long, hard years and not to distract us with the offer of short cuts and easy solutions begotten by good will out of the angels of man's better nature. "Until the Soviet leaders do genuinely accept a 'live and let live' philosophy . . . no approach from the free world . . . and no Trojan dove from the Communist movement will help to resolve our mutual problems," I said on one occasion; [18] on another: "The road to freedom and to peace which I have pictured is a hard one. The times in which we live must be painted in the sombre values of Rembrandt. The background is dark, the shadows deep. Outlines are obscure. The central point, however, glows with light; and, though it often brings out the glint of steel, it touches colors of unimaginable beauty. For us, that central point is the growing unity of free men the world over. This is our shaft of light, our hope, and our promise." [19]

These themes I repeated and elaborated from Massachusetts to Texas, on the Berkeley campus in California and at the United Nations in New York. What we expected to achieve by the creation of strength throughout the free world—military, economic, and political—to replace the inviting weak spots offered to Soviet probing was to diminish further the possibility of war, to prevent "settlements by default" to Soviet pressures, to show the Soviet leaders by successful containment that they could not hope to expand their influence throughout the world and must modify their policies. Then, and only then, could meaningful negotiation be possible on the larger issues that divided us. In the meantime the search for miracle cures for the earth's ills was a dangerous form of self-delusion, which only diverted us from the hard duties of our times.

In my speech at Berkeley in March 1950 [20] I told my audience that even though important settlements through negotiation would be impossible for long years to come, there were some quite simple things the Soviet leaders could do to make coexistence a great deal more tolerable to everyone, while leaving much yet to do. For instance, for five years the Soviet Union had blocked all efforts to

18. *Ibid.*, Vol. XXIII, July 3, 1950, p. 16.
19. *Ibid.*, October 16, 1950, pp. 615–16.
20. *Ibid.*, Vol. XXII, March 27, 1950, pp. 473–78.

move toward ending the state of war and occupation in Germany, Austria, and Japan. Granted that peace treaties presented difficulties, some progress toward relaxation of tensions, return of prisoners, a peaceful settlement of Korea's problems would not seem impossible. Similarly, some relaxation of rule by Soviet force in Eastern Europe and lessening of Soviet obstruction in the United Nations or in continued discussion of atomic energy problems would be welcome. Perhaps on the most primitive level of international intercourse—the treatment of diplomatic representatives and the language of international communication—some improvement in debased Communist standards might be possible. "I must warn you not to raise your hopes," I told my listeners. "I see no evidence that the Soviet leaders will change their conduct until the progress of the free world convinces them that they cannot profit from a continuation of these tensions."

X

EUROPE AND THE
SCHUMAN PLAN

ON MAY 6, 1950, after participating in a three-day state visit to Washington by Prime Minister of Pakistan Liaquat Ali Khan and Begum Sahiba, we climbed wearily aboard the presidential plane, *Independence*, for Paris en route to London and a ministerial meeting of the North Atlantic Treaty Council. Again the President came to the plane to see me off. We had been through a long, strenuous, wearying winter and spring. Colleagues in the State Department thought I might get a few days' rest and please Schuman by starting early and going via Paris for some friendly talks with the French before plunging into the series of meetings that always clustered about the North Atlantic Council. It turned out quite otherwise. The days in Paris, from the moment of my arrival on Sunday morning, May 7, were far from restful; and my presence there, in view of what occurred, convinced Bevin of a Franco-American conspiracy against him.

Scene 1: Paris

In the formal reception room in the American Embassy residence on the day of my arrival, Schuman, through an interpreter, disclosed to Ambassador Bruce and me his Coal and Steel Plan for Western Europe, which he and Jean Monnet had been developing in such secrecy that they had not yet discussed it with the French Cabinet. It was, indeed, as Bruce called it in a cable a week later, "the most imaginative and far-reaching approach that has been made for generations to the settlement of fundamental differences between France and Germany." The whole French-German production of coal and steel would be placed under a joint high authority, with an organization open to the participation of other European nations.

Schuman urged the utmost secrecy upon us. A leak before the Cabinet was aligned could wreck both the plan and the Government, so we were asked not to inform our colleagues in Paris or to send cables or to have memoranda transcribed for two days. Since the President was in the Far West, the matter of informing him did not arise for at least a day. Meanwhile, we agreed that Jean Monnet and John McCloy should be brought in to discuss the plan further with Bruce and me. This was a great help to us, especially to me. Training in the common law concentrates one's attention on the specific. The civil lawyer thinks in terms of principles. Those who have really great constructive ideas are often vague about what they mean specifically. To pin them down tends to frustrate them. In addition to this handicap, Schuman and I were talking through an interpreter who was not familiar with the subject matter of our talk. Ideas had a hard time getting through in either direction.

Jean Monnet was soon revealed as the plan's originator. In him fanatical zeal for supranational points of view and organization was combined with shrewd business judgment and experience. During the First World War he had been impressed, through the work of the Allied Maritime Transport Council, by the degree to which an international staff could transcend national considerations, and even pressures, in administering the use of the merchant fleets of all the allies to achieve an agreed common purpose through agreed procedures. He firmly believed that the thinking of groups, even those as tightly indoctrinated as business communities, was conditioned and confined by the frame within which it takes place. Once the small, restricting frame is broken, thought rapidly expands and accommodates itself to a wider setting. After that the effect is most unlikely to be undone. This belief, which I share, helped us both to survive General de Gaulle.

The Coal and Steel Plan was Monnet's reaction to a rather grandiose idea of Prime Minister Georges Bidault's put forth in a speech at Lyons on April 16 calling for an "Atlantic High Council for Peace." This appeared to combine propaganda, in the use of the word "peace," with the urge to pile machinery on machinery in an effort to form a holding company to "coordinate" the North Atlantic Treaty, the Western Union, the Organization for European Economic Cooperation, and the Council of Europe. Whatever idea may have lurked within this proposal was stillborn. Monnet's apparently more limited and modest plan was, in reality, more imaginative and far-reaching, because it picked out the basic materials of Europe's industrial economy, coal and steel, to put under the supranational control of an organization of the participating European states, with governmental powers and clearly defined purposes. The High Authority's immediate powers and effects would be great; its potential ones, still greater. Only by the patient coaching of Monnet and McCloy and their answers to our questions did this come home to us.

All sorts of questions at once arose. To begin with, was the plan cover for a gigantic European cartel? We became convinced that this was not the intention of its founders and that provisions to guard against this result would be incorporated in the charter. The more we studied the plan, the more we were impressed by it. Nothing better expresses the purpose and method of the proposal than the first two paragraphs of the French Government's announcement on May 9, as it appeared the next morning in *The Times* of London:

> World peace cannot be safeguarded without the making of efforts proportionate to the dangers which threaten it. The contribution which an organized and living Europe can bring to civilization is indispensable to the maintenance of peaceful relations. In taking upon herself for more than 20 years the role of champion of a united Europe, France has always had as her essential aim the service of peace. A united Europe was not achieved; and we had war. Europe will not be made all at once, or according to a single, general plan. It will be built through concrete achievements, which first create a *de facto* solidarity. The gathering together of the nations of Europe requires the elimination of the age-old opposition of France and Germany. The first concern in any action undertaken must be these two countries.

> With this aim in view, the French Government proposes to take action immediately on one limited but decisive point; the French Government proposes to place Franco-German production of coal and steel as a whole under a common higher authority, within the framework of an organization open to the participation of the other countries of Europe. The pooling of coal and steel production should immediately provide for the setting-up of common foundations for economic development as a first step in the federation of Europe, and will change the destinies of those regions which have long been devoted to the manufacture of munitions of war, of which they have been the most constant victims.

The genius of the Schuman-Monnet plan lay in its practical, common-sense approach, its avoidance of the appearance of limitations upon sovereignty and touchy political problems. What could be more earthy than coal and steel, or more desirable than a pooling and common direction of France and Germany's coal and steel industries? This would end age-old conflicts. It was not exclusive but open to all European nations who wished to participate in a coal and steel authority designed for specific purposes and with powers adequate to accomplish its purposes.

The Times—and, indeed, it was not alone—was perplexed by M. Schuman's method of announcement before official soundings in other capitals. When it reported him as saying that "the subject had not been broached in his talks with Mr. Acheson yesterday [May 8], even in 'the personal' conversation with which the day opened," both The Times and M. Schuman were correct. It had been broached on Sunday, May 7, when all good people, including reporters, should have been in church.

When the President had returned to Washington, I sent him a brief for his "eyes only" message, asking that, should rumors come from Europe of an impending important development, he withhold comment until I could inform him further. He agreed. The next day, the French Cabinet having approved the submission of the Schuman Plan to the Chamber of Deputies, an outline of the plan, to be kept secret until Schuman's speech, was sent to him with a request that after the speech I be authorized to express sympathetic interest pending further elaboration from Paris. Again the President approved. This set at rest my apprehension that upon receiving partial information the Antitrust Division in the Department of Justice might stimulate some critical comments, which would have been damaging at that stage.

Scene 2: London

On reaching London on Tuesday, May 9, the day Schuman was to make his statement presenting the plan, I found Ernest Bevin in distressing shape when we met him and his staff in mid-morning. He had recently undergone a painful operation and was taking sedative drugs that made him doze off, sometimes quite soundly, during the discussion. His staff seemed accustomed to it, though I found it disconcerting. At any rate, our talk got nowhere, and not knowing what, if anything, had yet occurred in Paris, I did not feel able to inform our British friends of what Schuman might be doing at the moment. During luncheon with Bevin and Attlee word came to Bevin and me separately that early in the afternoon René Massigli, the French Ambassador, wanted an appointment with Bevin to convey an important message, and another with me an hour later. My embarrassment grew as the company speculated about this mystery. Again ignorance of what had happened or, perhaps, would be happening as Massigli talked still kept me silent. When he did call at midafternoon, it was to announce the proposal of the Schuman Plan to the Chamber, which had gone according to schedule and about which I quite obviously knew far more than Massigli did.

Waiting for us at the Foreign Office, Bevin was in a highly emotional state, very angry with me and, what was much worse, rapidly working himself into bitter opposition to Schuman and the Schuman Plan. He at once charged that Schuman and I had cooked up the whole plan, purposely keeping him in the dark, and that I had gone to Paris to put the finishing touches on it and get it publicly announced before he ever heard of it. The circumstantial evidence in support of this reconstruction of the crime was strong indeed. Clearly we had managed things badly. Schuman, understandably absorbed in the problems of piloting his plan through his own government and parliament, saw my presence as a windfall of encouragement before, and help after, it was accepted. But I had been stupid in not foreseeing both Bevin's rage at his apparent exclusion from the circle of consultation and the old socialist's difficulty with the problem the Schuman Plan presented to a socialist government of Britain. If it joined a freely competitive system in the basic commodities of coal and steel, how could it isolate and manage the rest of Britain's economy as a welfare state? If it did not join, how could Britain retain her basic markets on the Continent?

This was Bevin's dilemma. After the first flush of anger had passed, I think he did accept the innocence of my motives in going to Paris. But damage had been done. Despite my most earnest arguments, in the next few days Britain made her great mistake of the postwar period by refusing to join in negotiating the Schuman Plan. From the bitter fruits of this mistake both Britain and Europe are still suffering. If I had not gone to Paris, Schuman would have had a tricky problem of acting unilaterally or of coming to London to consult us both before going to his own parliament. But the better course would have been for him to have authorized me to run what risks there were in trying to persuade Bevin and Attlee to give the plan their support. That course might not have worked, but, as it was, anger was added to bad judgment to insure the triumph of the latter.

The next day both Bevin and I put out short statements. His was noncommittal, but not so hostile as it had threatened to be. I welcomed "a most important development" prompted by the desire to further "a rapprochement between Germany and France and progress toward the economic integration of Western Europe," objectives favored by the United States Government. Specific comment must await development of the proposals; meanwhile we "recognize[d] with sympathy and approval the significant and far-reaching intent of the French initiative." [1] A week later the President called the proposal "an act of constructive statesmanship" and a "demonstration of French leadership in the solution of the problems of Europe . . . in the great French tradition." He was "gratified at the emphasis the proposal places upon equal access to coal and steel products to all Western European countries . . . [and] the full benefits of the competitive process." [2]

In this way we both did our best to back the launching with a fair breeze. But Bevin was still growling.

Scene 3: Lancaster House

On May 11 Schuman arrived in London for tripartite meetings to precede the North Atlantic Council, both being held at Lancaster House. We both got word from Bevin asking to see us a half hour before the full meeting at a private session in my office. This was a pleasant room in a southern corner of Lancaster House looking out on a charming lawn with a flowered border and golden-chain trees in bloom. But my office seemed to me a strange place for Bevin to hold a meeting and might seem even stranger to Schuman. Bevin might be thinking of giving him some of his own back. This suspicion grew when Bevin launched into a strong attack upon the announcement of the Coal and Steel Plan without prior agreement, or even consultation, among the powers occupying West Germany. He spoke slowly and forcefully, Schuman's interpreter translating as Bevin spoke. He had a good case, but rather overdid it. I knew that Schuman could take care of himself, but did not want him to get the impression from the meeting's being in my office that it was so by reason of collusion between Bevin and me. There had been enough misunderstanding among us without creating more.

When Bevin finished, I asked to be permitted to say a word to make my own position clear since Mr. Bevin was not speaking

1. *The New York Times*, May 11, 1950.
2. *Department of State Bulletin*, Vol. XXII, May 29, 1950, p. 828.

The author, British Foreign Secretary Ernest Bevin, and French Foreign Secretary Robert Schuman at Lancaster House for a NATO meeting. WARDER COLLECTION

for me. I had not, I said, told Mr. Bevin or anyone about the plan, in accordance with M. Schuman's request, until Massigli's message released me. Then I had explained our talks in Paris. These had annoyed Mr. Bevin, which was understandable. But Mr. Bevin was exaggerating their significance. We all understood our duty to one another as allies. Sometimes domestic and international matters became pretty much intertwined and occasions arose when each of us had to take his own line without consultation because of the exigencies of domestic politics. On this occasion M. Schuman had done this. I happened to think he had taken a brilliant line and was in favor of it. But quite apart from that I understood why M. Schuman had thought that secrecy was more important than consultation. "Similarly," I said, "last autumn at the time of the Bank and Fund meeting in Washington, Mr. Bevin and the British Government found it advisable to devalue the pound. That was a serious problem in which secrecy was also important. It affected France. M. Schuman and Maurice Petsche, the French Finance Minister, were in Washington. The impending devaluation had been discussed with Secretary of the Treasury Snyder and me but not with M. Schuman and M. Petsche. They had not complained, since they understood the need for secrecy." Bevin had had enough. "Let's join the others," he said, getting up. As we left the room, Schuman took my arm. "You have a large deposit in my bank," he said.[3]

On May 25 the French Government invited six governments to join in negotiating the Coal and Steel Plan, and in doing so asked that participating governments accept the main principles of the plan including the binding effect of the High Authority's decisions. Five nations accepted the invitation on these terms—the Benelux nations, Germany, and Italy. The British Government did not "feel able to accept in advance, nor do they reject in advance, the principles underlying the French proposal." They wanted a detailed discussion first to "throw light on the nature of the scheme and its full political and economic consequences." [4] If the French would change their attitude, they would be glad to join in negotiations on procedures. The French were not willing to do so and a conference among the six nations began on June 20 without Britain.

Some decisions are critical. This decision of May 1950 was one. It was not the last clear chance for Britain to enter Europe, but it was the first wrong choice—as wrong as General de Gaulle's tragic rejection of the penitent in 1963.

In mid-June the national executive of the Labour Party made clear that the reasons for the Government's decision were not procedural. In a party pamphlet entitled *European Unity*, the trouble for doctrinaire socialists with the plan was shown to lie just where Schuman had suspected it would: in the binding effect of the High Authority's decisions. The issue was the sovereign right of a Labour Government to pursue democratic socialism. Important but secondary was the national policy of special ties with the Commonwealth and the United States.

3. In an earlier book I continued the anecdote:

But Bevin had his revenge. Some days later at the end of a day I got a message to stop in his room at Lancaster House before going home.

"I know you like a Martini," said Ernie, "and it's hard to get a good one in London." Something was definitely afoot. I expressed guarded anticipation. At Bevin's signal, an ancient butler began operations at a sideboard. With growing disbelief I watched him pour into a tumbler one-third gin, one-third Italian Vermouth, and one-third water without ice, then bring the tumbler to me on a tray.

Ernie was observing all this with what he thought was a Mona Lisa smile —but was more like the grin of a schoolboy up to deviltry.

It was clear that I could never drink this horror if I tasted it. The only course was to take it in one gulp, or call "uncle." I chose the former, and down it went.

"Have another," Ernie almost commanded.

"No, thank you," I said. "No one could make another just like that one."

(*Sketches from Life*, pp. 40–41.)

4. Raymond Dennett and Robert K. Turner, eds., *Documents on American Foreign Relations* (Princeton: Princeton University Press, 1951), Vol. XII, January 1–December 31, 1950, p. 88.

Behind the Scenes

The split between our principal allies over the Schuman Plan made it more important than ever that the forthcoming conference on the plan should be a purely European one without interference from the United States. Accordingly, a joint, circular instruction was sent out on June 2 by State and the Economic Cooperation Administration to our missions in Britain and the six countries concerned that there were to be "no further public statements except to reaffirm our general position. . . . The U.S. is not to be a party to negotiations and is to have no official association or observers. . . . We are to take no position concerning UK-French issues on the Plan." Immediately we put the instruction into effect by turning down a proposal from Bruce in Paris to put out a statement comforting to Paris after the British refusal to join the conference. Later on, the instruction continued, occasion might call for discreet aid to Schuman to avoid watering down his proposal or to retain "favorable economic elements . . . emphasized in [Truman's] May 18 statement," but State and ECA would instruct specifically on these occasions.

The Department kept in intimate touch with the negotiations, chiefly through McCloy and Bruce and their missions. This was most discreetly and skillfully done by those two masters of the diplomatic art. On July 25 Schuman announced that agreement had been reached on all major aspects of the plan. This perhaps contributed more to confidence in the negotiation than to dissemination of fact. Many hurdles remained and on these the quiet exercise of our influence was helpful. During the summer these issues were chiefly "watering-down" issues. One concerned broadening appeals from decisions of the Authority to those "affected" as against those "directly concerned." We supported the narrower right. Another raised the period during which subsidy payments would cushion marginal producers against the shock of a single European market. Again, we favored the shorter period. Perhaps the most important issue came in the autumn when, to anticipate, American proposals for German participation in the defense of Europe gave Bonn a stronger bargaining position than it had as an occupied country. Sensing this, the Germans began dragging their feet in Schuman Plan negotiations, trying to obtain two important objectives: a lifting of the ceiling on German steel production and a rescue of the German selling cartel for the Ruhr, Deutscher Kohlen Verkauf, from the operation of provisions of the occupation statute of 1949. Here the United States was directly concerned and acted clearly in support of the French position, which Monnet had been appointed to work out. They had taken the stand that the first German position was not only consistent with but required by the Schuman Plan, but that the second was totally at odds with it. In our view it was at odds also with the occupation statute and sound economic policy. The dispute was settled on this basis. The European Coal and Steel Community treaty was signed by the Six on April 18, 1951.

XI

BALANCED
COLLECTIVE FORCES
FOR EUROPE

ONCE BEVIN'S ANNOYANCE over the Schuman Plan had eased, our talks at the Foreign Office performed the useful task of identifying subjects for discussion with Schuman, and also the North Atlantic Council afterward, and an attitude of approach to them. Bevin quite frankly confessed doubts of his wisdom in recognizing the Chinese Communists. He foresaw little profit in it and urged that we prevent our different lines from causing a breach between us. I saw no reason why they should. Three matters seemed to me of the greatest importance: defense and economics in Europe; a peace treaty with Japan; and, of secondary but still great importance, the troubled situation in Southeast Asia.

The need for deterrent defense in Europe exceeded the strength of European economies and, therefore, they needed basic strengthening. Here we approached dangerous ground, but Bevin agreed. The then treaty structure was hopelessly deficient in producing drive for improvement. Work fell between committees; difficulties and weaknesses were accepted as insuperable. The French attitude that Germany could never contribute to the common defense was all wrong. The German economy and German participation in trade, aid to undeveloped countries, and—short of rearmament—common defensive arrangements were all essential. This was quite a program for our friends across the table, but Bevin did not dissent.

The Tripartite Meetings

The great progress already made under the Marshall Plan, I said, gave real hope that after 1952 Western Europe, except possibly Austria, would not need grants in aid of economic development. But in the subsequent period, equal or perhaps greater cooperation within Europe and between Europe and North America would continue to be necessary. The remaining goals would be increased production and productivity, convertibility of currencies, reduction of tariffs, increasing supplies of raw materials and markets for manufactured goods, freer movement of peoples, equality of treatment for Germany, and opening fields for investment. All this required new ideas and methods as well as more activity. Mentioning the unmentionable, I said that Washington was in favor of the Schuman Plan and of the association of the United States and Canada with the Organization for European Economic Cooperation.

Turning to Germany, I urged my colleagues to remember that time was running out in which the occupation could exercise a useful and beneficial effect in reshaping Germany. The relation of victors to vanquished was basically an unpleasant one and no matter how wisely administered was gathering resentment as Germany recovered from the war, developed a generation free of guilt, and lost some of the present fear of Russian threat. A democratic and economically sound Germany should move quickly to take its own place in the European community. The Allied High Commission's influence in Germany could not be expected to be great beyond a couple of years more. The real interest of Germany lay in Western Europe. We must begin at once to lead Germany to "entangle and integrate" herself there. We could not begin too soon to transform the occupying forces into a new concept and new organization, a force for the protection of Western Europe.

Because of this situation, the High Commission was entering a new phase in which speed, restraint in method, and wisdom in substance would be necessary in striking a balance between maintaining the respect and confidence of the Germans and moving ahead of events. Here the implications of the French Coal and Steel Plan were particularly relevant and important. These were somber thoughts.

In the ensuing discussion it soon became evident that even Schuman had not fully appreciated that as the plan went into effect it would have far-reaching effects on the status of the occupation and the Ruhr Authority. Although my exhortations produced no immediate results in agreement, they acted as a useful spur to action that was soon to begin in earnest. Ratification of the Schuman Plan took rather more time than I had expected, but my estimate of the effective life of the occupation and the High Commission was accurate. Just two years later we concluded in Bonn and signed in Paris the agreements that began their end. Similarly, though not strangely, the occupation of Japan ended by the ratification of the Japanese peace treaty in the same summer.

Our talks on Germany produced two other useful results. In response to a formal inquiry from Chancellor Adenauer, we agreed and replied to him that an attack on our forces in Germany would constitute an armed attack within the meaning of Article 5 of the North Atlantic Treaty. To be sure, this was clear enough from a reading of the treaty, but few people read it and a statement from the three ministers gave reassurance in Germany. Our communiqué [1] also inspired hope and confidence there. It outlined the impressive record of German progress in the past twelve months and asserted our hope of maintaining the pace of free development while holding open offers made to the Soviet Union a year before to join in a treaty establishing a government for all Germany.

The Fourth NATO Council Meeting:
Basic Problems Emerge

At the fourth meeting of the North Atlantic Council, the last at which I was to preside, the basic problems, which NATO has never been able to solve, began to emerge. Both our third meeting and the Mutual Defense Assistance Program had recognized two goals—economic recovery and military defense—the first of which had been given priority. Meanwhile our studies in Washington earlier in the year, leading to the hydrogen bomb decision and NSC-68, had convinced us that a far greater defense effort on both sides of the Atlantic than either side had previously contemplated would be necessary. How could this be done in Europe without jeopardizing economic recovery, or leading Europeans to believe that it would be jeopardized? One thing was clear. Congress would not bear the cost of both economic recovery and rearmament in Europe as well as our own, and should not be asked to do so. And yet the obvious threat that had led the Europeans to want the North Atlantic Treaty was the threat of Soviet military power already greatly superior to anything Western Europe alone could produce.

1. *Department of State Bulletin*, Vol. **XXII**, May 22, 1950, pp. 787–88.

Nor was this the only problem becoming daily more clear and destined to be equally recalcitrant. The North Atlantic Alliance was a body—or more accurately twelve bodies—without a head. The congressional requirement of an "integrated defense" had produced a system of committees. They met, but failed to produce continuing or authoritative direction. American military supplies were already moving across the Atlantic, but the council was experiencing the frustrations of the Continental Congress in 1776 before the appointment of General Washington. It recognized the need of forces in being and in position, but saw little possibility of getting either without organization, a command, and a strategy. The first, most pressing need seemed to be to replace the intermittent attention of committees with the continuing preoccupation of a permanent body.

When the meeting was called to order around a large circular table in the great hall of Lancaster House, the members tended to fly off to headlined international problems of the moment—the Soviet boycott of the United Nations and the increasing troubles in Southeast Asia. In time, they became persuaded that we could do little or nothing about these and might better concentrate on the closer but no less perplexing problems of our own area. We had before us reports of our Defense and Economic committees. Both pointed out distressing gaps: the former, between the defense forces we had and those we needed; the latter, between the needs and the ability to meet them. The Defense Committee urged a progressive increase in defense forces, based on the creation of balanced collective forces rather than balanced national forces. By this was meant a force for the defense of Europe, complete and balanced in its components when viewed as a collectivity, rather than a collection of national forces each complete with all the necessary component arms. The latter was beyond the economic means of Europe, even when supplemented by large grants of military aid from the United States.

This proposal produced a lively debate. Lange of Norway raised the point, later to become the center of General de Gaulle's creed, that the committee's recommendation would leave a nation imperiled if the collective force should not come to its aid. This was, of course, true but incomplete. Such a nation would be imperiled, however its individual defense force was constructed, if the aggressor should be the only likely one, the Communist bloc. In that case, both deterrence and effective defense could be provided only through the collective force, which would include all the power of the United States. Schuman was inclined to gloss over this point, saying that the two conceptions were complementary and not incompatible. To take this view seemed to be unwise. The issue was real and should be faced—how real became clear a few years later when the mistaken Eisenhower-Dulles doctrine of "massive retaliation" gave vogue to the idea that security in Europe lay in the threat to use nuclear arms and that conventional arms were obsolete. Then France broke away from NATO in favor of developing her own balanced national forces, including the *"force de frappe,"* independent of the collective force.

Intervening in the debate, I urged that this most important issue should not be masked, but it must be understood. Exposed portions of the area would need forces in position adequate to the danger. Nations with responsibilities outside the area would need forces for these purposes. All would need to meet the requirements for peacetime security and order, none of which were in question. The sole point at issue was that in raising the forces for the defense of the area, economic necessity required that all duplication of effort be eliminated. Neither considerations of prestige nor of attempting to achieve a stronger defense position than a neighbor should be permitted to impair the common plan, the common effort, the common strategy. Any such attempt would prove self-defeating both to the nation engaging in it and to the whole effort.

Concluding, I agreed that there was incompatibility between a balanced collective force and a collection of balanced national forces. It sprang from the limitation of our means. I would rather see a clear division in the council and find myself in the minority supporting the recommendation until my colleagues could be won over to it than go home with some ambiguous words masking a disagreement. By the end of May 17 the recommendation to governments for balanced collective forces, still a rather vague concept, was unanimously voted.

The council passed on to set up a continuing body of deputy members of the council to remain in continuous session in London in the attempt to push forward the development of the collective defense. Our representative was Charles M. Spofford of New York. The deputies were instructed to examine as one problem the adequacy of forces and the availability of means to provide them. Each member was to "make its full contribution through mutual assistance in all practicable forms." [2]

Accomplishments at London

The fourth meeting of the council was a useful one. It took the most important steps yet taken to move from mere agreement

2. *Ibid.*, May 29, 1950, p. 830.

to do something in case of trouble toward the creation of a new factor in international relations to prevent trouble. The meeting first brought moments of truth which pierced illusions and revealed the gap between ideas and reality. In this candid light the "strategic concept" was seen to be little more than a division of functions, which, beyond what could be done by our strategic bombing and naval capabilities, had little prospect of being performed. The requirements as calculated by the soldiers "from a strictly military point of view" were so great as to discourage our allies, particularly the French, already engaged beyond their strength in Southeast Asia. While we Americans talked of balanced collective forces, our own military planning and budgeting were undertaken aloof and apart from Europe. Neither we nor the British had undertaken any force commitments to Europe. Finally, Germany, central politically and militarily to any defense of Europe, as the place both where our troops were stationed and where trouble might be expected, was unmentionable in this context.

All these unmentionables were mentioned in London. Taboos were lifted. Where we were naked we began to admit it. It was at London that Schuman burst out with the remark that considered as a treaty contemplating the "liberation of Europe" the North Atlantic Treaty was of no use. None of the Europeans there present would live for that event. Discussing the London meeting some years later, Averell Harriman remarked that it laid the foundation for NATO; in fact, it put the "O" in NATO.

What Harriman meant was that London began the creation of an organization and the outlines of a charter to guide it. Perhaps what we all felt at London was something even more basic—an act of will, a decision to do something. We had planned and adopted resolutions long enough. Even though the most modest plans seemed hopeless of achievement, the time had come to start trying. At London we fashioned the first crude tools.

The council in permanent session was always something of a disappointment. Unlike the high authorities of the European communities, it lacked powers. But it did not lack persistence. While the principles laid down to guide it also lacked the clarity and authority of those given the communities, they had the same germinal seed. They contemplated a common effort, jointly managed and directed toward a common end. When the next step toward integration was to come—and it was to come much sooner than any of us suspected —the London meeting had provided the basic organization and ideas. These were worth a good many divisions and made those we soon got a good deal more impressive as evidence of a common will made flesh.

XII

GERMANY AND THE
DEFENSE OF EUROPE

WE AND OUR European friends had had in the years since the war
stern instruction that events, even more effectively than theory,
can take a hand in the shaping of policy. As we have seen, conditions and events in Europe had played their major part in the
greatest change in American foreign policy since President Washington's Farewell Address, when the sudden and violent attack on
the Republic of Korea on the other side of the globe was to
complete the process.

The Need for German Participation

For some years the Defense Department had held that Europe
could not be defended without the willing and active participation
of Western Germany, but the State Department had not yet gotten
that far. Indeed, as late as June 5, 1950, after returning from London, I had said, in asking for Mutual Defense Assistance funds,
that the United States would continue the policy of German de-
militarization. "There is no discussion of doing anything else," I
said. "That is our policy and we have not raised it or revalued
it." [1] Some doubt should have been cast on my familiarity with the
subject, however, when the next day General Bradley said: "From
a strictly military point of view, I do believe the defense of western
Europe would be strengthened by the inclusion of Germany,
. . . because we do know that they have great production facilities

1. House Committee on Foreign Affairs, 81st Congress, 2nd Session, *Hearings
on Proposals to Amend the Mutual Defense Assistance Act of 1949*, p. 22.

that we could use and we know that they are very capable soldiers and airmen and sailors." [2] He added that there were political considerations on which he did not feel qualified to pronounce. A few, very few, voices had been raised in Europe to express the same thought. Field Marshal Viscount Montgomery, General Lucius Clay, and Konrad Adenauer early in 1950 had all seen a place for a German contribution toward a general European defense effort.[3] During the summer a steady stream of cables came from our missions in London, Paris, and Bonn, urging greater participation by Germany in European defense. In mid-July McCloy put it most dramatically. The probability was that we would lose Germany, politically as well as militarily, without hope of getting it back, if we did not find means for that country to fight in event of an emergency. If there should be a real war, we would have lost a most valuable reserve of manpower—a reserve the Russians could certainly use against us. Even though planning for German participation would require radical changes, it was time to consider our plans for European defense in the light of Korea. His thoughts, McCloy added, were preliminary ones only.

The need for increased military strength was in the air, given a renewed fillip by the Korean attack. In July General Bradley noted that "communism is willing to use arms to gain its ends. This is a fundamental change, and it has forced a change in our estimate of the military needs of the United States." [4] During the same month both the Germans and the French, looking with apprehension at the sixty thousand East German military police and twenty-seven Russian divisions also in East Germany, with more behind them, found little comfort in NATO's twelve ill-equipped and uncoordinated divisions with little air support. Both Adenauer and the French Cabinet inquired about additional American help. Our missions kept up a steady drumfire of recommendations for more American and new German additions to European defense. At the end of the month we asked through the NATO deputies what our allies were prepared to do to strengthen their

2. *Ibid.*, p. 54.

3. In November 1949, on a visit to the United States, Field Marshal Viscount Montgomery said that the only plausible solution to the inadequacy of forces planned at the moment was the use of German manpower (*The New York Times,* November 29 and 30, 1949, and December 6, 1949). On November 20, 1949, General Lucius D. Clay spoke up in favor of a limited German contribution to a composite European force (*The New York Times,* November 21, 1949). On December 9, 1949, Konrad Adenauer said that if German troops were to be raised, it must be on equal terms and in a European army (*The New York Times,* December 10, 1949).

4. House Committee on Appropriations, 81st Congress, 2nd Session, Subcommittee, *Hearings on Supplemental Appropriation Bill for 1951, Department of Defense and Mutual Defense Assistance Program,* p. 20.

own defense. When the replies were tabulated, even including substantial British and French efforts, the total available on the central front in Europe fell far short of any candid military view of an adequate defense.

French Desire for U.S.–European Integration

The French circulated with their reply a memorandum that gave us pause. They proposed to apply the principles of integration to the political, military, economic, and financial institutions supporting a NATO defense system. Integrated organs for foreign policy decisions, military command, military budget, and munitions and economic supply should be established, binding together all the member states. I paled at the thought of bringing so vague, unexplored, and enormous an idea before the Congress. The proposal, I told Ambassador Henri Bonnet, raised issues of such fundamental character, requiring consideration and decision at the highest level of government, that it would not be possible for the United States to reply during the present crisis on both sides of the world. We must have time for study.

My conversion to German participation in European defense was quick. The idea that Germany's place in the defense of Europe would be worked out by a process of evolution was outmoded. Korea had speeded up evolution. If there was to be any defense at all, it had to be based on a forward strategy. Germany's role must not be secondary, but primary—not only through military formations, but through emotional and political involvement. On the last day of July in a long talk with the President, I reported that some were urging that we first ask him for a decision on whether Germany should be rearmed and then, if he approved, go into methods. This seemed to me the wrong way to go at the problem. The real question was not whether Germany should be brought into a general European defense system but whether this could be done without disrupting everything else we were doing and giving Germany the key position in the balancing of power in Europe. To create a German military system, complete from general staff to Ruhr munitions industry, would weaken rather than strengthen European defense and repeat past errors. The President agreed and illustrated the point from European history in the last century. We went on to discuss some way of merging Germany's military contribution into a European Army or North Atlantic Army with an integrated command and, perhaps, supply. The latter could move German industry further into a European system already started by the Schuman Plan. The President was enthusiastic about this approach and wished to have the matter brought back to him through the regular channel of the National Security Council when further work had been done on it.

The "One Package" Proposal

First, however, the United States Government must come to grips with the basic problem involved in the defense of Europe—what were we prepared to do? So far we had made no commitments of ground and air forces for which we were being pressed by our allies. So far, also, we had done nothing to give reality to the strategic concept of an "integrated defense." When in August we turned to serious discussion with our colleagues in the Pentagon, we found ourselves confronted by an ugly dilemma. The Defense Department required no persuasion that the defense of Europe needed, in their phrase, "beefing up," nor did its officers doubt that the beef would have to be provided by increased allied forces, increased American troops and military aid, the inclusion of armed German units, and—to integrate and direct the whole effort—a unified command. But—and here came the rub—they wanted all of these elements in (their phrase again) "one package." They would not recommend any more American forces in Europe, or the responsibility of this country's assuming the unified command, unless the whole scheme should be made a viable one. To do this required wholehearted German cooperation. I knew that this was the stiffest fence on the course. To make it the first and the *sine qua non* of the rest seemed to me to be going about the project the hard way with a vengeance.

Two weeks or so of debate across the Potomac ensued. The Pentagon stood united and immovable. I agreed with their strategic purpose and objective but thought their tactics murderous. Once we established the united command and had a planning center, the inevitable logic of mathematics would convince everyone that any plan without Germany was untenable. To insist on requiring the inclusion of Germany at the outset would delay and complicate the whole enterprise. I was right, but I was nearly alone. McCloy had won over Colonel Henry Byroade, Director of the Bureau of German Affairs, and the German bureau early in August. The creation of a European defense was moving too slowly, he cabled; there was a real chance to solve the problem of a genuine European Army with Germany in it; we should start immediately to work it out; there must be no delay in German participation. Ambassador

Lewis Douglas and Charles Spofford joined in the bombardment from London. On August 11 the Consultative Assembly of the Council of Europe, with West Germany participating for the first time, called for the immediate creation of a unified European Army under a European Minister of Defense.

The President called a meeting for August 26 to discuss the differences between State and Defense. On the eve of this meeting a new factor entered the situation, already complicated enough. Sir Oliver Franks reported Prime Minister Attlee's wish to come to the United States to talk with President Truman. Although the Ambassador was vague about subjects to be discussed, it was not hard to see that NATO pressure for rearmament in Europe and the United States, as well as the possibilities of the war in Korea, was raising serious questions for the British exchequer and the British economy. On the one hand, increased military expenses would add to already high British taxes; on the other, general rearmament would raise the price of the raw materials that Britain must buy. However, the President, with the best will in the world, would be in no position to consult with Attlee helpfully until the necessary preparatory work was done and the general extent of rearmament was clearer. I explained enough of this discreetly and confidentially so that Ambassador Franks could keep the matter on an informal and personal basis for a few days more.

The next day the President pointed out that at the ministerial meeting of the NATO Council, due within a month, the most urgent problem would be how to strengthen the defense of Europe and the nature of the German contribution to it. He gave Secretary Johnson and me a list of questions upon which he wanted our joint recommendation by September 1, later extended to September 5.

The position outlined in the answers called for additional U.S. ground forces for Europe in the neighborhood of from four to six divisions, on the assumption of substantial increases in French forces and in British troops on the continent. All forces of European members, if possible, and the British and U.S. forces in Europe should be combined into a European defense force with an international staff and a Supreme Commander. A German contingent should be added at the divisional level without a German general staff. An executive group should be established in the NATO Military Production and Supply Board to coordinate and increase European military production and supply. The United States would accept the responsibility of supreme command (1) only if our allies requested it, (2) only if they undertook the obligations of the plans as outlined, and (3) only long enough to discover whether they could and would perform them. We hoped, also, that in time the Standing Group could work out a combined-chiefs-of-staff function.

After three days of study and further discussion, the President, on September 8, approved the plan as set out in a rewritten document. The next day he issued a public statement to dispel some of the uncertainty about our governmental position: "On the basis of recommendations of the Joint Chiefs of Staff, concurred in by the Secretaries of State and Defense, I have today approved substantial increases in the strength of United States forces to be stationed in Western Europe in the interest of the defense of that area. . . . Our plans are based on the sincere expectation that our efforts will be met with similar action on their part." [5]

Because of these maneuverings, we were running out of time. Although I kept Sir Oliver Franks informed of developments, Schuman and Bevin were to come to New York by sea, arriving on September 12. It was essential that they should know as soon as possible the position the President would approve. On September 2 our embassies were instructed to tell them of the "tentative" conclusions we had in mind. Sir Oliver was also told that the President thought it better for me to talk these over with Bevin before the Prime Minister and the President met. Schuman replied urging us not to put our plan on the NATO agenda because discussion of it might reveal such differences, especially on German rearmament, as we might not wish to disclose to our other colleagues. This ominous message boded ill for our meeting in New York. Moreover, it boded correctly.

The "one package" decision—to lump together the united command, increased American military forces, and an armed German element—has been called a mistake. I am inclined to agree, and held out against it until convinced that it was the necessary price for Pentagon acceptance of a united command. Even that conclusion was proved to be unsound when General Marshall succeeded Louis Johnson. Indeed, the united command was approved by NATO in December with German participation accepted only "in principle." Six years were to pass before principle matured into fact. During that period the European Army was conceived and miscarried. At the time, however, the danger to Europe seemed to us great and immediate, and these decisions were not being made in the unhurried calm of an academic study. In the first three weeks of September not only was the enlistment of Germany

5. *Department of State Bulletin*, Vol. XXIII, September 18, 1950, p. 468.

in European defense put forward, but General Douglas MacArthur landed at Inchon and began the rout of the North Korean Army, the "Uniting for Peace" proposal was made in the General Assembly in New York, the President authorized us to proceed with a peace treaty with Japan, Louis Johnson was removed as Secretary of Defense, and the primitives in the Senate reached a crescendo of vituperation over General Marshall's nomination to succeed him. Those were noisy and active days.

General Marshall Returns to the Pentagon

Never have talks been so dominated by offstage action as were ours in New York. No sooner had we arrived at the Waldorf Towers, where the Secretary of State lives during sessions of the United Nations, than a half dozen telephone calls—Averell Harriman's among them—informed me that Louis Johnson had resigned as Secretary of Defense and that the President had obtained General Marshall's agreement to succeed him.

At the New York meetings in the Waldorf-Astoria are, from left to right: Ernest Bevin and Emanuel Shinwell from England, Robert Schuman and Jules Moch from France, and the author and George C. Marshall. ACME

Before coming to New York I had met in executive session with the Senate and House foreign committees to outline for them what we were going to propose. This had been a great success; everyone had approved, wished me well, and expressed full confidence in me. The meetings in New York did not accomplish their purpose. Only three months later, when I was starting off for another meeting in Europe on the same subject, the congressional opposition voted that I had lost the confidence of the country, could not regain it, and should be dismissed. That meeting turned out to be a complete success. Thus one learned that congressional approval is pleasant but largely irrelevant to the outcome of international enterprises, unless they call in one way or another for congressional votes.

The "One Package" Proposal Stalls

With us on our mission to New York went Rear Admiral Thomas H. Robbins, Jr., known as "One Package" Robbins, to keep watch over me to see that I never wandered from the straight-and-narrow "one package" path. It was said that he neither slumbered nor slept.

From the outset Schuman took the indivisible proposal very hard. He embraced every part of it enthusiastically except German military participation, wishing to go even further toward allied integration along the lines of his mid-summer memorandum. For days his opposition to the central German provision was skillfully obscured by a kind of filibuster in which various elements of the plan were elaborated and wholly unacceptable roles for the Germans proposed in contributions, material and financial, and in service of supply functions, indicating an all too obvious second-class status. Finally, his opposition became flat and absolute. The French Government would be willing to discuss the formation of German military units only when the NATO allies had first been rearmed and an integrated defense force had been created into which the German units could be merged.

Bevin, on the other hand, though cautious at first for lack of a Cabinet decision, found himself in the position in which I had been earlier. His own Chiefs of Staff, I learned from him, were like ours ahead of the Foreign Office. They too had concluded that no defense of Europe was feasible without German military participation. But Bevin had foreseen French opposition, the danger of Soviet reaction, and anti-German resistance in Britain. He favored following up Adenauer's request to the High Commission to form a gendarmerie, or Bereitschaften, to counter the forces already created in East Germany and which he very much feared. This, he thought, avoided most of the difficulties. "You've got the right idea, me lad," he said to me, "but you're goin' about it the hard way." But to us a Bereitschaften could too easily develop into a separate German army.

Since the three of us could not stay locked in secret stalemate while our other NATO allies fretted on the leaking edges of discussion, we alternated meetings. On September 12, 13, and 14 the three ministers met without agreement. Both Schuman and Bevin then asked their governments for instructions. NATO meetings began on Friday, the fifteenth (D Day plus one at Inchon), and, skipping Sunday, continued through the eighteenth. The three ministers met again on the eighteenth and nineteenth. At this point all meetings recessed to permit me to make the "Uniting for Peace" speech at the General Assembly on the twentieth. The three agreed to resume on the twenty-second, this time with the help of the French and British defense ministers, Jules Moch and Emanuel Shinwell. General Marshall and they joined us on Friday and Saturday. All Monday I spent privately with the Benelux ministers, and on Tuesday, the twenty-sixth, the NATO Council met again and put the "one package" proposal in suspense with comforting phrases until we could make arrangements with the French in which both of us would yield something.

The notable fact about these ten days of discussion was that, frustrating and inconclusive as they seemed at the time, they comprised the first real debate NATO had had about the twin subjects of Germany and European defense and greatly advanced the thinking in all allied countries on both subjects. In May we had talked long and earnestly but about abstractions and phrases. In September we closed with facts and brutal comparison of aims and capabilities. Discussion in the two groups followed the same course, the smaller group preparing the way for the larger one. To begin with, I laid out the subject of debate in a series of propositions, each of which received careful examination:

1. The Korean attack had shown that the USSR was prepared to use force (initially, at least, through satellites) to achieve political ends, and had also shown the vital importance of strength in being and in position and of a plan of campaign.

2. The significance of the President's announced willingness to increase American forces stationed in Europe was its acceptance of the European aim of a defense of Europe as against a liberation of Europe.

3. A defense of Europe required more forces than any proposed plans provided for and a united command, with staff, commander, and agreed strategy.

4. The United States would join in such a defense if—and only if—it was to be a viable defense capable of achieving its purpose.

5. To achieve its purpose the defense would require not only increased forces from its members in being and in position, but also the enthusiastic participation of Germany and armed German units.

6. The United States was opposed to a separate German army and a German general staff.

7. The United States would agree to any plan the allies wanted to give their forces a lead—say of two years—in rearmament over the German formations, but the plan called for them to begin rearmament at once and at the same time to agree definitively to the creation of German units.

8. Finally, the plan was a single entity, to be considered as such; it was not a series of proposals, any one or more of which could be accepted apart from the others.

As the debate progressed, and with it opportunity for the foreign ministers to communicate with their governments, it appeared that five shared our views—Britain, Canada, Italy, the Netherlands, and Norway. The rest hung back, watching the French. With the arrival of the defense ministers each of the foreign ministers was strengthened in his position. Moch, whose son had been captured by the Germans while working for the French underground and garrotted, passionate in his hatred of the Germans, strongly backed Schuman. Shinwell brought solid Cabinet backing for Bevin to urge acceptance of the unprecedented offer of the United States to become permanently integrated into the defense of Europe.

To me General Marshall brought immense help in two ways. His great prestige and calm, compelling exposition left no doubt in any mind, including the French minds, that without Germany the defense of Europe was not possible. He also became convinced himself, and was able to persuade the Pentagon, that the tactic of the rigid and brusque "one package" proposal would not work. "Don't press so hard," said Hervé Alphand, Schuman's assistant; "we will find a solution." And wise old Joseph Bech, Foreign Minister of Luxembourg, drew me aside during a recess in one of the meetings, urged me to be more relaxed, and told me that Paris was working on a European military system based on the Schuman Coal and Steel Plan. (It later emerged as the Pleven Plan.) When I asked why Schuman did not tell me so, he answered, "He doesn't know it yet." Bech had gotten word from an associate of Jean Monnet in Paris. General Marshall also did useful work in private talks with Moch by getting him off generalities and onto specifics, the matching of needs and resources.

Adjournment with Progress

To General Marshall and me it had become clear that to press further at the time would only harden differences and that the better course was to record the progress made and put over

further discussion until the meeting of the NATO defense ministers in October. The President, who had been kept in intimate
touch with each day's discussion and by periodic appraisals of the
situation, agreed with our view. Despite the rhetoric over German
participation, a good deal of progress had been made both by the
council and by the ministers. The former announced on September
26 [6] agreement upon the establishment as soon as possible of "an
integrated force under centralized command . . . to deter aggression and to ensure the defense of Western Europe." The force
would be organized by NATO and under its political and strategic
guidance. It would have a Supreme Commander with power to
organize and train it in time of peace as an integrated force for
the event of war. The commander would be supported by an
international staff and subject to the strategic direction of the
Standing Group. The "finalization" by the council of these arrangements would await recommendations by the Defense Committee regarding the force's organization, command, and strategic
direction. Decisions regarding allocation of forces would be sought
from member governments at an early date, and recommendations
made by the Defense Committee of methods by which Germany
could most usefully make its contribution.

The fact of progress had become evident even earlier. When
Bevin, Schuman, and I had prepared our tripartite communiqué of
the nineteenth [7] we had been surprised at how much had been hammered out in the rough-and-tumble of frank and honest talk. A
series of measures was being inaugurated to move Germany further
from the position of defeated and occupied enemy to that of ally.
In the field of foreign relations the Federal Republic was recognized as the only German government freely and legitimately
constituted and hence entitled to speak for the German people.
To that end a Ministry of Foreign Affairs and the authority to
enter into diplomatic relations with foreign nations would be
authorized. Furthermore, the necessary steps would be taken to
terminate the state of war with Germany. In internal affairs far-
reaching reduction in economic and political controls was announced and limitations were relaxed on steel production and
shipbuilding. Regarding security, the ministers noted the creation
of outright military units in the Soviet zone of occupation, pledged
an increase of their governments' forces in the Federal Republic
to protect and defend it and Berlin, declared that any attack on
the Federal Republic or Berlin would be treated as an attack on

6. *Department of State Bulletin,* Vol. XXIII, October 9, 1950, p. 588.
7. *Ibid.,* October 2, 1950, p. 530.

their own nations, and authorized the establishment of mobile police formations on a Laender basis capable of being called into federal service to meet exigencies. Recently expressed German sentiments in favor of participation in an integrated force for the defense of European freedom were at the time the subject of study and exchange of views. Altogether this amounted to no small record of achievement.

The day after these communiqués were completed the President summoned me to Washington to go over with him and General Marshall definitive orders to General MacArthur.

October 1950 was a month of journeyings in which none of the wayfarers found what each sought, nor did serendipity put in their way anything else useful. President Truman flew to Wake Island in search of understanding with General MacArthur; the NATO foreign ministers came to Washington to find a role for Germany in the defense of Europe; the unlucky United Nations Command trudged toward the Yalu in pursuit of General MacArthur's mirage of victory. It was a frustrating month.

French Epilogue and the Pleven Plan

While the President and the General were meeting in the Pacific, Secretary Marshall, Secretary Snyder (of Treasury), and I stayed home for discussion with two French ministers, Jules Moch of Defense and Maurice Petsche of Finance. After that General Marshall was scheduled to meet with the assembled defense ministers of the Atlantic Treaty countries. Before the French arrived on October 12, preliminary plans were worked out with Robert A. Lovett, who had been recently appointed Deputy Secretary of Defense. Lovett and I agreed that if the French still opposed our "interim plan" for getting on with the defense of Europe we would not accept the burden of thinking up a new one, but leave the ball in their court. Unfortunately, they had thought of this too, and put forward a proposal designed for infinite delay on German participation.

Our financial talks proved not only a failure but a future source of misunderstanding. This happened all too frequently with Franco-American discussion on finance, partly because of language difficulties and partly because even when our language was clear our governmental position was not. Four departments and the Congress were all involved—State, Defense, Treasury, and the European Recovery Administration were all putting forward ideas. To increase confusion in this case the French wanted a commit-

ment for aid beyond the period for which funds had been appropri-
ated, which we could not legally give. Due to their war in Vietnam,
they would run into a budget deficit for the calendar year (also
their fiscal year) 1951 of about a billion dollars, a sizable portion
of which was in foreign exchange deficits. In addition to aid in the
form of military hardware, they wanted dollar aid to help on these
deficits and on manufacture in France of military items necessary,
they said, both to speed up rearmament and to furnish employ-
ment there.

At best it was a complicated puzzle. When four departments
had explained in two languages what could and could not be done
under existing law, with the French choosing to believe what
pleased them most, a deep, serious, and lasting misunderstanding
had been created. So far as the written word went, we made
commitments for the period January to July 1951, the first half of
the French fiscal year 1951 and the last half of the U.S. fiscal
year 1951. We could make no commitment of funds beyond that
time but would review the situation with them before July 1, 1951.
To the French our talk of the need for congressional appropriations
appeared to be pure legal formalism. They believed, and later
insisted, that for the months July through December 1951 we had
promised them *at least* as much dollar aid as in the preceding six
months, and more if we could get it out of Congress. Attempts to
explain our true and only possible position struck them as a rather
shabby descent into sharp practice. This long-dead and unimportant
quarrel is worth mentioning only to warn that all diplomacy does
not deal with great principles and broad policies and that our
constitutional separation of powers is not a pure boon to the State
Department.

We had hardly finished these financial talks and heard the
reports from Wake when the French announced in Paris a counter-
proposal for German participation in defense, which caused us
consternation and dismay. It came to be known as the Pleven Plan,
after its alleged originator, Prime Minister René Pleven. In essence
it proposed that, in addition to the elements of their national
forces that the European allies would pledge to the defense of
Europe under the command of a Supreme Commander in time of
war (but which would remain under national control in peacetime),
a special European force would be created under a European
Minister of Defense and its own command and staff structure,
in turn under the Supreme Commander. Into this army would go
contributions from the allies and German contingents at the bat-
talion level, the whole army amounting to some one hundred

thousand men. To the French the Pleven Plan had the attraction of a German contribution to the defense of Europe, though a small one, without "the rearmament of Germany"—that is, without the creation of a German Ministry of Defense, armament industry, or general staff. Aside from the minimal accretion to European defense that the plan offered, the second-class status accorded Germany was all too plain. There the Social Democratic opposition through Schumacher denounced the plan, while Adenauer for the Government more moderately pointed out the subordinate position into which it sought to place the German contingents.

Announcement of the plan in Paris was followed by ringing endorsement of it by the Council of Ministers and by the National Assembly with a vote of 349 to 235, remarkable in the Fourth Republic. We issued phrases of "welcoming the initiative" and "sympathetic examination," and I received copious explanations from M. Bonnet, the French Ambassador; but to me the plan was hopeless, a view confirmed by General Marshall and concurred in by the President, and protracted discussion of it dangerous. The French were united and dug in. While our Paris embassy believed that discussion in NATO might bring modification of the plan by threatening the French with isolation, that seemed to me too blind and dangerous an alley to enter. Better, I thought, to modify our own position—the "one package" proposal, which I had never liked—and proceed as I had originally wanted to do in August, by accepting the Supreme Commander in return for a unanimous agreement "in principle" for German participation, and to try to get it with united allied military support on our side.

Here General Marshall, in complete agreement, was of immense help in the Pentagon, and the President had always thought the State Department's plan the better course if not undercut by military opposition. The soldiers, too, were ready for a change of strategy. We had loyally supported the "one package" plan through a hard-fought and bloody campaign. It had not worked. They were now in a mood, led by General Marshall and General Bradley, to try it our way. Since the Pleven Plan had made obsolete our ideas of compromise through the defense ministers' meeting of October 28–31, it was decided to relax tensions by more easy discussion, reference of the problem to the NATO Council deputies for further study and preparation of our change of attitude at a meeting of all NATO ministers in December. This was done. It was a relief to get myself unstuck, if only briefly, from the cloying problem of German participation in defense.

XIII

A SUPREME COMMANDER
ALLIED FORCES EUROPE
IS APPOINTED

In the middle of December 1950, the disaster in Korea [1] and General Marshall's influence in the Pentagon had mitigated the rigidity of the military view sufficiently to permit the appointment of an American as Supreme Commander of an integrated force in Europe—provided the principle of German participation in it was accepted and steps inaugurated to bring it to pass. The French had also accepted "the Spofford Plan"—a proposal that the unit for incorporation of German troops into the unified command should be the regimental combat team, a self-contained unit of approximately six thousand men, on condition that this be

1. From the brilliant and lucky landing at Inchon on September 15, 1950, to October 24 the campaign in Korea was wholly successful. Seoul, the capital of South Korea, was taken between September 25 and 27. On October 1 South Korean troops moved across the 38th parallel in pursuit of the routed North Korean army. With the crossing, the first goal set by the Resolution of the United Nations in June—to repel aggression—had been fully achieved. The second—"to restore international peace and security in the area"—was vague and had been much discussed in the United Nations, in the U.S. Government, and among our allies. Should the aim be to seek assurances that North Korea would not renew the attack, or to achieve an independent, united Korean Government and, if so, how? The question had become urgent.

On September 27 General Douglas MacArthur was advised, with the President's approval, that his military objective was "the destruction of the North Korean Armed Forces," provided that there had been no entry by major Soviet or Chinese Communist forces, and that as a matter of policy no non-Korean forces were to be used in the northeast provinces or along the Manchurian border. On the next day, under instructions, he filed an acceptable plan of operations and reported there was no indication of major Soviet or Chinese entry. On October 1, with the permission of Washington, he issued a demand for surrender. This was answered by the Chinese Foreign Minister, Chou En-lai, with dire threats.

On October 7 the United Nations passed a resolution calling for "unified, in-

combined with approval of the longer-term goal of a European
Army, a refinement and improvement of the Pleven Plan. We
had obtained Attlee's grudging acquiescence in this compromise.

---

dependent and democratic government" of Korea. Its terms were ambivalent but
did not authorize the UN forces to impose such a government. MacArthur on
October 9 broadcast a second surrender demand, threatening to enforce by arms
this purpose of the UN.

During this period of optimism and confidence, General MacArthur, while
meeting with President Truman at Wake Island, predicted the end of fighting probably by Thanksgiving, and the return of most troops by Christmas, and also that
there was little danger that Chinese or Soviet forces would intervene in the fighting.

By mid-October General MacArthur's forces had reached the line established
in accordance with his plan of operations approved September 29. North of this
line the plan contemplated as a matter of policy the use of Korean troops only.

On the twenty-fourth General MacArthur without warning or notice to Washington ordered his commanders to "drive forward with all speed and full utilization
of their forces." The restraining line in the north was disregarded and with it the
inhibition against other than South Korean troops in the border provinces. The
Army moved swiftly. One element of the Eighth Army, the 7th Regiment of the
South Korean 6th Division, reached the Yalu near Chosan on October 26 without
opposition and turned back. Then things began to happen.

On October 26 the 7th Regiment, returning as reported from the Yalu,
blundered into a large concentration of Chinese troops, which had already crossed
the river, and was destroyed. The next day the South Korean II Corps to the
north of Unsan in northwest Korea and the 5th and 8th U.S. Cavalry to the west
of it were attacked by overwhelming force. At the end of four days and nights
of incessant and often hand-to-hand fighting the II Corps was no longer an organized force, and the 8th Cavalry had lost half its strength and most of its equipment.
The enemy broke contact and General Walton Walker regrouped II Corps back
at the Chongchon River, reporting to General MacArthur that he had been am-
bushed by "well organized and well trained units."

Through the next weeks the fighting would flare and die down and flare again;
information was difficult to get and confused and conflicting as to the course of
the battle, the Commander's intentions, and the extent of the Chinese commitment.
But the fact of the fighting and the bad situation of the UN forces were clear.

On November 17, with his forces widely separated, MacArthur informed the
Chiefs that on the twenty-fourth he would start a general offensive to attain a line
on the Yalu River, so as to clear the country of enemy forces before the Yalu
froze. He rejected the JCS's urging that he stop on high ground commanding the
Yalu valley.

The Army moved forward into apparently deserted mountain areas of Northwest Korea, unaware of the massive numbers of Chinese soldiers in the area. Four
days later Chinese counterattacks exploded all around the many columns. A series
of fiercely fought and separate battles developed, and General MacArthur reported,
"We face an entirely new war."

The disaster was apparent in Washington, at the United Nations, and to our
allies. But how great it was was not immediately evident. A line was urgently
sought that could be held and to which the troops could fall back and regroup.
It became evident that even such a line might not be possible and that the army
might be forced back onto dangerous beachheads.

By December 5 the rout and retreat had resulted in the loss of North Korea.
By December 15 the Eighth Army was back at the 38th parallel, having withdrawn a hundred and twenty miles in ten days. On December 16 President Truman
declared a state of emergency. At home and in the field morale was shattered; the
next Chinese offensive was awaited with dread and confusion. When it came on
New Year's eve, the situation had changed in one most important respect. On
December 23 General Walker had been killed when his jeep crashed on icy roads,
and General Matthew B. Ridgway had taken command of the Eighth Army on
Christmas Day. He found the demoralized army believing it had been irretrievably
beaten and without faith in fighting. Within a month the longest retreat in American
history ended and the army, its fighting spirit restored, "started rolling forward,"
to use its Commander's words. (For a fuller account of the crisis in Korea in the
fall of 1950, see Dean Acheson, *The Korean War* (New York: W.W. Norton &
Company, 1971).

While a Supreme Allied Commander had precedents in both world wars, including Marshal Foch in France and Field Marshal Sir Henry Maitland Wilson in Italy, we now had to face a critical and censorious opposition, which forced attention to the chain of command from our constitutional Commander in Chief, the President, through the Supreme Allied Commander in Europe to our forces in the field. The prevalent supposition that the Supreme Commander would be General Eisenhower did not assure acquiescence in the scheme of command, as his Republicanism was not then a matter of public knowledge. Each of our allies also had its own technical political problem.

Our difficulties were solved by the "two hat" theory. General Eisenhower as Supreme Commander Allied Forces Europe would also be appointed Commander U.S. Forces Europe, receiving the latter authority directly from the President. With our allies we arranged that the NATO Council should ask the President to make available a United States officer to be Supreme Commander, adding that due to its great respect for and confidence in General Eisenhower, the council would be happy if the President's choice should fall on him. The President would acquiesce. The council would appoint General Eisenhower Supreme Commander of the integrated force and each government would put under his command its troops assigned to the integrated force. Appropriately enough, the code name for the proposed message from the council was "Courage," and for the President's reply "Unity."

"Courage" and "Unity" in Brussels

With Frank Pace, Secretary of the Army, as my companion and colleague, we took off in the President's plane, *Independence*, for Brussels and the beginning of five strenuous days. The atmosphere was tinged with fear of Russian moves. George Perkins, Assistant Secretary for European Affairs, reported that Hervé Alphand, Schuman's assistant, took him aside to ask, "Do you really think we are going to be in war in three months?" The assembled company also was puzzled and worried about our country's state of mind. The NATO meeting on the nineteenth began at ten o'clock and went so smoothly that we were able to send cable "Courage" shortly after noon and make our way to the palace to be received by young Prince Royal Baudouin, to whom King Leopold had recently transferred his royal powers. I found him very touching. Barely twenty years of age, his father a storm center in Belgium, his mother killed in a motor accident, he bore great responsibilities looking solemn and vulnerable in heavy spectacles. I thought of my own son, ten years older, as the Prince drew me aside to ask me shyly Alphand's question to Perkins—did I think war was coming? I did not, but assured him with even more conviction that I had that this cup would not come to him.

At one-fifteen the council met again to receive the President's reply, "Unity." By four o'clock we had established the integrated force, assigned troops to give it substance, and appointed General Eisenhower to command it. We also set up a Military Production and Supply Board, which subsequently proved to be a failure. At five, refreshed by a hasty lunch, I met with Schuman, Bevin, and our three High Commissioners from Bonn in a four-hour discussion of German participation. Here, too, results of the Russian blitzkrieg were apparent. Bevin wanted to go slowly on defense arrangements with the Germans. (God knows we had done so and would continue to do so without need of exhortation!) Schuman kept finding impediments in the four-power agreements on Germany. I lost patience with this attitude and argued that we must beware of being mesmerized into accepting the Russian position that we were bound by these agreements but they were not. We must get on with the rest of our program and not be tied up by Yalta or Potsdam—documents outmoded and dead. On the other side, we must make no further concessions to the Germans until they carried out the New York decisions, acknowledged their debts, and shouldered their proper burdens, but then be ready to move ahead toward equality and modification of the occupation.

We authorized two simultaneous approaches to German participation: one, by the High Commissioners to Adenauer on the Spofford Plan for the raising of German forces (these discussions began on December 21); the other, to provide the institutional framework of the European Defense Community, of great promise and ill fate. Thence we took ourselves back to our embassy residence for an excellent ten o'clock dinner.

The Great Debate Opens

On December 12 our former Ambassador in London, Joseph P. Kennedy, described American policy as "suicidal" and "politically and morally bankrupt," denounced a weak United Nations and ungrateful allies, and demanded withdrawal from Korea, Berlin, and the defense of Western Europe, a refrain not unfamiliar years later. The main statement of the charges, however, was made by former President Herbert Hoover. Briefly put, Mr. Hoover laid down certain postulates, from which he derived governing principles.[2] The postulates:

1. A land war by sparse non-Communist forces against the Communist land mass would be a war without victory—we could never reach Moscow.

2. The United States alone by air and sea power could prevent Communist invasion of the western hemisphere.

3. Atomic weapons were far less dominant than once thought.

4. The United Nations had been defeated in Korea by Communist China.

Based on these postulates, Mr. Hoover proposed "certain principles and action":

First and fundamental, "preserve this Western Hemisphere Gibraltar of Western Civilization."

Second, with air and sea forces hold the oceans, with one frontier on Britain and the other on Japan, Formosa, and the Philippines.

Third, arm our air and sea forces to the teeth.

Fourth, after this initial outlay, reduce expenditures, balance the budget, avoid inflation.

Fifth, aid the hungry of the world.

Sixth, no appeasement, and no more Teherans and Yaltas.

Seventh, the prime obligation to defend Europe should rest with the nations of Europe—America could not create or buy spiritual force for them.

Europe, as seen on my recent visit, had been worried and frightened, but had responded to leadership and action. The stench of spiritless defeat, of death of high hopes and broad purposes, given off by these statements deeply shocked me.

The best way of explaining what was done at Brussels, I said at the press conference, was to describe it as the conclusion of a chapter in a book in which the previous chapters were history and chapters to come would be written by future action. The book dealt with our search with others for means and methods to bring about peace and security. Each chapter recorded a struggle between those who believed in the search and the effort and those who thought it futile, who urged retirement to our own continent, there to isolate ourselves from world problems and secure ourselves from world dangers. The decision was never unanimous and

2. Herbert Hoover, *Addresses Upon the American Road* (Stanford: Stanford University Press, 1955), pp. 3–10.

the debate would doubtless go on, as it was going on at that very moment. These debates had brought our government and, so far, a majority of our people to a number of conclusions, which had seemed controlling:

First, American withdrawal to this hemisphere would give to the Soviet Union such a dominating position over so vast an area, population, and military and economic resources as would make our problems unmanageable.

Second, placed in such a position, the Soviet Union would have the capability and desire to nullify such power to impede Soviet plans as we might possess.

Third, such developments would minimize the possibility through evolution or negotiation, or both, of a peaceful adjustment of interests on any basis other than Soviet desires.

Fourth, the alternative to acceptance of Soviet will would appear to be an appeal to the ultimate violence of nuclear weapons.

Fifth, in the meantime, however, it appeared likely that isolation in Fortress America or the "Gibraltar" of the western hemisphere would so change the spacious freedom of American life as to undermine its cultural, moral, political, and constitutional bases.

These conclusions had led Government and people to reject "any policy of sitting quivering in a storm cellar waiting for whatever fate others may wish to prepare for us." We were resolved to build our strength side by side with our allies, calling upon the entire free world to maintain its freedom, also.[3]

In other words, having put our hands to the plow, we would not look back but remember that "he that ploweth should plow in hope." Thus the pleadings were filed and the case was ready for argument at the next term of court.

It Flares and Fizzles

Even before debate on stationing American troops in Europe opened, there were hints that it would not be a purely party battle, but rather an assault by the bipartisan right upon the Administration's postwar foreign policy. As 1950 closed, Mr. Dulles in a nationwide broadcast pointed out flaws in the thesis that the undoubted Soviet threat called for abandonment of the whole idea of collective security and concentration upon building western hemisphere defenses. Later, when the debate was well launched,

3. Press Conference, December 22, 1950. *Department of State Bulletin,* Vol. XXIV, January 1, 1951, pp. 3–6.

Governor Dewey took a more forthright position that more troops should be sent to Europe and the home front mobilized more quickly. Former Governor Harold Stassen and General Lucius Clay also supported sending the troops.

The leader of the opponents was Senator Robert Taft. He it was who opened their argument by a long speech in the Senate on January 5, 1951. The Senator's attack was no narrow argument against the deployment of troops abroad, but a smashing attack against the whole position. It suffered from a defect of Taft's otherwise excellent mind, which Justice Holmes found also in that of Justice John Marshall Harlan the elder. "Harlan's mind," he said, "was like a vise, the jaws of which did not meet. It only held the larger objects." Taft asked and gave answers to three questions: Could the United Nations maintain or restore peace? How should we prepare militarily for a Russian attack against us and our allies? Could a proposed policy be maintained without inflation and a loss of liberty at home? A fourth—how to win the battle for men's minds against communism—seemed to disappear in the delivery.

His answer to the first question, a flat no, was and is hard to quarrel with; the proposed remedy was not so clear. The United States should "formulate . . . an ideal organization, insist upon a full discussion . . . and if . . . finally blocked by Soviet Russia, bring about the dissolution of the United Nations and the formation of a new organization which could be an effective weapon for peace." [4] What this ideal organization was to be, how it was to be brought into existence, and how this proposal squared with his next were matters not disclosed; presumably they were details to be worked out.

The Senator's military policy, like Mr. Hoover's, was based primarily on air and sea forces. Superiority in these arms throughout the world, he argued, could achieve other purposes than defense of America: assistance to free nations in preserving their freedom and maintenance of a balance of power under which more peaceful relations could be developed. He did not argue for a complete abandonment of the rest of the world, but rather that we interest ourselves in areas from which Communist influence could be excluded by means of effective control of air and sea. This, he believed, had been done for the past five years in Europe.

On the immediate question the Senator took the position that the soldiers had just abandoned and added his own notion that the President had no power to send troops abroad without con-

4. 97 *Congressional Record*, 82nd Congress, 1st Session, pp. 54–61.

gressional authority. If, he argued, we assumed responsibility for leadership and command in NATO, we would be constantly called on to increase our commitment. Furthermore, we would add to the likelihood of war by provoking the Russians to anticipate suspected aggression. The better policy would be to encourage the Europeans to develop their own forces and to let our air and sea forces cooperate with them in the defense of Europe. Later on, if and when our allies showed the capacity to develop a defense with a good chance of success, he would "not object to committing some limited number of American divisions to work with them in the general spirit of the Atlantic Pact." [5]

President Truman used to say that budget figures revealed far more of proposed policy than speeches. The Senator gave his own figures in the January speech: twenty billion dollars for a Navy and Air Force of seven hundred thousand men each, the money equally divided between current operations and new equipment; twenty billion dollars for an army of one and a half million men; and twenty-five billion dollars for all other expenditures, including foreign assistance, a total national budget of sixty-five billion dollars. The President's budget for fiscal 1952 (July 1, 1951–June 30, 1952) went to Congress on January 15. In it he asked for appropriations of seventy-two billion dollars and new contract authority (under which payments and hence appropriations would be required in later years) of ninety-four billion dollars. The appropriation request was divided forty-one billion four hundred million dollars for the military services, seven and a half billion for foreign assistance, and twenty-three billion for domestic purposes. Of the ninety-four billion dollars for contract authority, seventy-one billion was for military and foreign procurement, as was a good deal of the increase of ninety per cent of the appropriations requested for these items over the prior year. Whereas the Senator posited his figures upon a military establishment of two million nine hundred thousand men, the President's were based upon one of three and a half million. The difference between these conceptions of our need for rearmament was as great as the change recommended by the National Security Council paper of the preceding spring, NSC-68, discussed in Chapter 9.

Senator Taft, on the day of the President's budget message, called on Congress to assert itself and its right to determine fundamental principles of foreign policy, adding that he was "quite prepared to sit down with the President . . . or anyone on the majority side, and try to work out a program which could com-

5. *Ibid.*, p. 60.

mand the unanimous and consistent support of the people of the United States." [6]

All through January the debate continued with mounting intensity, the Government gaining encouragement from speeches by two important Republicans, Senators Lodge and Knowland, in favor of troops for Europe. The opposition was aided by the argument of two Democrats, Senators George and Douglas, that the President should obtain congressional approval, by the panic in the United Nations caused by the Eighth Army's loss of Seoul and continued retreat to the Han River line, and by "A Declaration of Policy," signed by a hundred and eighteen Republicans in the House, which called upon the Administration to revise its "tragic" and "costly" foreign programs, to adopt in essence the Hoover policy, and (their own idea) to "conclude peace treaties with Germany, Japan, and Austria," though with whom and how they did not reveal. General Eisenhower's report on his tour of NATO capitals was given to an informal joint session of the House and Senate on February 1,[7] followed up by a private session with the Armed Services and Foreign Relations committees.

The General reported favorably on the spirit of determination and will to resist in Europe, recommended that in the absence of any other acceptable leader the United States should take the leadership, that American troops in Europe should be increased but that no rigid formula or limit should be laid down, and that "the great crying need today . . . is equipment." Within the limits of solvency we should "go to the production of equipment exactly as if we were preparing for an emergency and war." This support of the Administration's proposals and budget caused Senator Taft to waver; he "would not object," he said, "to a few more divisions, simply to show the Europeans that we are interested and will participate in the more difficult job of land warfare while we carry out also our larger obligations."

Into this gap in the line General Marshall, testifying before the joint committees on February 15,[8] drove his counterattack with devastating effect. How many was "a few more"? With the President's consent, General Marshall revealed in public testimony what the Administration had in mind. It was four more divisions, making a total of six. Neither he nor General Bradley would be led into making that number a ceiling. It was, at the time, the meeting point of need and convenience; that point could in the

6. *The New York Times,* January 16, 1951.
7. *Department of State Bulletin,* Vol. XXIV, February 12, 1951, pp. 245–51.
8. *Ibid.,* February 26, 1951, pp. 328–30.

future move up or down. They refused to speculate. Senator Taft was neatly caught. "A few" was more than two, three anyway, which reduced the great strategic issue, as had been stated by President Hoover—of holding the oceans by air and sea power versus involvement on land—to an argument over one division to Europe.

Realizing his predicament, Senator Taft tried to shift his front under attack, a difficult maneuver at best, to the issue of constitutional policy. He did not object, he said after General Marshall had finished his testimony, to the four divisions, which was "about what [he] expected." But "no divisions should be committed to an international army until an agreement is reached with the other countries of the Atlantic Pact . . . and approved by Congress."

In the end the Republicans dropped all thought of legislation in favor of a Senate resolution merely expressing the sense of the Senate without force of law. The resolution had in it a present for everybody, which gave it the comforting majority of 69 to 21, though one provision unpalatable to the Administration was adopted by the close vote of 49 to 43.[9] The main provisions of the resolution voiced Senate (not legislative) approval of General Eisenhower's appointment, of sending abroad such armed forces as might be needed to contribute to European defense, but not more than four divisions "without further congressional approval," desire that the President should consult with the Joint Chiefs of Staff and that they should certify that the other allies were making a "full and realistic" effort toward collective defense before our troops were sent, and a request for semiannual progress reports and consideration of using the military resources of West Germany and Spain.

9. The provision was that "no ground troops in addition to . . . four divisions should be sent to Western Europe in implementation of article 3 of the North Atlantic Treaty without further congressional approval" (97 *Congressional Record*, 82nd Congress, 1st Session, p. 3095).

XIV

A YEAR OF GLOOM
IN THE ORIENT;
STAGNATION IN EUROPE

FROM THE END of 1950 through 1951 was a grim time in the Far East and a frustrating time in Europe. Only the latter concerns us here; but events do not occur in isolation, though separated by half the globe. It is enough to say of troubles in Asia that in the winter of 1950–51 American arms suffered their worst defeat since the battle of Bull Run in 1861. With it came loss of confidence in American leadership and prestige at home and abroad. Two compensating actions prevented this loss from being as great as it might have been: the negotiation and signature of the Peace Treaty with Japan, and the relief of General MacArthur followed by the performance of his successor, General Ridgway.

On the other side of the world American-European relations following the appointment of the Supreme Commander saw the NATO allies still recoiling from the unresolved problem of German participation in the defense of Europe into a sort of paralyzed absorption with problems too great for them: France facing the fast-approaching loss of her positions in Indochina and North Africa —in short, her status as a "great power"; Great Britain facing her loss of Empire and especially the Indian army, becoming thereby a middle-sized European state; and the United States, through its Congress, resentful of—yet barely perceiving—enormous problems of the whole free world headed her way for lack of any other. In the United States, too, those who had thought in 1948 that it was "time for a change" were prepared to make sure that in 1952 there would be no mistake about it. They were, however, not so inspired about the nature of the change that was wanted. The promises of the New Deal, of the welfare state, had given way long enough to the sterner demands of a world in dissolution. Soon they would come flooding back demanding once more the center of attention.

France in Two Minds

Early in the new year a succession of Franco-American meetings evoked a variety of French viewpoints, depending on the participants, which varied from deep suspicion of Germany to great hopefulness of Soviet tractability. President Auriol held both. M. Schuman, however, looking to the future, saw European unity in Franco-German rapprochement and in unity a reduction of tension with the Soviet Union. Some viewpoints held contradictions, which the French were quite able to see but not so able to resolve. The Russian pressure for a four-power meeting on "the German question" was, without doubt, for the purpose of defeating German participation in defense. Each of our French visitors wished —or said he wished—to discuss European defense with the Germans and the German question with the Russians. The phrase was "to close no doors," yet each visitor had different sympathy for each discussion. The President, General Marshall, and I had no sympathy for four-power discussion on Germany, which we regarded as purely a spoiling operation. Recognizing it as meant to cause trouble between us and our European friends and, more generally, to depict us to the world as warmongers, we had to tread warily. Mere opposition would have aided Russian propaganda.

Since talks with the French, into which the British were drawn, and negotiations between the three and Moscow went on through the late winter and spring, the results gave a basis for appraisal. In Germany, the Soviet notes and demand for discussion of the German question had the expected effect. Chancellor Adenauer on February 10 rejected any "neutralization" of Germany as "a disaster for Europe . . . and the German people." He pressed for ten to fifteen divisions as the German contribution to defense. Denying that "neutralization" was under consideration, we pressed the French hard to expedite agreement between the High Commission and Adenauer on liberalization of the occupation. Important agreement was announced on March 6, 1951—the formation of a German Ministry of Foreign Affairs and a diplomatic and consular corps, the abolition or reduction of many reserved powers, and negotiations for a German international debt settlement.[1]

Under the "Spofford Plan" a regimental combat team had been adopted as the "national unit" for the German contribution to the NATO united command. While French President Vincent Auriol and Schuman were with us, from March 25 through 30, we approached them, on military advice, to consider a larger unit. The French in June agreed with the Germans on a divisional unit of ten thousand men. While Schuman was working toward this solution, Auriol was telling Harriman that the Germans were revengeful, nationalistic, and could not be trusted, a view.he was pressing with passion a year later. France was not of one mind on policy toward Germany, as the defeat of the European Defense Community three years later was to make unmistakably clear.

Pleven in his turn raised on two occasions a signal of future trouble, which I was not acute enough to recognize. It was a proposal for a three-power consultative body (with Britain) to coordinate policy on a worldwide basis. This was later, when not accepted, to be one of General de Gaulle's aims and chief grievances against "les Anglo-Saxons." In 1951 my difficulty was in getting from Pleven what he wanted the new body to do. What specifically did he want to coordinate? In Europe our tripartite responsibility for Germany and constant meetings to discharge it, as well as our tripartite position in the Standing Group of NATO, already gave the three such pre-eminence in the alliance as to cause painful jealousy. In the Far East, France refused to (and could not) assume responsibility beyond Indochina and was deeply suspicious of any intrusion by others there. The impression left with me was that the appearance of France on a worldwide tripartite body, rather than the functioning of the body, was what interested our guests. However, all in all, our discussions on German and defense matters had useful results.

The same cannot be said about our talks on France's predicament in Indochina. Here the trouble seemed to spring from the lack of any practicable French policy and their refusal to face that fact squarely and devise one. They were engaged in the most dangerous of all activities—deceiving themselves. General Alphonse Pierre Juin, Commander-in-Chief Allied Land Forces Central Europe, explained that the drain in Indochina was so great as to threaten France's European and African positions. He spoke of the possible need of help should an emergency evacuation be necessary, a panic theme with which General MacArthur had familiarized

1. *Department of State Bulletin*, Vol. XXIV, March 19, 1951, pp. 443–49.

us. Their immediate needs were for military material, especially planes, the loan of another aircraft carrier, and monetary assistance to pay local forces. The last we could not do and what we could do fell a good deal short of their needs.

At this time we began an effort—a frustrating and unsuccessful one—to get our friends to see and face the facts in Indochina. France was engaged in a task beyond her strength, indeed, beyond the strength of any external power unless it was acting in support of a dominant local will and purpose. To us this meant a much more rapid transfer of responsibility and, authority to indigenous institutions than the French had in mind, and this, in turn, required administrative and military training applicable to local needs and capacities rather than adapted from French methods. We urged them to observe and use methods we had found effective in Korea. Although talks of this sort went on for three years, they had no effect and the drain on France continued until the effort failed in 1954.

As already pointed out, all through the first half of 1951 Moscow pressed for a four-power conference on "the German question." When the French came to think about this, their two main preoccupations emerged. The first concerned the French political situation. The public must be convinced, said Pleven, that we had met the Russians halfway in an effort to resolve our differences with them over Germany. Only if convinced that the Soviet Union remained obdurate would the French public support a movement into the dangerous waters of German rearmament. The second preoccupation lay in the persistent hope in France that Russian policy, faced with this alternative, would so change as to make possible re-examination of German rearmanent. Such an idea was exactly what the Soviet maneuver was designed to plant in European minds. Moreover, if, by what would seem almost divine intervention, Russian policy did so change as to make German rearmament unnecessary, this might renew a fast-fading wartime hope of the practicality of disarmament. General Marshall was inclined to believe that it could be ruled out and strongly supported steadiness and continuity of policy rather than a start-and-stop approach attuned to Russian moods and propaganda.

When, however, we all turned our minds specifically to what an agenda of a four-power conference should contain, real difficulties began to appear. I have already referred to the importance that the Russians attached to the agenda of a meeting and the tendentious purposes for which they would use it. They would refuse to discuss matters not specifically included, argue that language used in describing items limited the discussion in various ways, or use the language in propaganda before the conference to cause concern. They would attach great importance to the order of items, sometimes refusing to go from one to another item until the preceding one was completed and then refusing to return to it. We discussed this agenda problem with the French and the British for a whole month through Phil Jessup and Ambassadors Bonnet and Franks until an idea occurred to them. Why not precede the four-power ministerial conference by a four-power meeting of deputies to try to work out what their principals should later meet to discuss? In this way the Western allies would not be put in the position of refusing to meet and would have an excellent opportunity to find out whether the Russians had serious proposals in mind or only propaganda.

The meeting of deputies opened at the Palais Rose in Paris on March 5, 1951. Ambassador at Large Philip C. Jessup represented us; Alexandre Parodi, Secretary General of the Foreign Office, France; Ernest Davies, Under Secretary of State for Foreign Affairs, the United Kingdom; and Andrei Gromyko, Deputy Minister of Foreign Affairs, the Soviet Union. The conference held seventy-four sessions and adjourned on June 21 without accomplishing its purpose—preparation of an agenda for a conference of foreign ministers.

Ministers in Search of Solutions

During the second and third weeks of September 1951 we turned from the high achievements of the Japanese Peace Conference during the first week in San Francisco to that mixture of frustration and progress that is the daily grind of foreign affairs. During these weeks, first in Washington and then in Ottawa, Herbert Morrison, who had succeeded Ernest Bevin as Foreign Minister, Schuman, and I with our ministerial and official colleagues tackled problems so intractable that they still bedevil our successors. The futile weeks at the Palais Rose had convinced even the reluctant French that agreement with the Soviet Union on Germany was not possible. This threw us back on the immensely difficult problems of bringing Germany into the European community and its defense and of finding a fair and workable division of the economic and financial burdens of European defense. The Middle East also was presenting its own insistent problems. The very toughness of these problems acted as an abrasive upon our personal relations, a process exacerbated by attitudes of mind in all three of our countries, long-suppressed—among the British and French these attitudes were the result of their humiliating retreat from empire; among us, of an unsought war in the Far East and a frustrating attempt to rally our harassed allies to an effort in Europe beyond their strength and will. In retrospect I wonder that the frustrations did not seem to be greater at that time than they did; perhaps it was because some matters, such as the European Defense Community, then appeared to offer hope, which would be dashed in the clouded future.

For German and Defense Problems

There was nothing buoyant about Morrison. He could be counted on to deepen the gloom that surrounded our talks. European integration was all very well, he told us, provided it was done right. But was it? The United Kingdom was impatient with the irresponsibility of the Council of Europe, and could not accept the Schuman Plan. So far, the political containment of the Soviet Union had been a success. He would not deny that. But it could go too far and precipitate world war. So far as Germany was concerned, he discerned a tendency to exploit the allies, to squeeze them into paying occupation expenses that the Germans should carry. He had said flatly, he told us, to the German and Austrian chancellors that the occupation forces were providing their defense and that the beneficiaries must pay for it.

Here was something with which Schuman could agree. The Germans were always harping on equality of treatment, he added; let them learn that it should include equality of burdens. The national incomes of Germany and France, he went on, were about the same; hence the Germans should spend the same amount as the French for defense, including the French overseas expenditures. However, the Germans should not be allowed to have a greater contingent in the European Army that he was devising; the difference should go to pay allied occupation costs in Germany. This neat theory would go far to kill any prospect of an adequate German contribution to defense. Sometimes Schuman's ingenuity in devising original solutions to problems seemed exceeded only by his cleverness in circumventing them.

My colleagues set about driving another nail in the coffin of the European Army by their concern for the preservation of democracy in Germany. As they saw it, the threat came not only from the East but from resurgent nazism within Germany. The constitutional order in Bonn might be overthrown as it had been

in Weimar; therefore, the occupation must retain power to intervene whenever constitutional or public order might be in danger—
in other words, the Germans must be persuaded to pay not only
for an allied occupation to protect them against the Russians and
themselves, but for a German contingent as great as the French,
but no greater.

As Chief Justice Edward Douglass White used to say, to state
this proposition was to answer it. My colleagues did not really believe it. They were partly blowing off steam and partly countering
what they thought was my too favorable view of Adenauer. But
form at least required that I respond to this dialectical departure
from reality before trying to get from the British more understanding support for Schuman's European Army and for a further
easing of the occupation. This we were able to do despite the in-
auspicious start.

During the summer of 1951 I had come to the conclusion
that the best way to an adequate German contribution to defense
lay in strong support of the French proposal for a European Defense
Community. The negotiations in Paris about this had become so
involved that the only two Americans who claimed to understand
them were Ambassador David Bruce and a Treasury attaché named
William M. Tomlinson who had forsaken foreign exchange problems
to become a passionate supporter of and expert on the Community.
Neither of them could impart understanding of the negotiations
to the rest of us; indeed, Bruce would not try. The Europeans, he
said, liked to do things in a way that seemed to us like beating up
a soufflé of generalizations. It would come out all right, if we would
leave it alone and worry about something else. I accepted the first
but not the last part of his advice and, therefore, worried alone and
in the clarity of ignorance. Two ideas helped me to my conclusion.

The adoption of our Constitution, I reflected, was aided by
the delusion of innocuousness created by its simplicity. The Congress, said the Founding Fathers at Philadelphia, should have
power to regulate commerce with foreign nations, among the
several states, and with the Indian tribes. They either did not foresee or were not telling what complexities these few words con-
cealed and what powers the Supreme Court would produce from
them as a magician the unexpected from his hat. And the vast
authority contained in the war power was even more modestly
clothed. If the states had been able to foresee all this, the Constitution would never have been adopted. It might be that, intentionally
or not, Schuman was cloaking incursions upon sovereignty by complexity instead of simplicity and, it might be, with equal success.

But what was he up to? And was it sensible? Studying General Eisenhower's chart of the integrated command of NATO, I got a glimpse of what he might have in mind and reassurance that it might be sensible.

Under General Eisenhower's supreme authority were to be a Northern Command, a Southern Command, and a Central European Command under General Juin. Into this last would fall the Benelux, French, and British forces and most of the American with responsibility for dealing with any military thrust across the Eastern European plain toward Germany. Here was the nucleus of the European Army with a European commander, in which European troops could be incorporated in times of both war and peace, for training and operations, and with American troops attached as at present. Add to this a civilian organization for supply and finance and some cooperative recruiting functions in Germany, and one had a European Army with German divisions but no German defense department or general staff. The civilian politico-economic additions should not be allowed to become too complicated or specific or they would create alarm and concern about infringements of sovereignty; they should be developed as need and experience required. The main stress should be on the military aspects of the problem.[2]

These ruminations I incorporated in a memorandum which suggested that only by prompt and vigorous action along these lines could we make progress with the interconnected problems of bringing Germany into European defense, ending the occupation of Germany, and moving into a constructive phase of the integration of Western Europe, all of which were now stalemated. After some discussion in the Department my memorandum on July 16 became the agenda for a meeting at the Pentagon with General Marshall, Bob Lovett, General Bradley, Frank Nash, and Colonel Beebe, their German expert, to which Phil Jessup and Deputy Under Secretary of State H. Freeman (Doc) Matthews accompanied me. Unanimous agreement and a State-Defense paper signed by Lovett and me was taken to the White House at the end of the

2. These were the essential ideas of the European Defense Community, evolving from M. Pleven's 1950 suggestion. During the four years of negotiation that preceded the defeat of EDC in the French National Assembly, it passed through a number of forms, but maintained the idea of providing an international-supranational army for the defense of Western Europe which would include the West Germans but in such a way that the international organization could control German rearmament; it also continued to provide for supranational organizations operating in the political, economic, and financial fields. For an interesting account of why the EDC was defeated in France, see Daniel Lerner, "Reflections on France in the World Arena," in *France Defeats EDC*, eds. Daniel Lerner and Raymond Aron (New York: Frederick A. Praeger, 1957), pp. 198–225.

month and received the all-important endorsement, "Approved, July 30, 1951, Harry S. Truman."

In many respects this was an epoch-making series of decisions, removing many important matters from the realm of discussion to that of execution and enabling the Administration with clear instructions to carry out policy. In later years the prevailing doctrine of "preserving options" precluded this continuity of decisive action so typical of the Truman years. My memorandum and the interdepartmental one based on it concluded that an effective defense of Europe, ending the occupation in Germany, and integration in Western Europe were all interrelated and all waited upon a solution of the allied military problem acceptable to France and Germany. The only one in sight seemed to be the European Army. We proposed, therefore, that the United States go all out for it as I had deduced it to be, without stirring up trouble by asking for clarifications from Paris.

With the President's decision in hand we went into the Washington talks in September united on pressing hard for progress with the European Army and for the inauguration of another even larger plan, which became known as the "contractual relation" with Germany. Since the Russians were blocking a treaty of peace with Germany such as we had just made with Japan, our plan was to enter into a "contract" with West Germany which would end the occupation and clothe that government with as many of the attributes of sovereignty as we safely could in view of the situation in East Germany. The Germans should be given full power to run themselves. Our mission there should cease to be that of occupation of a defeated enemy's territory and become that of an ally contributing by agreement to mutual defense. We should retain authority in four fields only: the protection of our troops, Berlin, the unification of Germany, and subsequent peace settlement and territorial questions.

To work out this agreement would be a colossal job, for the United States Government did not have in Germany, as it had had in Japan, the last decisive word. Many vested interests in the occupation had grown up beyond our control. Fortunately our High Commissioner, John J. McCloy, possessed the tireless persistence, persuasiveness, and force that the task demanded. He was to find a vigorous coadjutor in Adenauer.

The correctness of this analysis and strategy seemed borne out by the Washington meeting. Assured of strong American support for the European Army, Schuman grew more flexible and forthcoming on the "contractual program" and together we moved the British ahead, if not to enthusiasm, at least to an attitude of friendly cooperation with the European movement, as exemplified by the Schuman Plan and the European Defense Community.

For Economic and Rearmament Problems

For some time in 1951 it had been dawning on us that we were trying to move our allies and ourselves faster toward rearmament for defense than economic realities would permit. The gap between goals and performance, both on the part of the separate nations and of the group, was daily more apparent and more painful. In Britain Mr. Churchill, of all people, was criticizing Mr. Attlee for overstressing the military program; and in April, Aneurin Bevan resigned as Minister of Health in the Labour Government, protesting against cuts in his programs to find funds for rearmament. In France the press and elections of June 17 reflected similar sentiments, and in Washington on June 21 a major meeting took place to discuss a paper revealing a shortfall in European defense programed through June 30, 1952, by all the allies and Germany of about twenty-five billion dollars. With Generals Marshall and Bradley concurring, we anticipated Mr. Churchill by several months with a stretch-out of the program to achieve by mid-1954 what we had hoped to accomplish by mid-1952. In this discussion that least militant of soldiers, General Marshall, pointed out how much closer the people of Europe were to personal sacrifice than we were. A cut of five per cent, he said, in the European standard of living meant the difference between white bread and black on the table, while in similar American homes such a cut would mean forgoing a radio or television.

Secretary of the Treasury Snyder hoped that we need not go into lagging European performance with Congress until after it had passed the tax bill. This, however, involved another danger, and I opposed his suggestion. Congress was moving toward a course that would cause us more harm than increased hesitation in raising taxes. This was to cut off aid funds to any of our allies whose restrictions against exports to Communist countries were less stringent than our own. As usual, Congress saw this issue in moralistic terms of black and white; but it was not as simple as that. Our exports to Communist countries were of negligible importance to our businessmen and Government, but this was not so in Europe, as the most extreme examples—British trade through Hong Kong and Portuguese through Macao—were cited to show. To interrupt this, except in the case of strategic materials, could have grave political and military, as well as economic, results. Then, too, views regarding what materials were strategic differed; and, finally, as in the case of Germany's trade with Communist and satellite countries, the State Department believed that persuasion and bargaining was a more effective and less damaging method of reducing it than blunt coercion.

To steer Congress away from petty squabbling with our allies when increased help to them was more than ever necessary, we should not avoid mentioning the gap but explain it fully. Since the beginning of the Korean war, European military budgets had doubled (though ours had trebled); their industrial production, including military, was up twenty per cent, necessitating a sharp rise in high-cost imports, prices, and the cost of living. Their trade deficit had widened, and their reserves had fallen. Congress should be educated, I believed, not appeased like a testy old lady continually revising her will as some of her nephews and nieces met her standards of good conduct and others fell from grace. The Kem Amendment, punishing recalcitrant allies by withholding aid—and thus slowing defense—was already in the offing and gaining strength. Our legislators' exasperation with foreigners (whose weaknesses are very much like their own) has a strong influence on their views of foreign policy.

As a result of this work and talk at home we were prepared and sympathetic when Hugh Gaitskell and René Mayer joined us with their tale of woe in mid-September. Even our own Treasury head, who had glumly said to us a few weeks before that while we were willing to put a ceiling on what Europe should be asked to do we never took the same lenient view toward our own country, had softened a bit. Gaitskell, Chancellor of the Exchequer, reported an estimated deficit between Britain's foreign receipts and payments of a billion dollars, half of which came from the increased cost of raw materials brought on by our purchases for rearmament. A substantial part of the balance would come from diverting manufacture of exports into manufacture of arms. The British were already behind in their own program for 1951; the increased requests of General Eisenhower were out of the question. Not only was it impossible for them to do more, but they could not long continue the present rate of rearmament.

Mayer, Minister of Finance, corroborated from French experience. Industry was working a forty-five-hour week, in some cases up to fifty-two hours; already shortages were developing in power and coke. The nation faced a deficit in foreign payments of six hundred million dollars and rising inflation. He enlarged upon

Schuman's complaint that defense requirements were being fixed by military men without knowledge of economic and financial realities. France would press at Ottawa for a full review of the economic capacity of the NATO countries. It made no sense to destroy them in the name of defending them; new ideas must emerge.

Thoroughly convinced, I drew Harriman, Nitze, and the Pentagon into talk with our allies about methods and means and with the President for his authority to follow up the French suggestion. This he readily gave. Thus the week of talks ended with a surprising degree of agreement on the general line of action we should seek in the economic and rearmament field.

Two Futile NATO Meetings
and One at the General Assembly

The last quarter of 1951 appeared to mark the nadir of international effort for both security and arms control. The NATO Council led off a succession of efforts without substantive results by its September meeting in Ottawa. There it took up, since the association of Germany with the defense of Europe was not ripe for further action, consideration of a Temporary Council Committee to correlate ends (defense) to means (resources) and invitations to Greece and Turkey to join the alliance. In both efforts it ran into sulky resistance from the smaller associates, caused by a belief that the three larger allies arrogated too much to themselves, that the U.S. Congress was trying to control their trade with the Communist bloc, and that their economic troubles flowed from U.S. pressures for rearmament. The bloom was off NATO, the fears of a year before had faded as music wafted westward from the World Festival of Youth and Students for Peace in East Berlin. All this led politicians and writers in Western Europe to question the danger from the East and the need for rearmament upon which the Americans so continually harped.

A press leak in May that Britain, France, and the United States were consulting together about invitations to Greece and Turkey alarmed and annoyed the other allies. The "North Atlantic" had been stretched in 1949 to include Italy; now we were trying to take in the eastern Mediterranean, a snake pit of troubles. How could Northern European statesmen convince their people that attacks in the Levant should be regarded as attacks on Scandinavia or the Low Countries? In carrying the debate for the invitations, I pointed out the absence of any feasible alternative. A year before, recognizing the importance of Greece and Turkey as an eastern flank of European defense, the NATO Council had decided to associate the two countries through a defense planning agency, but it had not worked. They wanted full membership, which from our point of view had the advantage of mutuality of obligations. The idea of a Mediterranean defense treaty including Greece and Turkey and some but not all of the NATO allies (which some had advocated) really made no sense, because if some of us got to fighting, the other NATO allies could not escape danger of involvement but would have no voice in the initial decision, surely a poor position for them. Finally, if Greece and Turkey became allies and were attacked, not every ally would be called upon to fight in the eastern Mediterranean. Action there would have to be geared into a strategic plan for European defense as a whole. All these decisions would affect their security and require their participation. Frank Pace, Secretary of the Army, supported me with military arguments. On the last day of the Ottawa sessions, after much private exhortation, the NATO Council unanimously voted to extend the invitations.

The idea of a small committee (the "Three Wise Men") to bring rearmament more in line with capabilities was the French one, broached in Washington by Schuman and René Mayer. Morrison and I, while approving, left it to them to make the running, a wise decision as our French friends ran into solid resentment against Anglo-French-American "guided democracy." Our allies approved the end but were determined to broaden the means. They wished a committee of the whole to undertake the survey. The highlight in the discussion of the economic problem was Dirk Stikker's speech. "Any further lowering of the present standard of living in Europe," said the Netherlands Foreign Minister, "without the prospect of a rise in the near future, will endanger the social peace on the home front which is so essential to our defense effort." Others eagerly caught up this theme.

John Snyder, Secretary of the Treasury, believing that he saw where the discussion was likely to end, intervened with more bluntness than tact to tell our allies not to expect the United States "to foot the bill" for their defense. During this week he was chiefly concerned with the possible effect of Ottawa decisions upon pending Treasury refunding operations. At last the unruly flock entered the fold, a twelve-man Temporary Council Committee was created with authority to set up a three-man working group and with instructions to report by December 1 in time for another discussion at a meeting to be held that month in Rome. So the idea of the "Three Wise Men" survived and became incarnate in the persons of Averell Harriman, Jean Monnet, and Sir Edwin Plowden, men of outstanding ability and common sense.

Soviet Hostility Increases

To add to the depression of late 1951, the Russians contemptuously rejected an arms control proposal put forward by the three western allies at the United Nations meeting in Paris in November. This seemed the signal for intensification of the propaganda war that had been raging all the year between the principal powers. President Truman launched the joint British-French-American proposal from Washington on the evening of November 7, passing the exposition of it to the three ministers in Paris. This I took up the next morning before the General Assembly to be supported by Eden and Schuman. But before they could speak, Vishinsky got the floor to say during a diatribe of two hours that "I could hardly sleep all night last night having read that speech [President Truman's]. I could not sleep because I kept laughing." The sheer bad taste of this boorish remark shocked both the Assembly and press. Speaker after speaker rose to rebuke Vishinsky and to welcome the proposal.

It is no longer important, however, since it was soon apparent that the Soviet Government would have none of it. Its purpose was to press on with the increase of its armaments, not to limit them. The talk dragged on in Paris for many weeks, but ministers had to turn to measures for their countries' security and the mounting hostility of the Soviet Union.

We Meet with Adenauer

After the presentation of the disarmament proposal to the Assembly, Chancellor Konrad Adenauer came to Paris to meet with Schuman, Eden (who had succeeded Morrison), and me. This was his first visit to Paris since the war and the first joint meeting of the four foreign ministers, a landmark in German-allied relations. The three allied High Commissioners in their negotiations with the Chancellor had already begun granting to the Federal Republic increasing control of domestic affairs and advancing association of the Republic with the defense of Europe.

Adenauer seemed to have grown in assurance over two years and to have become an impressive figure. He and I met for our first discussion at lunch at the embassy with Ambassador Bruce,

High Commissioner McCloy, and Assistant Secretary of State George Perkins. The Chancellor had with him State Secretary Walter Hallstein, operating officer of the Foreign Office, which Adenauer himself headed. After lunch, while we talked in the living room, the Chancellor bluntly stated what was clearly his principal concern. Would the occupying powers, he asked, use Germany as a pawn in attempting to reach a settlement with the Russians? He had the gravest worries about our British and French associates. Both public and governmental opinion in those countries, shown in press and parliaments, was deeply suspicious and hostile toward Germany, and understandably so. What attitude could he expect from the United States? Not merely from President Truman, who had made his position and his Government's very plain, but over time from the country? He was aware, he said, that we would have an election within a year and of the speculation regarding it that our press carried.

The question seemed a fair and honest one, deserving a forthright and honest answer. Due to our different position and experience, I said, the American people did not share the suspicion and hostility toward Germany that existed in France and Britain. However, this attitude existed among us toward the Soviet Union and Communist China to a far greater extent than in either of the other countries. He could be sure that neither the present U.S. Government nor any now-discernible successor from either party, in asking Western Europe and Germany to join with us in common defense arrangements against Soviet aggression, would countenance the sacrifice of one of our allies in an attempt to appease the Communist powers—an effort as futile as it was immoral. McCloy and Perkins, I pointed out, were members of the Republican Party and I asked them to express their own views, which they did to the same effect. We all analyzed the winter debate on "troops for Europe" to point out the weakness of the isolationist position in America at the time.

We went on to argue that the attitude of not only the occupying powers but of all Western Europe toward Germany would depend upon German conduct. If Germany pressed on, as it had been doing, to be a good European neighbor and to carry its weight of the cooperative defense burden, it could and would be received as an equal partner with an equal voice in policies and decisions. In rebuilding mutual confidence in the West after the experiences of the past two and a half decades, suspicion was natural on both sides, but Adenauer should remember that ground for suspicion was far more plentiful to the British and French than to the Germans. We proposed to deal openly and honorably and insist that others do the same. If that sort of relationship should break down, the principal sufferer would be all of Europe.

Afterward McCloy told us that Adenauer was much impressed by the frankness of this talk. He was also impressed, McCloy said, by the relations he observed in the meeting the next day between Eden, Schuman, and me—the informality, the friendliness, and the mutual understanding that existed among us. It was, McCloy added, a completely new idea to Adenauer—whose experience in international affairs had been very limited—that representatives of important powers could conduct themselves as understandingly, indeed warmly, as we did. He gained a sense that he was dealing with people among whom everything was frank, friendly, and aboveboard. After that, discussion between Adenauer and the High Commissioners went better than ever.

Before our meeting with the Chancellor on the afternoon of November 22 at the Quai d'Orsay, the three of us had conferred with the High Commissioners to get a common view of several matters to propose to the Chancellor. The High Commissioners had gone far in working out with him the contractual relationship, consisting of a general agreement and four or more subsidiary agreements, which would supersede the Occupation Statute, the Allied High Commission, and the various Land Commissions with their powers of intervention in German affairs. Some questions remained for discussion by the Chancellor and ourselves. In general, these were either theoretical, impossible to be settled without Russian agreement, or not yet ripe for solution. They were dealt with in different ways.

In the first category, for instance, was Adenauer's worry that the allied reserve power to resume authority in Germany in the event of danger to the state from foreign invasion or civil disorder might be unduly prolonged. He wanted some arrangement for appeal. This, I pointed out, was wholly unrealistic since a danger from invasion could not be foreseen in advance and dealt with judicially, and one from domestic disorder would either be clearly terminated or not. In one case we would be only too eager to return authority; in the other we could not. But to resolve any doubts of our good faith, I suggested a review on request by the NATO Council, which all were ready to accept.

Of the same nature was Schuman's desire to have in the agreements a list of armaments that Germany should be prohibited from producing. Here again was the question: Was Germany an ally or an enemy? To take an ambivalent attitude would be fatal.

We must either leave to the European Defense Community the matter of allocating weapons manufacture among its members or work out with Adenauer a unilateral declaration of what weapons Germany would not produce. Important steps along these lines were taken a few months later in London at our second quadripartite meeting.

In the second category was the Chancellor's desire for some statement on Germany's eastern boundary. Here the solution was found not in an unwise attempt to draw or define it but in agreement "that an essential aim of the common policy of their [four] Governments is a peace settlement for the whole of Germany freely negotiated between Germany and her former enemies, which should lay the foundation for a lasting peace. They further agree that the final settlement of the boundaries of Germany await such a settlement." [3] This met one of Adenauer's principal worries, already mentioned, of a dictated peace treaty on the Versailles Treaty model, worked out among the three of us and the Russians and forced upon him.

Questions of German contribution to defense both in the support of allied troops in Germany and through German military formations were just as difficult for the Germans at this stage as for the French. With the latter we went again, as we had done in 1950, through the anguish of probing their budgetary position to discover whether the six hundred million dollars they asked of us was to meet a foreign exchange deficit or a budget deficit or both. Insofar as it was the former, we could not spend dollars in France until the French had provided the land and facilities to house our ground and air forces, which for internal political reasons they were agonizingly slow in doing. We had our own troubles, too. Our funds were all expendable through three men who, although good friends, were also good poker players and not eager to assume one another's just obligations—Harriman of Mutual Aid, Lovett of the Defense Department, and Snyder of the Treasury. Added to this was the infuriating American practice of reviewing every decision to death. One never knew when a commitment could be regarded as final and not subject to review by some group not conversant with the facts. In the end, however, we gave the French assurances which, although unsatisfactory and productive of future misunderstandings, enabled them to strengthen their forces.

The problem of the German contribution to defense was

3. For text of Joint United States, United Kingdom, French, and West German Statement on Germany, issued at Paris on November 22, 1951, see *Department of State Bulletin*, Vol. XXV, December 3, 1951, p. 891.

complicated by a difference in approach by the French and British on one side and the Germans on the other. At the moment it was clear that amounts paid by Germany for the support of occupation forces were too high to be continued as aid to allied defense garrisons. But a reasonable figure was not yet ascertainable. Nor was it possible at that time to determine the cost of German forces still not agreed upon. The French and British proposed agreeing on a total figure of thirteen billion deutsche marks, a reasonable total figure for German defense costs, and working back from that to an appropriate division. The Bundestag, like any parliament, would have great trouble with authorizing so large an amount with so little knowledge of its precise uses. Our discussions, *à trois* and *à quatre*, brought out these difficulties but not solutions for them. It would take another meeting of the three at Lisbon and of the four at Bonn in 1952 before sufficient precision could be provided to make agreement possible.

I summed up my impressions in a cable to the President: Our meeting had been held in a good atmosphere. The specific agreements we had reached were of less importance than the fact that we had met on a basis of equality. We had satisfactorily reassured Adenauer as to his main fear, which was that the allies might, at German expense, conclude a deal on German unification with the Soviets. On his concern about eastern borders, he had been assured that Mr. Byrnes' position still held. We had not been able to move beyond bare fundamentals when it came to the problem of Germany's defense contribution. The High Commissioners had been authorized to start negotiations on a total figure of thirteen billion deutsche marks for the fiscal year beginning April 1, 1952. We had also repeated the security declaration for Germany of September 1950, which should tide us over until Germany could be formally linked to the North Atlantic Treaty.

Another Council Meeting Stalls

The Rome meeting of the NATO Council in December 1951 like that in Ottawa continued to stall, through lack of progress outside NATO circles, on the two fundamental obstacles to European defense: an arrangement for enlisting a strong German contribution to it and a reconciliation of the military needs of defense with the capabilities of the European economies and political structures. The arrangement for a German contribution had made more headway in the negotiations between Adenauer and the High Commission at Bonn than in Schuman's negotiation of the Euro-

pean Defense Community. The Three Wise Men of the Temporary
Council Committee were hard at work on the second—reconciling needs and capabilities—but were not yet ready to report
and would not be for two or three months. So the meetings were
destined to frustration. "The big problems remained unsolved,"
I cabled the President in a personal appraisal of the session, "and
will need most energetic work for the next sixty days if we are to
solve them. In the international field we are experiencing what
the production people call 'slippages.'" Both Eden and I, the
report added, believed, and had impressed on Schuman, that he
must aim for some conclusion of his efforts by the end of the year.
Otherwise we would be threatened by a permanent deadlock and
would have to drop the European Defense Community. Eden was
a most stalwart ally, despite ambivalent attitudes expressed by
Mr. Churchill in London.

The depressing attitude of the meetings themselves was height-
ened by a revolt of the Benelux ministers and my getting what a
Roman doctor regarded as ambulatory pleurisy with occasional
relapses into bed. General Alfred Gruenther, General Eisenhower's
Chief of Staff, opened the meetings with a hair-raising description
of how devastating a Soviet attack on Western Europe would be
if the Russians brought their full power into play. Whether or
not the accuracy of the figures Gruenther used was borne out by
later intelligence, this sort of exegesis tended to discourage rather
than encourage the European defense effort, since failure to speak
frankly of the deterrent factor of American nuclear weapons made
the task of defense seem impossible. While the ministers were
digesting this somber report, General Eisenhower gave an in-
spirational address on the pressing necessity of the political unification of Europe. After this speech the council took a coffee
break, during which the American group mingled with the others
to gather impressions created by the addresses. These were almost
uniformly critical of the effect created by the military command
apparently trying to bring pressure for a political result, European
integration. Unknown to the General, the political lecture was
delivered to a group already heatedly divided on this very issue.

My wise, shrewd, and humorous friend, Joseph Bech, Foreign
Minister of Luxembourg, added another comment. "Before long,"
he said, "I think we shall lose our Supreme Commander." I was
puzzled. "Yes," he went on, "the signs are unmistakable. Our
commander will soon leave us to run for President of your country." And so he did, less than four months later.

In the Paris discussions of the Defense Community a considerable fissure had opened between the Benelux countries, led by Paul van Zeeland of Belgium, and France, Italy, and Germany regarding the degree and scope of integration to be sought in the Community. The issue was framed in terms of Benelux reluctance and constitutional difficulty in placing all their military forces in peacetime as well as war under supranational command. The problem, however, ran deeper. They believed that in the economic field their Benelux integration was working well in a tidy, small area with largely similar conditions. If sucked into the larger, more confused, and disparate economic affairs of France, Italy, and Germany, they would be submerged and powerless. Furthermore, they were being drawn into these problems not primarily for economic reasons but because of military problems, where their part must necessarily be small.

These were very valid objections. For the time being they were postponed by provisions for approaching integration in non-military fields by stages. Later when the Defense Community idea collapsed in 1954 and was followed by the Messina negotiation of the European Economic Community (Common Market), these same problems required a great deal of patient discussion and adjustment. At the moment, however, they were in the phase of generating heat.

XV

SMOG LIFTS OVER EUROPE

Crisis in the Alliance

On February 6, 1952, King George VI died. When it was decided that the King's funeral would be on February 15, followed a week later in Lisbon by the NATO Council meetings, the President concluded that I should attend the funeral as his representative and use the following week for a supreme effort to remove the obstacles blocking the establishment of a defense for Europe. The situation there, particularly between France and Germany, had worsened materially since the turn of the year. The Bundestag, sensing Germany's rising importance in Europe, sought to raise German conditions for contributing to defense, and the French Chamber amid increasing fears pushed harder to impose discriminatory restrictions on German rearmament and arms production. French ambivalence between treating Germany as potential ally or enemy was paralyzing action.

Issuance from the impasse depended entirely upon the United States. In February the French Cabinet was once again in trouble, and within it Schuman in deeper trouble. Adenauer could control the Bundestag but not lead in Europe, though both McCloy and Bruce reported to me in January that he was the most stalwart supporter of the European Defense Community in Europe. Italy and the Northern European allies were deeply worried, fearing Franco-German domination if the Community succeeded and German adventurism if it failed. British opinion, hostile toward Germany and apathetic toward Europe, received no lead from the Prime Minister. A lead—and perhaps a push, too—had to come from the United States. Ever since the past midyear our Govern-

ment had brought pressure on the French and British to get on
with the German program theoretically agreed at Brussels in December 1950. General Eisenhower had hammered away at European governments through Chiefs of Staff and defense ministers,
especially for the European Army; John McCloy had put all his
great energy into pressure on the Chancellor and the High Commissioners to move the contractual arrangements; Harriman had
done the same to bring all military programs, including the German, within the limits of economic and financial feasibility; and I
had harried the foreign ministers, sometimes to the point of revolt.
The crisis had only increased, to reach its peak in this period of
prelude to Lisbon.

At the end of January I had had a disturbing letter from Schuman in which French fear of Germany was discernibly destroying
French hope for the Defense Community. The French Government,
he wrote, could see no possibility of a German defense contribution
except through the Community, but Bonn insisted that the Community not discriminate against Germany. Therefore, the restrictions and prohibitions upon German rearmament could not be
written into the document, but must be accomplished by the contractual arrangement between the three occupying powers and
Germany. Moreover, the German military force in the Community
must be limited to one-fifth of the whole, so that it should not
exceed that of France (which, of course, would not include her
forces outside Europe). Germany must agree to an economic union
between France and the Saar and must be precluded from seceding
from the Defense Community and from joining NATO.

The idea that Adenauer could accept such a position was, of
course, absurd. Plainly Schuman's excellent judgment had been
overborne in the Cabinet and Foreign Office. In the effort to
strengthen Schuman against instructions that would destroy any
possibility of success at London or Lisbon, I replied that NATO
could not survive another failure, another postponement of hope
for a defense of Europe. A conference was pointless unless our
friends were determined to join us in making it a success. Germany
could and would contribute to the support of allied troops stationed
there for her and Europe's defense if her position was made consistent with her self-respect. What armaments she produced should
not be determined by imposed prohibitions but by agreement
within allocations of production by strategic areas through the
European Defense Community.

The Saar issue must be removed from current discussions by
an initiative from Schuman and Adenauer. Germany should not be

precluded from future membership in NATO, a dangerous and destructive idea; Adenauer would accept an intermediate and temporary association. "I do not believe that the way to solve a difficult question is to inject one which is presently insoluable."

I pleaded with Schuman not to risk all with irritations and unnecessary problems, but to reach agreement in London so that the contractual arrangements and EDC (European Defense Community) could be concluded; and in Lisbon NATO could be reorganized, Greece and Turkey admitted; the TCC (Temporary Council Committee) recommendations adopted, and the establishment of EDC, its relationship to NATO, and the contractual relationship with Germany, all pushed forward. It was a big agenda.

"Either we must guide the events we have set in motion to the goal we have chosen," the letter concluded, "or they will move themselves, we cannot tell where." Lisbon was to be the supreme gamble upon which we would stake our whole prestige, skill, and power.

Even as we prepared to fly to London the Bundestag and the French Assembly further exacerbated the situation. The more fully Schuman and Adenauer fashioned the principal features of the Defense Community, the more parliamentary interest quickened in each country. Soon each body sought to instruct its negotiator on conditions, qualifications, and desiderata—all reducing maneuverability, hardening positions, and making compromise more difficult. On February 8 the Bundestag set German conditions to membership in the Community. The French National Assembly soon after recommended the restrictions and limitations to be imposed on Germany and a guarantee by the United States and United Kingdom against German secession from the European Defense Community. With these unhelpful contributions overhanging us, we took off for London in the *Independence* on February 12.

No one ever went to a funeral so fully staffed and prepared for negotiations with so many on so many critical and perplexing problems. The method lay in creating a momentum of agreement; a week of ceremonies among which meetings of different people on different subjects could be interspersed, without apparent plan, provided an excellent opportunity to do so. Eden and I, with our staffs, were on the scene first for ceremonial reasons; Schuman came a little later, and Adenauer joined us after the funeral. Our plan was to prepare an agenda of the essential items for the four, agree on the substance ourselves so far as possible, try for French acquiescence in ameliorating major problems before Adenauer came, and enter the final discussion as united as possible.

We soon convinced our British colleagues on two important points. As we had told Schuman some time before, unless he could quickly make progress on the European defense treaty, we would withdraw our support from it. It was now or never with that idea. Secondly, the United States would not consider a guarantee (which would have to be a treaty) against German secession from the Community. Such a withdrawal, I pointed out, contemplated another civil war in Europe—an impossible contingency on which to build a defense alliance. Schuman raised this same point when he arrived later in the day for the funeral on the morrow. With Eden, we had the issue out. The proposal was unwise; Adenauer would not accept it; and the President would not propose it to the Congress. The defense of Europe must be worked out within the limits of existing congressional commitments. We thereupon dropped that subject and agreed to invite Adenauer to join us for our discussions after the funeral.

While Schuman briefly returned to Paris, Eden and I agreed that Eden would reassure Schuman of Britain's solid support in case of any such drastic change in the European situation, should it occur. We also agreed to press both Schuman and Adenauer to stop agitating the Saar issue and postpone a decision for the present. We would ask Schuman to approve the review of sentences for war crimes imposed by occupying authorities in their zones which would have to be carried out by German authorities. A review board of three allied and three German members—with a neutral member if Adenauer wanted one—could do this. On the troublesome problem of civil aircraft production in Germany the happy thought occurred to us of putting the problem up to Adenauer, who might decide that with military aircraft production not permitted it would be more economical to buy than to build planes for civil use—as, indeed, he did.

Finally, we agreed to press Schuman for a relationship between the European Defense Community and NATO by which joint meetings of their councils should take place at any time by mutual agreement or on the call of any member of either claiming the existence of a threat to its security.

When Schuman joined us, he had gained enough latitude in Paris to agree with most of what we had to propose, but the complex and tangled question of German contribution for the support of allied troops to be stationed in Germany for the common defense remained. Three decisions helped greatly to simplify this:

First, to consider only the next two German fiscal years beginning in April, in the first of which we would assume that the

Defense Community would not yet be in effect and in the second that it would be;

Second, to appoint a work group under the High Commissioners to review the charges and practices that the victorious forces had imposed on occupied Germany and reduce them to what a host ally might properly contribute to guest forces come to aid in the joint defense;

And, third, to assume for discussion that the total German budget item for defense (including provision of its own forces and support of allied) should be the amount recommended by the Temporary Council Committee report, ten billion deutsche marks.

For the first year the issues for ultimate decision would be to fix a total sum for support that would be less than Germany was now paying and that would fall well within the budget figure, since German military forces would not yet have been organized. For the second year the issues would be in one respect simpler and in another more difficult. French forces in the Defense Community would be chargeable to the Community budget, as would those of other members, and contributions to the budget would be worked out by its own procedures. German contribution to support of British and American forces would have to be determined by a negotiation among the United Kingdom, the United States, Germany, and the Defense Community. Difficult as some of these issues were, they were now understandable.

Turning to security controls over German production of certain war materials, the French had now adopted the British idea of what they called a binding unilateral declaration not to produce certain items. We preferred the less discriminatory method of having the Defense Community establish "forward zones" in which these items would not be produced by anyone. More important to us, however, was striking "gun barrels" and "propellants"—i.e., explosives—from the list. Twenty per cent of the military aid asked of us by our European allies was for ammunition, a substantial amount for artillery. To exclude Germany from production of both continued the burden, wholly unnecessarily, on us. Schuman's plea not to rebuild Krupp was not persuasive if Germany was to rearm herself for the common defense.

Adenauer Joins Us

My admiration for Adenauer continued to grow during the London meeting. He was quick in understanding through the welter of interpretations, wise in judgment, and decisive. Often I found myself agreeing with him contrary to the views of the other two. When working groups brought in drafts of proposals, he would accept, reject, or propose specific change at once. My impression, too, was that his judgment was based on long-range views of purposes and consequences and not on immediate political convenience. Schuman disclosed—it became much clearer three months later—a consciousness of diminished authority with the Cabinet and Assembly and a hesitance to move from authorized positions. Eden then, and even more at Lisbon and later in Bonn, could be counted on to end up on the side of angels, which I tended to identify with my own.

Adenauer and his German aids increased both the tempo and the size of the meetings. Quick agreement was reached on the review of war crimes sentences, as the three of us had proposed. Discussion of German contribution to allied troop support was put off a day to permit Adenauer to consult Finance Minister Fritz Schäfer on the Temporary Council Committee's revised report available only the day before. Adenauer accepted readily the proposal for joint sessions of the NATO and European Defense Community councils and for a declaration by him that Germany would not produce certain war materials if we could agree on the list. He went further and stated his willingness to accept a Defense Community decision not to have materials produced in a forward zone, which would include Germany and all or parts of other countries. Schuman began a speech on the adverse psychological effects of the rebuilding of German war factories. To avoid creating troubles for ourselves I suggested putting a group to work on a memorandum combining these ideas for the ministers to consider in the morning.

The next day, when the quadripartite meeting resumed, Eden read a new draft about security controls, which would deal with the problem by an added provision in the European Defense Community treaty giving that organization authority to decide what should be produced in various areas. Adenauer would write two letters: one to Defense Community countries saying that provided that the equipment of German troops was the same as that of all other contingents, Germany would not regard as discriminatory a decision not to allocate to forward areas the production of weapons to be stated in an annex to the treaty; the other was to the United States and Britain saying that the Defense Community treaty would become domestic law in Germany.

When it came to the contents of the list, I again vigorously opposed the inclusion of gun barrels and explosives. Eden proposed suspension of these items from the list for a limited time pending reconsideration by experts and a report to the ministers by spring. This was agreed. Regarding civil aircraft, Adenauer disposed of the matter, as we had hoped, by saying that Germany had no intention of producing planes. It would be far too expensive; Germany would purchase them.

Turning to the most critical of all our issues, the financial ones, Adenauer said that Bonn agreed to publication of the Temporary Council Committee's report and saw no difficulty to agreement on the total German contribution before ministers concluded the Lisbon meeting. He thought our plan for negotiation excellent. On this cheerful note we adjourned to fly to Lisbon.

Although the President had been kept informed day by day of our talks in London, they had been too kaleidoscopic to permit a personal appraisal until they ended. This I gave him from Lisbon. At first, I cabled, it had been doubtful whether Schuman could meet with Adenauer at all since his Government might fall at any moment. But with Adenauer in town for the King's funeral, arrangements were made. Another hazard lay in discussing, as we had to do, matters just debated and voted on by the Bundestag and which the French Assembly was debating and did vote on while we talked. Adenauer felt that he had preserved enough latitude for maneuver, while Schuman, though fatigued and worried, gallantly took a chance on the leaks and went further toward compromise than I had thought possible. This delicate situation explained why our communiqués were so restrained. Some important, indeed critical, matters—such as German support for allied troops in Germany and the prohibited list for German war production—must await decisions during that week in Lisbon, but we were in much better shape to make a good showing than we had been a week earlier. Much had been decided; much had been advanced toward decision; irrelevant obstacles like the Saar and the war crimes sentences had been removed from the stage.

Success at Lisbon

At Lisbon we received the cheering news that Chancellor Adenauer was already carrying out his part of the London agreements. Germany, he had announced, would not engage in the production of nuclear energy, missiles, or heavy warships. The Government would ask for legislation to carry out the antitrust program.[1]

---

1. In meeting with Eden and Schuman in London we had agreed that Adenauer must stop procrastinating over the decartelization program and complete it by spring.

The last obstacle was cleared from the way of the Temporary Council Committee's level of forces report. The committee wished to say that the level would provide an adequate defense for Europe. The military advisers believed that it was not adequate but was the best that could be done at the time and would have a strong deterrent effect on any aggression. A suitable form of words was found.

French and German Military Finances

We began at once to wrestle with our most baffling as well as our central problem—French and German military finances and their interrelation. We continued to wrestle with it all through the conference and the night that followed its adjournment. The new Prime Minister, Edgar Faure, had proposed a military budget that would raise French military expenditures from ten to twelve per cent of French gross national product, the highest ratio in Europe. Because of the war in Indochina, however, French divisions in the European Defense Community would be cut from fourteen to twelve and its air-power contribution would be cut also. The cost of his proposal would be higher than the Temporary Council Committee recommendation and higher than the current budget. France would need American help. Reports of his plan, which promptly leaked, brought predictions in the Paris press that Faure would fall and a charge by General de Gaulle of a "sellout" and a policy of "bankruptcy and debasement" on the part of French leaders.

On the last scheduled day of the conference (Monday, February 25, 1952) continuous meetings by ministers and technical assistants charged with special aspects of the problem brought us within sight of solutions. Faure's budget, with its twelve divisions and twenty-seven air squadrons for service with NATO-EDC could be financed with approximately six hundred million dollars of U.S. aid and the German contributions to allied troop support under discussion with the High Commissioners in Bonn. We were prepared to furnish the aid provided all other questions could be worked out.

In Bonn, however, discussion had stalled over two questions: first, whether, as Adenauer claimed, such expenses as frontier police, veterans' care, and defense of Berlin already in the West German budget should be included in the eleven-billion-deutsche-mark military budget to which he had agreed on February 21; second, whether a definite figure for allied troop support could be settled before the four governments had agreed what items of support were allowable. Adenauer was ready to liquidate the claim at half a billion deutsche marks a month. This seemed sensible.

Since these unsettled questions would undoubtedly be appealed to the three ministers in Lisbon, we would do well to get all other matters agreed before this occurred.

While the talks with the French delegation went on day after day and the wires were busy between Lisbon and Bonn, we worked at putting together other segments of our puzzle. Starting on February 21 with a meeting between the Benelux ministers and those of the occupying powers, we reported on the great progress of the London visit, the relations being worked out between the European Defense Community and NATO, and the continuing interest of the United States in the movement toward European integration. This cheered Stikker. I met with Halvard M. Lange of Norway and Ole Björn Kraft of Denmark to bring them relief from pressure by our Air Force to station units on the NATO-built airfields in their countries. This publicized demand had brought countervailing pressure from the Soviet Government. A solution was found in Air Force visits and a system for quick occupation upon alert.

Most important of all, however, was the adoption on the twenty-second by the council of a resolution approving the establishment of the European Army [2]—which we had been unable to get at Rome—followed by a buoyant press conference by Lester Pearson, Chairman of the NATO Council, supported by Eden, Schuman, and me, pointing out how far NATO had come in its three years of life.

On the same day, the Temporary Committee's report on the economic and military goals for NATO and its individual members during the next three years was adopted and an annual review procedure established to call attention to successes and failures. The military goals, as experience proved, were not achieved, although in my view they were achievable. The cause was the receding tide of political will that became discernible in 1952 and unmistakably obvious in later French repudiation of the European Defense Community after Schuman left the scene and Pierre Mendès-France took over leadership in 1954.

Eden reported on the progress of the arrangements being made with Germany to bring the occupation to an end, obtaining council endorsement. The difficult matter of infrastructure financing, patiently and ably guided by Lovett, was agreed, reducing

2. For text of communiqué, see *Department of State Bulletin*, Vol. XXVI, March 10, 1952, pp. 367–68.

the U.S. share of the cost from forty-eight to forty-two per cent. Finally, after a great deal of private discussion the troublesome problem of the headquarters of the council and the selection of a Secretary General was resolved. After dinner at our embassy on Sunday evening, February 24, Eden told me that if the consensus was in favor of Paris for the council headquarters, he would not object.

The next morning the council voted to establish the headquarters in Paris and after our meeting had adjourned, Lord Ismay was chosen its Secretary General.

The Grand Slam

The ninth meeting of the NATO Council adjourned at seven o'clock on Monday evening, February 25, but a long night's work remained for the three ministers and their assistants, who had been hard at it all day, for on that morning Adenauer's memorandum of appeal from the High Commissioners on the two unsettled questions and a group from the High Commission arrived in Lisbon. We met at the British Embassy residence at ten in the evening. Long reports were made by the High Commission group on ways to pull together Adenauer's figures, Faure's budget, and our aid proposals. With everyone tired and nerves on edge, quibbling arguments broke out, which confused an exhausted Schuman and bored Eden, who was catching cold. I was relying on midnight weariness to solve them. This it did, whereupon a working group instructed by the three of us retired to the dining room to draft a closing proposal, and Schuman went to bed.

While Eden and I were waiting for the message, the group returned to us, deadlocked over a matter on which the French had understood the instructions differently than their colleagues. We could not move them; they would not wake Schuman and proposed to call the night session off. Then Anthony Eden exploded in a most spectacular and satisfying pyrotechnical display, accompanied by animadversions upon French national deficiencies. In one telling sentence, he observed that no sooner did a crisis occur than some damned Frenchman went to bed. If the staff did not straighten this out, he would go to the embassy himself and set it straight. That did it. A puzzled Schuman confirmed our understanding and told his people in case of further doubts to accept our word. When, soon afterward, Eden himself decided to go to bed, I reminded him of his observation about Frenchmen in a crisis and demanded and received supreme power by right of survivorship. Fortunately, it was not necessary to test it. By four o'clock the message was completed and dispatched, accompanied by a private one from me to Adenauer, urging him to accept the comparatively minor adjustments and complete our remarkably successful work at London and Lisbon.

The next morning word came back that he had done so. To the President I sent an exultant final report on the conference, ending, "We have something pretty close to a grand slam." The four ministers immediately issued a statement confirming our agreement.[3] To a press conference that afternoon I added, "This clinches it." We seemed to have broken through a long series of obstacles and to be fairly started toward a more united and stronger Europe and an integrated Atlantic defense system. The world that lay before us shone with hope. The momentum of the past month would carry on to midsummer before it slackened, as some, wearied by the pace, fell behind and the shadows of a change of governments fell across France and the United States.

However, that lay ahead.

Four days after adjournment at Lisbon a cold wind came across the Atlantic from Paris. Faure's government had fallen. But the Lisbon decisions still stood.

3. *Ibid.*, March 17, 1952, p. 423.

XVI

ONCE MORE
UNTO THE BREACH

THE THREE MONTHS between the Lisbon and Bonn meetings were a time of growing weaknesses in the alliance and a supreme effort in Washington to achieve the European Defense Community and end the occupation of Germany before ebb tide in Europe and America lowered the level of will too far. In Germany Adenauer was having trouble with the opposition parties, Schumacher in his bitterness declaring that anyone who would sign the contractual arrangement was not a German. In France the shaky government of Antoine Pinay, which followed Edgar Faure's, staggered through increasing troubles in Indochina, North Africa, the United Nations, and with the value of the franc—all of which increased French resentment against the United States. Curiously, Arab-Asian hostility to us also increased, because of our asserted support of French policies. Eden was calm and helpful throughout.

Hardly had we returned from Lisbon when a clap of thunder on the left warned that Moscow had been disturbed by the results achieved at London and Lisbon and was determined to prevent the further integration of Germany into the West and into a unified Western Europe. Already the wholly false charges of our use of chemical and biological weapons in Korea were being recklessly issued from Peking and Moscow when on March 10 Vishinsky handed identical notes to the British, French, and United States ambassadors calling for four-power talks about a peace treaty with a new all-German government.

To the foreign ministers this was a familiar Russian gambit. They had been through this same maneuver before when Stalin had used it to block the formation of the West German Government. The sterile debate at the Palais Rose in the summer of 1951 used the same plays to preclude the inclusion of Germany in the defense of Europe. Here again was a spoiling operation intended to check and dissipate the momentum toward solutions in the West brought about by three years of colossal effort. Old and obvious as this gambit was, it had strong appeal to timid and wishful thinkers—in France, those who feared a reunited and strong Germany and hoped for a "matured" and "satisfied" Soviet Union; in Germany, those who grasped at a chance of reunification, however slim, and hoped for security without the cost and risk of alliance with Western Europe and America.

Schuman also saw the note as aimed at the Germans. It provided something for all elements in Germany—for the Socialists, unity; for the industrialists, markets; for the soldiers, an army; and for the Nazis, reinstatement. This amounted to an attack on Adenauer and his policies. A second objective was to break up the unity of Western Europe. The French public, Schuman believed, had seen the danger in the military provisions, which had caused embarrassment even to the French Communists. He hoped to meet with the British and ourselves at an early date to coordinate our replies.

Adenauer took two attitudes toward the Soviet note. To disarm the opposition in Germany he favored four-power talks; to reassure his allies and his own right, he rejected a number of expected Russian demands.

Eden made the largest contribution. He agreed that the Soviet note was their counter to our meetings in London and Lisbon, and believed that if handled adroitly it might be turned to our advantage. The heart of the matter lay in the extent to which the Soviet Union was prepared to depart from prior positions regarding the creation of an all-German government. If it was not prepared to move from them, we need not even reach divisive discussion of the substance of a German peace treaty. The propaganda battle could be fought as before on the preliminary issue. If, however, the Soviet Government was prepared to pay the price of an honestly non-Communist government for all Germany in order to block German association with the West, we must tread very warily, as we could arrive at the same stalemate as in Austria, with a government for the whole country but no progress toward a peace treaty or the end of the occupation or stability of any sort in Europe. Based on his suggestions, identical notes were delivered to Vishinsky on March 26,[1] a little over two weeks after the delivery of his notes

1. *Department of State Bulletin*, Vol. XXVI, April 7, 1952, pp. 530–32.

to our ambassadors.

The notes made a few brisk points. First they pointed out that, as the Soviet Government itself asserted, an all-German government was a prerequisite to a peace treaty, free elections were prerequisite to an all-German government, and free conditions prerequisite to free elections. In order to ascertain whether these conditions existed, the United Nations had appointed a commission to carry out a simultaneous examination of the Federal Republic, Berlin, and the Soviet zone. Necessary facilities had been assured in the Federal Republic and West Berlin. Would they be assured in the Soviet zone and East Berlin? Second, the Soviet note did not state the international position of the all-German government. The allies considered that it should be free before and after the conclusion of a treaty to enter into associations compatible with the United Nations Charter. Third, it did not seem possible to enter into discussion of a German peace treaty until an all-German government existed capable of joining in those discussions. Forth, the Soviet note stated that Germany's frontiers were established by the Potsdam conference. However, that conference provided that the final boundaries of Germany must await the peace settlement. Finally, the notes observed that the Soviet proposal for the formation of German national land, air, and sea forces was a step backward and inconsistent with the achievement of German participation in a purely defensive European community designed to prevent aggression and preclude the revival of national militarism. (Adenauer had worried over the implications of this statement, should the European Defense Community fail to come to fruition.)

Although what Eden called "the battle of the notes" continued for two months—indeed, the last Soviet note burst among us when we were meeting in Bonn at the end of May—it was plain from the first response that Moscow was not prepared to wager high stakes in order to stop the Lisbon program.

Spring Thaw in Bonn

The central theme of our thought and work in the spring of 1952 was the negotiation in Bonn, conducted through and among the High Commissioners and Adenauer, to bring to fruition the contractual arrangement with Germany and the group-of-six discussion in Paris to conclude the European Defense Community. All the rest was obbligato. In the three months between the London and Bonn meetings a vast amount of work was done; issues were debated and agreements reached. It was a period not only of settling differences but of growth of understanding. In his final report High Commissioner McCloy put it this way: "The final conventions bear little resemblance to those which were initially proposed, and the differences are primarily due to Allied concessions to the German negotiators and to Allied recognition that in the new relationship the Federal Republic was justified in demanding full equality." [2] McCloy with great energy pushed the discussions in Bonn. He and the old Chancellor were inexhaustible, often wearing down argumentative colleagues and staff members to agreement as dawn broke over the Rhine. James Dunn, who had succeeded David Bruce as Ambassador to France, followed the European Defense Community discussions in Paris, keeping us informed and putting forward our suggestions for breaking deadlocks.

The major problems that remained after Lisbon were of two general types—those of high policy and those that, while involving policy, also involved vast and complicated detail. Of the first type, so far as the contractual arrangement was concerned, were the extent of allied reserved power to declare an emergency and resume authority in Germany and the extent to which a future all-German government should or could be bound by the present government; of the latter type, the division of the German defense budget between German military effort and allied troop support, and the review of items that might properly be charged to German support of allied troops stationed there. Lesser but still troublesome questions concerned an amnesty policy for war crimes and the period of preferential tax treatment for allied businesses in Germany.

In the European Defense Community discussions the insistent French demand for guarantees against German secession remained a major problem for the ministers. It represented the accumulation of all the French Government's neuroses—fear of inflation, of German economic recovery and domination of the Community, of the outcome in Indochina and North Africa, of French Communists on the left and General de Gaulle on the right, and of Moscow's "golden apple" policy, which appealed to both left and right. All these fears produced hesitation, suspicion, second thoughts, and, almost inevitably, irritation with the United States. We were the main force, as they saw it, behind their troubles, or most of them—behind the drive for European defense and the emancipation of Germany, behind impatience with stand-patism in North Africa and Indochina, behind their own ideas, which they were beginning to re-examine, of integration and suprana-

2. Office of the High Commissioner for Germany, *Report on Germany* (*Final*), September 21, 1949–July 31, 1952 (Cologne: Greven & Bechtold, 1952), p. 14.

tionalism in Europe.

Two matters in particular stimulated French annoyance. Faure had resigned when his cabinet refused to support the taxes necessary to finance his ambitious military budget. Pinay, who succeeded him, retained the budget but not the tax program. In looking for funds for military needs, he found increased American aid an alluring solution, and proposed another half billion dollars over the next three years in addition to the six hundred million for 1950. Since in addition to that, in the first six months of 1952, we would bear about a quarter of the cost of the French war in Indochina, we were able to find only a third of the new request. The French, arguing that they had taken on more than Harriman's Temporary Council Committee had recommended, believed that unwillingness to give all the help they asked amounted to "a raw deal." They also freely stated that our "meddling in Tunisia" was unhelpful. Nevertheless, the European Defense Community treaty was initialed in May, although the French Cabinet on May 22 voted to require a guarantee against German secession from the Community as a condition to French signature of the contractual arrangement with Germany.

In this negotiation, as in its Paris counterpart, progress while substantial had not been smooth. Adenauer characteristically had provoked trouble, then overridden it. At the end of April he informed the coalition parties of the state of the negotiations, hailing the progress made in securing equality of treatment for Germany, and proposed to conclude the discussions and sign the document in time for consideration by the United States Senate before its final adjournment, scheduled for July. This produced a storm of protest from the Bundestag, which claimed that its members were being asked to approve complicated and far-reaching measures "at five minutes before twelve." Two leading supporters of the Chancellor, Dr. Heinrich von Brentano, later Foreign Minister, and Dr. Franz Blücher, made public a letter demanding postponement of the signature to allow for careful re-examination by the Bundestag. This would have thrown United States legislative consideration into a new Congress and a new administration. Moreover, the Bundestag voted against the principle of a German defense contribution.

The Chancellor, however, only intensified his drive toward signature, skillfully using the opposition of the Bundestag to extract a few more concessions from the High Commissioners. After a week of night sessions the High Commissioners started redrafting in mid-May. Then work was begun on the vexed question of the amount of the defense contribution to be allocated to allied troop support. This had been exacerbated by unusually high occupation costs for March in a drive to clean up past accounts. A three-man team was sent over from Washington with power to act and the issue was prepared for ministerial action. Finally, a Social Democratic attempt to stage a long debate was beaten, and opposition in the Bundestag subsided as quickly as it had arisen.

At last, the nightmarish weeks of being held immovable by difficulties, as the clock ticked away the time for action, came to an end. On the afternoon of May 22 the President saw us off on the *Independence* for Bonn. This mission, the culmination of the effort launched at London and Paris, was to be the most critical one of my tenure of office.

Success in Bonn

On Friday afternoon, May 23, 1952, the ministers met at Bad Godesberg, a suburb of Bonn. Our meetings would be held in the conference rooms of the American chancery as the most adequate allied quarters, and I would act as chairman. This arrangement made available as staff McCloy's group, which had by far the best organization and knowledge of the material to be discussed.

Next morning the three allied ministers and the High Commissioners met; and, with interludes for lunch and dinner together and for a four-power meeting in the afternoon, they remained in session until the early hours of Sunday. The visible presence of French disquiet lay in Schuman's changed mien. In London and Lisbon he had obviously not been in assured command of French foreign policy. In Bonn he seemed not even to be in control of his own ministry and was obviously tired, nervous, and depressed. On Sunday Adenauer said to me, "Can't you give some confidence to our poor friend?" Adenauer himself needed no such help.

A good many questions in the numerous and complicated documents that ended the occupation and brought Germany into the defense of Europe required the final decision of the ministers. In most of these the various national staffs (and to some extent the High Commissioners) had acquired such vested interest and pride in divergent positions that compromise was difficult for them. Here the need was for decision. The ministers listened to statements of the issues and summaries of the arguments. As chairman I would propose a decision; my colleagues would amend or agree, or sometimes one would withdraw his staff's objection. In this way

At the four-power meeting in Bonn to discuss German defenses are, from left to right: Anthony Eden, Konrad Adenauer, the author, and Robert Schuman. WIDE WORLD

we covered a great deal of ground. However, four matters required national negotiation at the top. It was by no means a foregone conclusion that agreement could be successfully accomplished on three of them—those relating to the well-worn guarantees to the European Defense Community by Britain and the United States, to the division of the German defense budget, and to the binding effect of the agreements on a future all-German government.

The matter of the guarantees was reached Saturday night and continued far into the early hours of Sunday morning. We had already worked out with the Germans an exchange of treaty agreements among the signatories of the North Atlantic and the European defense treaties (who were the same except for Germany in the latter) by which each extended to the others the obligations of Article 5 of the North Atlantic Treaty (to treat an attack on one as an attack on all). This bound Germany into the common defense bond. But, as we have seen, the French wanted more, a guarantee by Britain and the United States against German withdrawal. Eden was ready to negotiate a treaty with France on the matter, but in discussions with the President before leaving for Europe, we had concluded that such negotiation was impossible for his dying administration and to attempt it might throw the whole effort we had worked on so long into the uncertainties of a new administration in 1953. We determined that on this matter we could go no further than the existing legislation permitted.

A suggestion by Philip Jessup, which the President approved, offered an escape from a dangerous impasse. Article 4 of the North

Atlantic Treaty bound its members to consult together should one or more believe its security to be threatened in order to find means to remove the threat. The Jessup suggestion was for a tripartite declaration by Britain, France, and the United States reciting the reasons why the three governments had "an abiding interest in the effectiveness of the [EDC] treaty and in the strength and integrity of that community." Then came the operative sentences: "Accordingly, if any action from whatever quarter threatens the integrity or unity of the Community, the two governments will regard this as a threat to their own security. They will act in accordance with Article 4 of the North Atlantic Treaty." It ended with a reference to our expressed resolve to station forces in Europe, including Germany, as might be appropriate to the defense of the area having regard to our obligations under the North Atlantic Treaty and our interest in the Defense Community.

This proposal we held in reserve, knowing that whatever we offered the French would want more. When I put it forward, Eden picked it up with great enthusiasm, telling Schuman what a great success he had had. If he would make the most of it instead of picking flaws in it, his own position and French morale would both have a lift. The proposal was cabled to Paris. While we waited, we took up other points. The evening wore on. Paris at last replied, wishing to leave out the reference to Article 4, calling for consultation, and saying merely that in event of any threat to the integrity or unity of the Community the two governments would act in accordance with the treaty. This change, I pointed out, would give (as it was intended to do) the impression that they would regard any threat to the integrity of the Community as an attack on themselves and would cause infinite trouble when the Senate came to ratify the exchange of guarantees between the two treaty groups. As the debate continued, with Hervé Alphand leading for the French, Robert Schuman kept going to sleep. Messages flew back and forth to Paris. Finally, with minor changes, our proposal was accepted and the largest obstacle overcome.

The next morning an early meeting with von Brentano and some of his colleagues from the foreign relations committee of the Bundestag found an escape from the theoretical problem that bothered them. They thought that an attempt to bind a future and as yet nonexistent all-German government was both impossible and wrong. I suggested avoiding the problem by having the present Federal Republic Government agree that it would not join in creating and transferring its power to any new government that did not agree to assume and abide by the international obligations of the Federal Republic. This happily resolved another source of difficulty.

At this point the Soviet Union, with a clumsiness to which it was more prone then than now, aided us greatly with German opinion. In West Germany, and especially among the Social Democrats, opposition to the contractual agreements, passionately voiced by Schumacher, grew out of the powers reserved by the allies because of the division of Germany, the Soviet occupation of the eastern zone, and the precarious position of Berlin. When, on May 25, Moscow delivered to Bonn a bullying, threatening note aimed at frightening the Germans away from completing any of the agreements under negotiation, it had quite the opposite effect. Almost before our eyes we saw German opinion solidified behind Adenauer, the reservation of allied powers abundantly justified, and the contractual agreements acclaimed. We were fortunate in our opponent.

The final meeting of the four was scheduled for Sunday morning, but weariness had adjourned the night session of the three before they had come to agreement among themselves. Our meeting with Adenauer was put off first until after lunch, then until four o'clock. Meanwhile time was running out. When we did meet, Adenauer made final agreements possible. He silenced his advisers and took over the discussion himself, making decisions without further consultation. The German defense contribution and its division were agreed, and he and I worked out the problem of the future all-German government's obligations, which the others accepted. A dozen or more difficult but unimportant problems were decided on the spot without further argument. The spur of the Soviet note was having a most beneficial effect. Our meeting adjourned in time to dress for a large and gala dinner given by the Chancellor in the Palais Schaumburg, the former residence of the Archbishop of Cologne, and later of the Kaiser's sister, situated on the bluff overlooking the Rhine.

Monday morning, May 26, was the time set to sign the considerable number of documents that made up the contractual agreements. The Social Democrats in the Bundestag had planned to boycott the signing ceremonies, but overnight the Russian note had turned German opinion strongly in favor of the new step toward closer ties with the West, and the bulk of them attended. We were not certain that some last-minute hitch would not occur in Paris. It was a relief to see Schuman appear smiling and relaxed. The signing took place in the room where the Bundesrat, the German senate, met, the glass side of which opened upon stands filled with spectators. Each minister in turn took his place at a small table covered with gray velvet and signed several master copies of the documents as attendants produced them.[3]

After lunching with the Chancellor, we all took off for Paris to complete that formality.

Apprehension in Paris

All the problems attendant upon the negotiation of the European Defense Community had now been worked out. Unfortunately, though we did not realize it at the time, those which ultimately blocked French ratification of it had not. All that remained for the present was to sign it and the appurtenant documents—nineteen altogether. This ceremony took place in the Clock Room at the Quai d'Orsay. Eden and I sat at either end of a long table with representatives of the other NATO nations along one side and a horde of photographers and newsreel men behind ropes on the other. After the signing, full of hope and elation, I expressed, ". . . my profound conviction that what we have witnessed today may well prove to be one of the most important and most far reaching events of our lifetime. . . . We have seen the beginning of the realization of an ancient dream—the unity of the free peoples of Western Europe." [4]

Brave words! And, in part, true, but spoken without reckoning on the ebb tide in France and the future roles of M. Mendès-France and General Charles de Gaulle. The apprehension in Paris began to appear as soon as the signing was over. For two days we listened to French complaints of the lack of understanding and appreciation in America of French sacrifices and efforts in Indochina (where we were providing from a quarter of the cost of the war in the first half of 1952 to a third in the second half) and in North Africa. All we said was of no avail. A bitter mood was growing in France. There all our interest was said to be reserved for Germany.

The note of pain and strain was echoed from the Elysée, where I called at President Auriol's request. He and Mme. Auriol had been very kind and friendly to my wife and me during our many visits to Paris. On this occasion I found him passionately and dramatically disturbed as he received me in his private study, alone save for his private interpreter. What had I done, he asked

---

3. For summary, see *Department of State Bulletin,* Vol. XXVI, June 9, 1952, pp. 888–94.
   4. *Ibid.,* p. 895.

tragically, mistaking the real danger in Europe and leading Schuman into the dreadful error of rearming Germany? For an hour
he reviewed the unchanging menace of Germany. To revive the
triple entente and add the United States to it was the only sound
policy. I was argued-out for the day.

Exhausted, we took off for Washington. There our elation
lasted a little longer. I presented for ratification by the Senate the
documents signed in Europe. The hearings and debate went easily,
though the political conventions to nominate candidates for the
Presidency impended. The Senate came through magnificently,
ratifying on July 1 the Bonn convention by a vote of 77 to 5 and
the protocol to the North Atlantic Treaty by 72 to 5. The past
six months had been for us a successful period.

AFTERWORD

In 1953 new governments came into power in both France and the United States. In France eight governments over six years hastened the decline of the Fourth Republic and the return of General de Gaulle in 1959 to inaugurate the Fifth Republic, and strong nationalist, presidential leadership. In the United States General Eisenhower had been elected President on the slogan, "It's Time for a Change"; but both the country and the originators of the slogan seemed unsure what sort of change was desired.

In March 1953, Stalin died. Immediately, jockeying for power began in the Kremlin. In East Berlin discontent grew among the workers over increased production quotas imposed upon them by East German authorities. In June strikes and defiance of the police spread throughout East Germany. Soviet troops hesitated; some even appeared sympathetic. Then the tanks moved. Their guns cleared the streets. Infantry arrested and executed violators of the curfew, leaders of the strikes. Appeals from East Germans to Western Germany brought no response. The United States Government chose to ignore declarations of intention, expressed in the 1952 presidential campaign to roll back the communist regimes. Twenty-five thousand Soviet troops held East Berlin; ten times that many the surrounding area. Three more divisions backed them up. The United States chose denunciation; there was no rollback in Eastern Europe.

In the next year occurred two decisions of unmistakable import—one in the United States, one in France. On taking office the new American Administration announced its intention to make a drastic reduction in its military budget. This would involve a revision of American military strategy. On January 12, 1954, Secretary of State Dulles disclosed the new strategic and budgetary policy.[1] It was reminiscent of the Hoover-Taft policy of 1950–1951.[2]

. . . If an enemy could pick his time and place and method of warfare [said Mr. Dulles]—and if our policy was to remain the traditional one of the meeting aggression by direct and local opposition—then we needed to be ready to fight in the Arctic and in the Tropics; in Asia, the Near East, and in Europe; by sea, by land, and by air; with old weapons and with new weapons.

. . . .

But before military planning could be changed, the President and his advisers . . . had to take some basic policy decisions. This has been done. The basic decision was to depend primarily upon a great capacity to retaliate, instantly, by means and at places of our choosing. Now the Department of Defense and the Joint Chiefs of Staff can shape our military establishment to fit what is *our* policy, instead of having to try to be ready to meet the enemy's many choices. . . .

After this policy had been in effect for a few years, and army strength had been reduced by six hundred thousand men, Mr. Hanson Baldwin observed that if we followed "to its logical con-clusion the road upon which we have started, we shall have sacrificed upon the altar of economy the capability of fighting non-nuclear wars. The result, if carried to the extreme could be dollar savings at the cost of national existence." [3]

Europe, also, was aware that, as America redesigned its military establishement to rely primarily on nuclear weapons, its willing-ness to intervene abroad on behalf of others would narrow. Euro-peans could not fail to notice, also, that Mr. Dulles, in stating the new policy, had underscored *our*. It was a Washington policy, and action under it would be taken in Washington. General de Gaulle, waiting impatiently at Colombey-les-deux-Eglises for the signal to return to power, saw a minor role for the European Defense Com-munity. In January 1954, the General confided to C. L. Sulzberger of *The New York Times*: [4]

The United States has walked along with this idiocy [the EDC]. Now you must extricate yourselves. . . . I guarantee that EDC will not go through. I will do everything against it. I will work with the Communists to block it. I will make a revolution against it. . . .

1. *Department of State Bulletin*, Vol. XXX, January 25, 1954, pp. 107, 108.
2. See pages 147–153, *ante*.
3. *The New York Times*, July 18, 1957
4. C. L. Sulzberger, *A Long Row of Candles* (New York, Macmillan, 1969), p. 950.

But such extreme measures were unnecessary. London and Washington granted the French almost everything demanded to placate the Chamber of Deputies. Yet, when the EDC was brought to a vote in the French National Assembly on August 30, 1954, it was defeated. Resentment against France was bitter in Europe and the United States. Yet only two years later distrust in Europe of Washington's reliability and good judgment equaled this resentment.

Troubles did not fall singly upon France. Her repudiation of the European Defense Community in 1954, after four years of leadership in creating it, was followed in the same year by the collapse of her eastern empire in Indochina. The United States turned away from extricating her from the resulting mess and "let Sir Anthony Eden and the [British] Foreign Office," as Mr. Drew Middleton of *The New York Times* put it, "do the donkey work in patching up European unity . . . and negotiating a settlement in Indochina. . . . Such a policy of limited liability in great affairs," he observed, was "not in accord with . . . the power of the United States. . . ." [5]

Two years later the United States abandoned both France and Britain in their hour of crisis in the Middle East, a crisis that the United States had a hand in precipitating. For some years Britain had been under pressure from Egypt to give up her bases in Suez, which supported her claims to an international status for the canal. In 1956 Mr. Dulles brusquely withdrew financial help for Egypt's Aswan Dam, undertaken during a period of American courtship of Colonel Gamal Abdel Nasser. The latter's riposte was the forcible seizure and nationalization of the Suez Canal. The British Government had long made clear their conviction that the water route to Middle Eastern oil and to Commonwealth countries to the east was a vital interest that it could not, without a fight, permit to fall under the control of another state. Some of its most powerful members stated this to us again early in 1956. But at a later stage the British Government did not inform ours of its plan to use force.

The French made no secret that short of the overthrow of Colonel Nasser they saw no end to their troubles in Algeria. They would use force to accomplish this if they could get the British to join them.

On the American side, it later became plain that the Government was prepared to accept what the British would not—

5. Drew Middleton, *These Are the British* (New York: Alfred A. Knopf, 1957), p. 172.

Egyptian control of the canal. It would not join in or tacitly approve
—but, on the contrary, would vigorously oppose—the use of force
to prevent it. This was not made clear to the British. Indeed, it is
fair to say that at the London conference of nations using the
canal our conduct in discussing sanctions such as a boycott of the
canal, whatever the intention may have been, led to expectations
that proved to be false. The blow fell as Nasser was preparing to
open discussions on September 3 of the recommendations of the
London Conference with a mission of representatives of five countries, headed by Prime Minister Menzies of Australia, and including
the United States. On August 31 at a press conference in Washington President Eisenhower stated that ". . . we are committed
to a peaceful settlement of this dispute, nothing else." [6] Thereupon
the whole international effort blew up.

In this situation the British, believing that the protection of
their interests must lie in their own action and that the Arab-
Israeli war offered a favorable opportunity to act, secretly joined
with the French in an expedition to seize the Suez Canal Zone.
This was unwise in conception and execution. The expeditionary
force was not constituted to be able to seize the canal quickly
before it could be damaged; nor had the consequences of damage
been accurately foreseen. The force was not strong enough, nor the
British public determined enough to have occupied Egypt against
continued resistance and the condemnation of non-Communist
states. If the effort bogged down with the British in possession of
a damaged canal and with Colonel Nasser still resisting, there
was no plan what to do next. The sole strategy rested on the
mistaken belief that, with the destruction of his air force by
bombing and with a threat of landings, Colonel Nasser would be
deposed and his successors in power would make a satisfactory
settlement of the canal issue. With the very best of luck, the
enterprise required speed and dash. It was marred by irresolution
and delay. Unexpected Soviet occupation of Hungary had a bearing
on this, for Britain and France were fearful of finding themselves
cast in the same brutal role as the Soviet Union.

At this juncture the Russians made threats that volunteers
would join the battle in Egypt and rockets would bombard Britain
and France. The United States Government joined the Soviet-
Arab-Asian bloc in raising a hue and cry in the United Nations.
Under this pressure Prime Minister Eden and Premier Guy Mollet
collapsed, agreeing to an end to the fighting and withdrawal of
troops; and Colonel Nasser emerged as the hero of the hour.

6. *The New York Times,* September 1, 1956.

Further blows were soon to fall both upon European unity and upon European confidence in the United States. In August 1961, the first summer of President Kennedy's brave new world, the Soviet Commandant in Berlin, over a weekend, shut off East Berlin, the Soviet zone, from West Berlin, made up of the three allied zones, and prohibited all transit from one to the other. At one stroke this cut off the escape route by which thousands of the ablest and most skilled East Germans had been fleeing to West Germany. It also violated the whole series of agreements by which Berlin had been set up as a unified city under a quadripartite Kommandatura with four separate zones of occupation, though with freedom of movement within the whole city.

What the consequences would have been had the three allied powers immediately knocked down the flimsy temporary barriers and insisted on free movement within the city, but not from East Germany into it, was not tested. By the time the Western governments had recovered from the stunning effect of the Soviet coup, its attitude had hardened and the possibility of treating that action as an unauthorized one by the local commandant had passed. A confrontation of military forces in Berlin appeared as dangerous and distasteful to the Western allies in 1961 as in 1953. So they did nothing, and accepted the division of Berlin.

The next two blows came from an ally who almost made enemies unnecessary. General de Gaulle had returned to power in 1959 and at once caused grave disquiet by his publicized dislike of the supranational organizations fathered by the Fourth Republic. It is curious, therefore, that his next two steps proved to be the shattering surprises that they were. The first came on January 29, 1963, when he vetoed the otherwise unanimous approval of Great Britain's application to join the Common Market. This and his continued maintenance of opposition delayed European development by a decade.

The more stunning one, however, fell on March 11, 1966, when the French Government delivered to the American Embassy in Paris an *aide mémoire* which in brusqueness and clarity left little to be desired:

For years, it noted, the French Government had pointed out that the North Atlantic Treaty Organization no longer corresponded to the conditions prevailing in the world. The threats to Europe no longer had the immediate and menacing character of 1949. The countries of Europe had reestablished their economies and regained resources. France had equipped herself with an atomic armament that excluded integration. Nuclear balance between the Soviet Union and the United States had

replaced the former nuclear monopoly held by the United States and had
changed the conditions of defense of the West. Europe was no longer
the center of international crises, which had shifted principally to Asia,
where the countries of the Atlantic Alliance were obviously not involved.

This evolution did not call in question the treaty signed at Washington on April 4, 1949. Barring events altering the relations between East
and West, France considered that Alliance in existence as long as
necessary.

However, the organization, agreements, arrangements, and decisions
made after signature of the treaty no longer met essential requirements.
Already the French Government had withdrawn French naval forces
from these arrangements. It would now do the same with its ground and
air forces stationed in Germany and assigned to the Allied Command
in Europe. France would, also, withdraw from this Command. The
Government would, in consequence, be prepared to discuss with its
allies the liaisons that should be established between the French Command and the NATO Commands. Moreover, the French Government
gave notice of its desire to terminate—within, as later fixed, one year—
all agreements for facilities within France for allied commands and
foreign troops, air fields, depots, etc. In short, the note concluded, the
French Government was led to resume in French territory the complete
exercise of its sovereignty, no longer agreeing to foreign units, installa-
tions, or bases in France under the control in any respect of authorities
other than French authorities.[7]

Within approximately the time allotted the ultimatum was
carried out and France had done its best to destroy its own conception—the conception of allied forces for the defense of Europe,
in being and in place, operating under unified command and in
accordance with an agreed strategy. De Gaulle pulled France out
of the Organization of the North Atlantic Treaty and expelled the
Organization and its forces and facilities, including the great American commitments, from France. It was an act of unbelievable stupidity and of harm to France, to Europe, and to the non-Communist
world.

Headquarters and other facilities were found for NATO in
Belgium. There the Organization continues and there we shall
leave it and its future for another generation to adapt, if possible,
to meet a future as yet so inscrutable.

It is tempting—but, I believe, a great mistake—to read the
history of the European movement since the end of the war as a

7. For complete text, see *Department of State Bulletin*, Vol. LIV, April 18,
1966, pp. 617–18.

history of failure. By the European movement is meant that series of gifted and original improvisations, of various origins, beginning with the Marshall Plan and continuing on through NATO, the Schuman Plan, and the Common Market, contemplating the rebirth of Germany and her reception into a unified European community, all of which would be joined closely with North America for mutual security. The failure is sometimes attributed to a good idea being betrayed by human weakness, error, and folly, exemplified by the actions recounted in this Afterword. The source of failure, as General de Gaulle saw it, was departure from the true faith that nationalism is the foundation upon which human affairs rest.

Whatever the thesis, a reading of these postwar years as years of failure can come only from excluding the overwhelming weight of the evidence. That shows almost unbelievable achievement. The great empires of Europe and the world order they had created in the nineteenth century, after having been destroyed by thirty years of civil war (1914–1945) brought on by Germany, had come to the verge of utter ruin. Only the Soviet Union, though sorely stricken, retained its power base and its social structure. The Ottoman and Austro-Hungarian Empires had disappeared, reverting to breeding grounds of trouble inviting penetration by ambitious empire-builders. Czarist Russia had been transformed from a stabilizing to a revolutionary factor. Germany by its division had ceased to be a great power and become two impoverished, middle-sized dependencies of hostile powers. In their loss of empires, both France and Great Britain had lost also the indispensable basis of their military power—France, in African troops; and Great Britain, in the Indian Army. All the Western European countries ended the thirty-year war period with their economies bankrupt and, except for Britain, their populations bitterly divided and their political systems overthrown. Furthermore, the war in Europe ended in 1945 not with a peace settlement but with the death of Hitler, the collapse of the German Reich, and the military occupation of all of Europe that had been under its power. The danger of a resumption of military conflict was by no means over.

A dramatically changed situation is presented in Western Europe today. Not of a recovery in the sense of a return to a European system of world powers dependent for economic, military, and social strength upon imperial positions. Rather, Western Europe is made up of a congeries of middle-sized states, self-organized into close political and economic cooperation. This con-

geries is capable of enlargement in numbers and in intimacy. Of
its own collective choice it joined with the great power of the
United States for mutual security against external danger from
the east. In Western Europe over the past twenty years the return
of vitality had been most phenomenal in the economic field. Here
imaginative genius has called forth the greatest effort and broken
the most restrictive limitations of the old European system. The
Marshall Plan provided new capital and the NATO system, the
security essential for the return of capital that had fled elsewhere.

Further political and military development in Western Europe was paralyzed by General de Gaulle. The General, however,
made an important contribution by presiding over the dissolution
of the French empire, without adding to it the dissolution of the
French state by civil war or of the whole European movement by
French withdrawal. Of his legacies, belief in military power to
deter the Soviet army, mobilizable by France from purely European sources, provided with a nuclear sting by France's *force de
frappe*, and under the umbrella of the North Atlantic Treaty, was
soon seen to be a fraud. But faith has lingered on in a *détente*
with the Soviet Union engineered either from London, Paris, or
Bonn, depending upon the domicile of the believer, which would
win security for Western Europe by the lure of lessening its ties
with the United States. It would seem that such a proposal would,
also, appear the fraud it is, yet the pilgrimages to Moscow continue, each leaving a residue of distrust, confusion, and frustration.

If Europeans were distracted from their basic interests and
weakened by "trips" under the influence of hallucinatory policies,
Americans were similarly diverted and weakened by the costly and
divisive expedition to Southeast Asia. This appears to have been as
ill-judged, but one hopes will not end as disastrously, as the
Athenian expedition to Sicily in 416 B.C. or Napoleon's to Russia
in 1812. Throughout this period a new change in circumstances
has been developing, noted by General de Gaulle in 1966—the
steady growth in nuclear capability of the Soviet Union to a position
approaching equivalence of destructive power with that of the
United States. The two superpowers could come close enough to
destroying each other to have every reason for avoiding a thorough-
going test of their respective abilities to do so. Hence, the direct
use of the military power of either against the other is dangerous
in the extreme.

Only a little less dangerous is a diplomatic-military maneuver
that suddenly develops into a military confrontation. Such a maneuver was the Soviet intervention in Cuba that resulted in the

missile crisis of October 1962. In this instance the Western allies
held together firmly in support of a United States position, contemplating the use of force if necessary. The Soviets withdrew
from the brink. Another such maneuver was the Soviet intervention in Egypt, culminating in the (October 1970) uneasy ceasefire
along the Suez Canal. Here the Western powers are very confused
and divided about the nature of the basic threat to their interests
in the Middle East and how to deal with it. Is the threat the
danger of an Arab-Israeli war in the Middle East with the possibility
of United States-Soviet involvement in it? If so, can a peace or
modus vivendi be devised acceptable to the states and groups in
that area or which can and will be enforced upon them by a major
group of powers?

If the answers to these questions is in the negative, does
Arab-Israeli hostility provide an enduring opportunity for the Soviet
Union to attempt to become the dominant power in the Middle
East and the controlling distributor of Middle Eastern oil upon
which all Europe and Asia depend and upon which the United
States depends for about a fifth of its needs? Such an analysis
might require different policies from the former one. To try to
muddle through upon a defective analysis of the problem might
bring about a shift of power and alignments that could be irreversi-
ble.

If Europe and America are to pull together again as their
common interests and security demand, and exercise the influence
of which, acting together, they are capable, both areas need time
and good management—but not excessive amounts of either—to
extricate themselves from obsessions that are now absorbing major
proportions of their energies. These are, on the European side, the
relations between the Common Market countries (France, Germany, Italy, the Netherlands, Belgium, and Luxembourg) and
Great Britain; across the Atlantic, the present involvement of the
United States in the Southeast Asia war. In the tangled affairs of
nations a breathing space for repairs can rarely be arranged. However, events in the Middle East and Southeast Asia may have so
shaped up as to permit the Atlantic allies, with luck, to get their
obsessional entanglements straightened out to a substantial degree
before they must face once more major crises from abroad or
paralyzing elections at home.

If these hopes could be approximated, the way might be
opened for the Atlantic allies to return once more, refreshed and
wiser, to their most vital common interests, and to pick up once
again the task of finding together the means of furthering them.

APPENDICES

Appendix 1: *Secretary George C. Marshall's Harvard Commencement Address, June 5, 1947* [1]

I need not tell you gentlemen that the world situation is very serious. That must be apparent to all intelligent people. I think one difficulty is that the problem is one of such enormous complexity that the very mass of facts presented to the public by press and radio make it exceedingly difficult for the man in the street to reach a clear appraisement of the situation. Furthermore, the people of this country are distant from the troubled areas of the earth and it is hard for them to comprehend the plight and consequent reactions of the long-suffering peoples, and the effect of those reactions on their governments in connection with our efforts to promote peace in the world.

In considering the requirements for the rehabilitation of Europe, the physical loss of life, the visible destruction of cities, factories, mines, and railroads was correctly estimated, but it has become obvious during recent months that this visible destruction was probably less serious than the dislocation of the entire fabric of European economy. For the past ten years conditions have been highly abnormal. The feverish preparation for war and the more feverish maintenance of the war effort engulfed all aspects of national economies. Machinery has fallen into disrepair or is entirely obsolete. Under the arbitrary and destructive Nazi rule, virtually every possible enterprise was geared into the German war machine. Long-standing commercial ties, private institutions, banks, insurance companies, and shipping companies disappeared, through loss of capital, absorption through nationalization, or by simple destruction. In many countries, confidence in the local currency has been severely shaken. The breakdown of the business structure of Europe during the war was complete. Recovery has been seriously retarded by the fact that two years after the close of hostilities a peace settlement with Germany and Austria has not been agreed upon. But even given a more prompt solution of these difficult problems, the rehabilitation of the economic structure of Europe quite evidently will require a much longer time and greater effort than has been foreseen.

There is a phase of this matter which is both interesting and serious. The farmer has always produced the foodstuffs to exchange with the city dweller for the other necessities of life. This division of labor is the basis of modern civilization. At the present time it is threatened with breakdown. The town and city industries are not producing adequate goods to exchange with the food-producing farmer. Raw materials and fuel are in short supply. Machinery is lacking or worn out. The farmer or the peasant cannot find the goods for sale which he desires to purchase. So the sale of his farm

1. *Department of State Bulletin,* Vol. XVI, June 15, 1947, pp. 1159–60.

produce for money which he cannot use seems to him an unprofitable transaction. He, therefore, has withdrawn many fields from crop cultivation and is using them for grazing. He feeds more grain to stock and finds for himself and his family an ample supply of food, however short he may be on clothing and the other ordinary gadgets of civilization. Meanwhile people in the cities are short of food and fuel. So the governments are forced to use their foreign money and credits to procure these necessities abroad. This process exhausts funds which are urgently needed for reconstruction. Thus a very serious situation is rapidly developing which bodes no good for the world. The modern system of the division of labor upon which the exchange of products is based is in danger of breaking down.

The truth of the matter is that Europe's requirements for the next three or four years of foreign food and other essential products—principally from America—are so much greater than her present ability to pay that she must have substantial additional help or face economic, social and political deterioration of a very grave character.

The remedy lies in breaking the vicious circle and restoring the confidence of the European people in the economic future of their own countries and of Europe as a whole. The manufacturer and the farmer throughout wide areas must be able and willing to exchange their products for currencies the continuing value of which is not open to question.

Aside from the demoralizing effect on the world at large and the possibilities of disturbances arising as a result of the desperation of the people concerned, the consequences to the economy of the United States should be apparent to all. It is logical that the United States should do whatever it is able to do to assist in the return of normal economic health in the world, without which there can be no political stability and no assured peace. Our policy is directed not against any country or doctrine but against hunger, poverty, desperation, and chaos. Its purpose should be the revival of a working economy in the world so as to permit the emergence of political and social conditions in which free institutions can exist. Such assistance, I am convinced, must not be on a piecemeal basis as various crises develop. Any assistance that this Government may render in the future should provide a cure rather than a mere palliative. Any government that is willing to assist in the task of recovery will find full cooperation, I am sure, on the part of the United States Government. Any government which maneuvers to block the recovery of other countries cannot expect help from us. Furthermore, governments, political parties, or groups which seek to perpetuate human misery in order to profit therefrom politically or otherwise will encounter the opposition of the United States.

It is already evident that, before the United States Government can proceed much further in its efforts to alleviate the situation and help start the European world on its ways to recovery, there must be some agreement among the countries of Europe as to the requirements of the situation and the part those countries themselves will take in order to give proper effect to whatever action might be undertaken by this Government. It would be neither fitting nor efficacious for this Government to undertake to draw up unilaterally a program designed to place Europe on its feet economically.

This is the business of the Europeans. The initiative, I think, must come from Europe. The role of this country should consist of friendly aid in the drafting of a European program and of later support of such a program so far as it may be practical for us to do so. The program should be a joint one, agreed to by a number, if not all, European nations.

An essential part of any successful action on the part of the United States is an understanding on the part of the people of America of the character of the problem and the remedies to be applied. Political passion and prejudice should have no part. With foresight, and a willingness on the part of our people to face up to the vast responsibility which history has clearly placed upon our country, the difficulties I have outlined can and will be overcome.

Appendix 2: The Charter of the North Atlantic Treaty [2]

The Parties to this Treaty reaffirm their faith in the purposes and principles of the Charter of the United Nations and their desire to live in peace with all peoples and all governments.

They are determined to safeguard the freedom, common heritage and civilization of their peoples, founded on the principles of democracy, individual liberty and the rule of law.

They seek to promote stability and well-being in the North Atlantic area.

They are resolved to unite their efforts for collective defense and for the preservation of peace and security.

They therefore agree to this North Atlantic Treaty:

ARTICLE 1

The Parties undertake, as set forth in the Charter of the United Nations, to settle any international disputes in which they may be involved by peaceful means in such a manner that international peace and security, and justice, are not endangered, and to refrain in their international relations from the threat or use of force in any manner inconsistent with the purposes of the United Nations.

ARTICLE 2

The Parties will contribute toward the further development of peaceful and friendly international relations by strengthening their free institutions, by bringing about a better understanding of the principles upon which these institutions are founded, and by promoting conditions of stability and well-being. They will seek to eliminate conflict in their international economic policies and will encourage economic collaboration between any or all of them.

ARTICLE 3

In order more effectively to achieve the objectives of this Treaty, the Parties, separately and jointly, by means of continuous and effective self-

2. *The Signing of the North Atlantic Treaty* (Washington: Government Printing Office, 1949), pp. 50–60.

help and mutual aid, will maintain and develop their individual and collective capacity to resist armed attack.

ARTICLE 4

The Parties will consult together whenever, in the opinion of any of them, the territorial integrity, political independence or security of any of the Parties is threatened.

ARTICLE 5

The Parties agree that an armed attack against one or more of them in Europe or North America shall be considered an attack against them all; and consequently they agree that, if such an armed attack occurs, each of them, in exercise of the right of individual or collective self-defense recognized by Article 51 of the Charter of the United Nations, will assist the Party or Parties so attacked by taking forthwith, individually and in concert with the other Parties, such action as it deems necessary, including the use of armed force, to restore and maintain the security of the North Atlantic area.

Any such armed attack and all measures taken as a result thereof shall immediately be reported to the Security Council. Such measures shall be terminated when the Security Council has taken the measures necessary to restore and maintain international peace and security.

ARTICLE 6

For the purpose of Article 5 an armed attack on one or more of the Parties is deemed to include an armed attack on the territory of any of the Parties in Europe or North America, on the Algerian departments of France, on the occupation forces of any Party in Eurpoe, on the islands under the jurisdiction of any Party in the North Atlantic area north of the Tropic of Cancer or on the vessels or aircraft in this area of any of the Parties.

ARTICLE 7

This Treaty does not affect, and shall not be interpreted as affecting, in any way the rights and obligations under the Charter of the Parties which are members of the United Nations, or the primary responsibility of the Security Council for the maintenance of international peace and security.

ARTICLE 8

Each Party declares that none of the international engagements now in force between it and any other of the Parties or any third state is in conflict with the provisions of this Treaty, and undertakes not to enter into any international engagement in conflict with this Treaty.

ARTICLE 9

The Parties hereby establish a council, on which each of them shall be represented, to consider matters concerning the implementation of this Treaty. The council shall be so organized as to be able to meet promptly at any time. The council shall set up such subsidiary bodies as may be necessary; in particular it shall establish immediately a defense committee which shall recommend measures for the implementation of Articles 3 and 5.

ARTICLE 10

The Parties may, by unanimous agreement, invite any other European state in a position to further the principles of this Treaty and to contribute to the security of the North Atlantic area to accede to this Treaty. Any state so invited may become a party to the Treaty by depositing its instrument of accession with the Government of the United States of America. The Government of the United States of America will inform each of the Parties of the deposit of each such instrument of accession.

ARTICLE 11

This Treaty shall be ratified and its provisions carried out by the Parties in accordance with their respective constitutional processes. The instruments of ratification shall be deposited as soon as possible with the Government of the United States of America, which will notify all the other signatories of each deposit. The Treaty shall enter into force between the states which have ratified it as soon as the ratification of the majority of the signatories, including the ratifications of Belgium, Canada, France, Luxembourg, the Netherlands, the United Kingdom and the United States, have been deposited and shall come into effect with respect to other states on the date of the deposit of their ratifications.

ARTICLE 12

After the Treaty has been in force for ten years, or at any time thereafter, the Parties shall, if any of them so requests, consult together for the purpose of reviewing the Treaty, having regard for the factors then affecting peace and security in the North Atlantic area, including the development of universal as well as regional arrangements under the Charter of the United Nations for the maintenance of international peace and security.

ARTICLE 13

After the Treaty has been in force for twenty years, any Party may cease to be a party one year after its notice of denunciation has been given to the Government of the United States of America, which will inform the Governments of the other Parties of the deposit of each notice of denunciation.

ARTICLE 14

This Treaty, of which the English and French texts are equally authentic, shall be deposited in the archives of the Government of the United States of America. Duly certified copies thereof will be transmitted by that Government to the Governments of the other signatories.

In witness whereof, the undersigned Plenipotentiaries have signed this Treaty.

Done at Washington, the fourth day of April, 1949.

INDEX